With Best Wishes June
28-10-2015.
Fr. Chris.

The rocky road to Paradise

By

Chris Conroy

ORIGINAL WRITING

Editor - John Fanagan
Legal adviser - Kevin Brophy, solicitor.

ISBNS
PARENT : 978-1-78237-637-8
EPUB: 978-1-78237-638-5
MOBI: 978-1-78237-639-2
PDF: 978-1-78237-640-8

A CIP catalogue for this book is available from the National Library.

Published by ORIGINAL WRITING LTD., Dublin, 2014.

Printed by CLONDALKIN GROUP, Glasnevin, Dublin 11

Dedication

To my sister in law, Margaret, my nephews and nieces, John, Richard, Cormac, Mary and Gráinne.

In loving memory of my parents Edward and Kathleen, my brothers, Eddie, Davy and Richie. May they rest in peace.

Contents

Prologue

When Sir Thomas More languished in the tower of London awaiting execution because he would not take the oath of allegiance to the King, his wife and daughters implored him to find a way to take the oath. He replied "The road to Paradise is not on featherbeds." It would appear that featherbeds were the epitome of luxury in those days as they were in Irish farmsteads down through the centuries until they were replaced by duvets. But the moral of the story is clear. There is no easy way to Heaven. We all have difficult choices to make. I live on the Rocky Road in Wicklow so the title of my book became obvious, "The Rocky Road to Paradise." It is not an autobiography, rather a series of memories and memoirs.

It contains a rare speech by President Sean T. O'Kelly about his meetings with Pope Benedict XV concerning Irish freedom. I also recall one of the last orders of the First World War obtained by my father in November 1918.

When I decided to live among the Inca Indians in the mountains of Peru I could never have realised the profound effect it would have on my life. I wrote about these experiences among the Indians in my first book "A Beggar In Paradise."

The Rocky Road to Paradise recalls the time before and after. I could never have foreseen that I would be falsely accused and my good name and reputation be taken away in an instant. Although I was found 'not guilty' in the civil court, I was betrayed by the Church.

I would like to thank John Fanigan for editing my book and my niece Gráinne for her expertise with computers.

An altar boy at 7 years.

1

Once Upon A Time

"Christy, are you awake? It's nearly seven, you'll be late for Mass." Bleary eyed I jumped out of bed and searched for a match to light a candle. It was black dark and freezing cold, it wouldn't be light for another couple of hours. I quickly dressed, shirt and tie, short trousers long stockings and hob nailed boots. The sound of the boots on the stairs reverberated around the house and woke everyone except my father. Breathing a sigh of relief, they turned over and quickly went back to sleep. "Don't forget your coat, you'll get your death of cold," my mother shouted. "And don't eat anything; remember you are going to Communion." I looked at the grandfather clock on the wall, it was just ten minutes to seven, I had plenty of time. The carbide lamp was out of carbide, anyway it took too long to prepare. "If you are bringing the storm lantern, don't use all the paraffin, we need it for the primus, I forgot to bring in sticks for the fire," came the voice from above. I settled for the lantern with the four glass sides and candle in the middle. It didn't give much light but it was better than nothing, anyway I could cycle from the Copse to the church in Rathdrum with my eyes shut.

I left my bike in Paddy's and Johnny's at the bottom of the steps to the church. The sacristan was ringing the second bell as I came around the back of the Church and into the sacristy. I was the first to arrive. I put on my soutane and surplice and lit the candles for Mass. There were two people in the church. I prepared the cruets with the water and wine and the little spoon. Now all I had to do was wait for someone to come. Tommy Mac always came at the last minute. I decided I would play a prank on him. I would climb up the press behind the door and jump down on him as he arrived. Soon I heard the sound of steps outside and the door opened slowly. I jumped and let out a mighty scream. As the light came on I suddenly realised to my surprise that it wasn't Tommy but Fr. Kennedy the parish priest.

His biretta went flying as I landed on top of him. He could have died of a heart attack. As he picked himself up he reacted very calmly, "You weren't expecting me, were you?" he said. I was still shaking as we proceeded out to begin the Mass. He placed the chalice on the altar and returned to the bottom of the steps. With his back to the people he began....

"Introibo ad altare Dei,

Ad Deum qui laetificat juventutem meam"

(I will go to the altar of God,

To God who is the joy of my youth)

***

I was born into this world on Tuesday the 20th of December 1932 at 8.30am, in the Rotunda maternity hospital. My father brought my mother to Dublin with Davy a few days previously and they stayed with my Aunt Molly in Sandymount. It was the festive season in the capital and the streets were thronged with Christmas shoppers.

It was raining cats and dogs. A month's rain fell in two days but this didn't seem to deter anyone from their Christmas shopping. Clerys was a veritable paradise brimful of lovely gifts. "Come and bring the little folk to Clerys town of toys" shouted Santa Claus at the door, "a fairyland to make their Christmas dreams come true." There were Christmas trees everywhere adorned with flashing fairy lights multi-coloured balloons and tinsel paper to wrap the many presents. Everyone was happy in spite of the rain. Aladdin was playing at the Gaiety Theatre while Jimmy O'Dea was starring in the Olympia on St. Stephen's Day. At Pims, Santa Claus with his two fairy attendants awaited all his little friends in Toytown. What a wonderful welcome for me into the world. In the Rotunda my mother too was overjoyed. Dr. Bethel Solomons the Master of the hospital, with the matron Miss Todd led a group of nurses around the wards singing Christmas carols. They stopped at the end of my bed and sang "Silent night, holy night, all is calm, all is bright...," another child was born into the world, a time for celebrating and rejoicing. I was baptized in the Star of the Sea church, Sandymount. The ceremony took place early in the morning at the back of the Church. I was named Christopher. My name just came naturally because I was born so near to Christmas.

So it was in the beginning.

Mam, Eddie, Davy, Me. In safe hands.

2

Arrival At The Copse

The Copse House has a long history. It began as a small 18th century farmhouse in the centre of extensive forests. Lord Ardee, the Earl of Meath, converted this into a shooting lodge in the early part of the 19th Century. Here the surrounding gentry of the time would be invited to take part in hunting parties especially the beginning of the grouse season in August. These parties were renowned for their wining and dining and lavish celebrations in the midst of the extreme poverty of the local peasants, some of whom were used as beaters. In the middle of the 19th century it was extensively enlarged and remodelled and given a mock Tudor frontage. Lord Ardee and his family would have come to stay here many times a year from their home in Killruddery in Bray. In the 1890's a further extension was added to the house consisting of a large billiard room and more bedrooms. In 1926 Lord Ardee sold Copse House to Mr. Thomas Joseph O'Neill. Little is known of his time at Copse House but he did not stay long as it was sold to Cuthbert Kingston Hackett in 1928. Mr. Hackett did not take up residence immediately but had further renovations carried out before his arrival in 1930. This is where my parents come in. They were employed by Mr. Hackett and arrived with my two older brothers Eddie and Davy at the Copse in 1930. My brother Davy had been born in Greystones two years before while they were waiting for the Copse to be ready.

Copse House, a beautiful home.

My father was demobbed from the British Army in 1919 and returned home to Ireland which was in the middle of the War of Independence. There was no victorious homecoming for the Irish soldiers coming home from the First World War. In England returning soldiers were being recruited to join the Black and Tans. The most notorious and uneducated soldier was attracted to join and it soon became the most hated and brutal group ever to come to Ireland. It wasn't a good time to be an ex British soldier in Ireland. The motto was "don't mention the war." My father returned to his home at Wellington Cottages Crumlin. He immediately set about trying to rehabilitate himself to civilian life. Before the war he had spent six years as a groom with Mrs Phillips at St. Anne's Terenure. He wanted to go further and enrolled in the Automobile School and Chauffeurs Employment Bureau at Dartmouth Place, Ranelagh Rd., Dublin. He completed a full course of motor-driving and mechanics at this school. With these qualifications there were great opportunities for work in the many big houses around the country. The manager of the Automobile School, Mr. Daly, immediately got him a job with Captain Bailey of Ballinderry House, Moate, Co. Westmeath. Captain Bailey had also been in the War and welcomed him as an old comrade.

The Baileys had inherited Ballinderry House and property from their aunt Sarah Kelly who had mysteriously been murdered on the land. She had been notorious for evicting tenants who couldn't pay their rent and it was assumed that it was one of these who did the deed. Captain Bailey had two cars as well as large stables with numerous hunters. My father was employed as chauffeur, mechanic and groom. As luck would have it my mother was also employed as a housemaid at Ballinderry House. She was Catherine Sheridan, the third eldest of ten children. She was from a place called Kilcurley near Tubber, a short distance from Ballinderry House. The Sheridan family had been evicted from their farm some years before, probably by Sarah Kelly herself.

My mother lived in the servants' quarters while in service. The housemaids were always dressed in uniform; they wore blue dresses with white collar, cuffs and aprons and a blue cap with a white band. In the afternoon they wore black dresses with white accessories until bedtime. The duties of the housemaids, apart from cleaning and dusting the rooms were to light fires in the bedrooms of which there was about fifteen in all, seven of these being for the staff alone. Fires had to be looked after, fire grates cleaned out and black-leaded, hot water to be taken upstairs in brass cans to the bedrooms, for the family and the guests who bathed and changed for dinner every night. It wasn't long before my father noticed this beautiful young twenty one year old girl and started courting her. Captain Bailey let my father have the car on his days off and he brought my mother on trips to the surrounding countryside.

On Sundays they went to Mass at the local Carmelite Church in Moate. My mother was already familiar with the Carmelites. A Carmelite priest from the Friary called to the family home each year on the quest (donation of alms). My parents were married within three years on the 21st of January 1922 at the Church of the Holy Family in Tubber. Honeymoons were not the custom at the time and so they celebrated late into the night with music and dancing. The Sheridans were very musical. Within ten days they had to leave Ballinderry as the I.R.A. had attacked the house and burned the stables. My father managed to save most of the hunters but two were burned to death in the blaze. The Baileys decided to leave Ballinderry for a while so my parents were reluctantly let go.

Within a month they were again in employment at Dunderry Park, in Navan by a Mr. W.E. Eccles. My father was his chauffeur, mechanic and of course groom to the horses. He also looked after the electric lighting and water pumping plant. At Ballinderry they had used carbide for the lighting. My mother continued her work as a member of the kitchen staff while caring for her first born Eddie.

Mr. Eccles also kept race horses and the whole family were regular visitors to nearby Fairyhouse. One evening as my father was leaving Fairyhouse he heard someone calling him. "Conroy is that you, how wonderful to see you." It was his old Sergeant Major from the war, over for the races. They had become great friends and the Sergeant Major admired my father's expertise with horses as they lugged a 60 pound gun through the battlefield of Flanders. Before they left France he offered my father a job. "Conroy, you are not going back to that awful place where everyone is killing one another. Come and work for me. I have a large farm in the north of England with plenty of horses. You would love it. I could do with someone like you to look after them." My father explained that his parents were still alive back home and he had a brother and sisters. "If you ever feel like coming to England there is always a place for you." As they left Fairyhouse that evening he wished my father luck. That very night he was shot by the I.R.A.

My parents stayed in Navan for almost four years and then they were on the move again. A Mr. Cuthbert Kingston Hackett had just bought the Copse House in Co. Wicklow and he was looking for a chauffeur. He interviewed my parents in Dublin and they got the job. For some weeks they lived in luxury in the Salthill Hotel in Monkstown before moving to a cottage in Greystones where they lived for almost a year while the Copse was being renovated. Mr. Hackett had just bought a beautiful new car, an Armstrong Sidley so they eventually arrived to their new home in style.

Armstong Sidley, a real classic.

3

The Copse Estate

There is something very special about the place where we are born and grow up. It is as though our first images of the world, our tastes and smells and sounds leave an impression on our minds that lasts forever. No matter how many other worlds we experience during our lives there is no place like where we were born. There is something of the salmon and the homing pigeon in each one of us. We always want to return to our roots. The world that I was born into was a little place called The Copse, just outside Rathdrum, in the county of Wicklow. It was on the main road to Glendalough surrounded by trees and woods and green fields. Here I grew up with my parents and three brothers. Eddie was the oldest, eleven years older than me. Then came Davy who was four years older; my younger brother Richie would not be born for another four years. Our nearest neighbours were more than a mile away along the road or over the hill. This meant that we grew up as a very united and close knit family who did everything together. It was here that I took my first unsteady steps and learned how to walk. I could never have imagined then where these steps would take me as I walked through life. Just across the road down through the woods, past the bluebells and primroses, along the plantation of newly sown saplings of fir trees was the Avonmore river. Here my father taught us all how to swim on hot summer days. He was a strong swimmer who was always called on by the Gardaí to recover the body when someone drowned. Very few could swim in those days. We learned the breast stroke, the back stroke and the dog paddle. We had to swim against the current so that if we were advancing we could stay in the one place. Afterwards when we went to Brittas Bay it was so much easier to swim in the salt water. Eddie and Davy were very keen fishermen. They spent hours fishing on the long evenings in May when the fish were rising. They arrived home with the fork of a hazel twig loaded with trout. I never really took to fishing. They say I hadn't the patience, but I loved to eat the freshly caught fish fried in the pan. The Avonmore river meandered its way to the village where it drove the giant wheel of Comerfords Flour Mill. It continued on to Avoca where it met the Avon Beg coming down from Glenmalure, one of the last strongholds of Fiach Mc Hugh O'Byrne and Michael Dwyer. Sitting under a leafy tree Tom Moore was to pen the beautiful song, "There is not in this wide world a valley so sweet as the Vale in whose bosom the bright waters meet." The tree has long since gone but the song remains (forever).

I grew up to love nature in all its forms. I knew all the birds and animals of the forest. At first by their names and then by their habits and characteristics. For them this too was their home and I soon learned that each had its own territory. The rabbits and the red squirrels as they leaped from branch to branch high up in the trees. In times of plenty they gathered their nuts and carefully hid them in the ground or in holes in the trees. They were decimated in 1947 when the big snow came and lasted for seven weeks. Soon after this the grey squirrels took over and the beautiful red became a thing of the past. We also kept a pet fox for a while. We kept it on a lead. It seemed perfectly at home until one day it escaped and went back to the wild, collar and all. Tom Meegan told us afterwards that he saw a fox with a collar and a chicken in its mouth crossing the road. It never lost its natural instincts.

***

*Minding Richie,
I was his big brother at 4yrs.*

Eddie, me and Davy 1933, a wonderful welcome into the world by my brothers.

Mam, me, Richie, Davy. Early days at the Copse.

Mam, Davy, Me, Dad.

Richie with Me in our Sunday best clothes.

In my Rolls-Royce pram 1933 on a winters day.

With Richie on his first Communion Day.

With Richie at the Copse on his Confirmation day.

Outside the Copse I mowed the grass and looked after the flowers. 1949.

With jeep outside home, it was wonderful on and off the road.

Growing up.

When I first went to school it was an old building on the fair green consisting of two classrooms. Mrs. Wedick taught the infants and Mr. Kinnane the seniors. Everything had to be learned by heart. We spent hours reciting our addition, multiplication and division tables, all through Irish. To this day I do my mental arithmetic in Irish. In the winter there was an open fire that had to be lit every morning. Sometimes this took quite a long time. Each pupil was expected to bring to school a block of wood or a sod of turf for the fire. While the fire was being lit we would all stand up and do our physical jerks to keep warm. I arrived in school one day in long trousers. This was most unusual as everyone wore short trousers in those days. To my embarrassment Mrs. Wedick brought me out in front of the class to model the trousers.

The new school was built at the back of the old school and was opened in April 1941 amid great celebrations. It was a lovely three classroom building with toilets and cloakrooms. It compared with any National school in the country at the time. Mr. Morrissey was the new principal with Mr. Gordon as assistant and Mrs. Wedick continued with the infants. By now I had moved into Mr. Gordon's class. He was a good teacher and had the interest of each pupil at heart (He was later to become a priest in England). He was also interested in amateur dramatics. He took part in many concerts and plays. These took place in the Court house which was originally the Flannel Hall. This building dated back to 1792. Mr. Gordon played a prominent part in all the plays and concerts. He gave a very amusing commentary on "The Ballyknocken Chase."

The point to point races at Ballyknocken had recently been revived by Major Ellison after a period of over fifty years. The cups were presented by Pierces of Rathdrum and Phelans of Clash. The Dramatic Society put on many productions that played to packed houses on long winter evenings before the age of television. Everyone was moved to tears by their production of "*Fr. Murphy,*" the hero of the '98 rebellion in Wexford.

Another highlight of the year was the arrival of Radio Eireann to Rathdrum to broadcast Question Time. In the early days Noel Hartnett was the compère. Later Joe Linnane made it the most popular radio programme on Sunday nights. All the local intelligencia put themselves to the test before the nation. It always followed the same format. Two two mark questions, two four mark and one six mark question. One's reputation could be destroyed if you missed a two mark question. The questions weren't always very easy but of course they are always easy if you know the answer.

"What colour is a Polar bear?"

"What is the difference between Flannel and Flannelette?"

(This question was especially for Rathdrum because Question Time was taking place in the old Flannel Hall.)

"Why is a bird not electrocuted when it lands on an electric wire?"

"What is nepotism.?"

"What famous Irishman lived in Ballymanus?" (Billy Byrne)

The first Tuesday of every month was fair day in Rathdrum. From early morning the animals converged on the fair green from all directions. When Jack Jordan had cattle for the fair I would run ahead and cover all the gaps to prevent them from escaping up lanes or into fields. Sometimes the buyers who had come from Dublin tried to waylay the farmers and make a bargain before they reached the fair green. But most of the farmers were wary of this practice and preferred to take their chances at the fair. As the farmers gathered around for a sale there was much shouting and bargaining and walking away before a deal was done. This was sealed by the spitting on the hands and slapping the seller. Then a large wad of notes was handed over and counted. Afterwards they all retired to the pub for the evening. Lessons that day took place in the midst of baah..ing and moo..ing and shouting. Later on in the town the following conversation could be heard between two farmers.

"Ah hello Tom are you not gone home yet?

No, not yet Jack are you not gone home yet?

How did you get on today?

Ah fair to middling. How did you get on?

About the same, fair to middling. It could have been better, I thought I would have got more.

So did I, but I suppose that's the way it goes. Some good days and others not so good and others middling.

Would you like a pint? Sure I might as well."

Everyone looked forward to the annual visit of the circus. The caravans and wagons began arriving from early morning. Most were pulled by horses but there was the odd steam engine for the heavier equipment. The big top went up like clockwork. Everybody gave a hand, the acrobats, the jugglers, the lion tamers, and the trapeze artists. I loved the animals. I couldn't wait to see the lions and the tigers as they paced up and down in their cages letting out a growl when they were disturbed. Two circuses came to Rathdrum each year, Duffys and Fossetts. Fossetts always seemed to have more animals. They claimed to be the only circus with performing wild animals, lions and tigers in an iron cage. Myself and Davy arrived early for the matinee. The music began as the piebald horses with their lady riders entered the ring. The ringmaster with his long whip kept the horses at a steady pace as the girls jumped from springboards to their backs. They performed all kinds of tricks on the horses' backs as they went around and around in the ring. I thought how wonderful it would be to be able to do that and one year I got my chance.

At the end of the performance the ringmaster came to the centre of the ring. There was a wooden arm extending from the centre pole with a rope hanging down and a harness at the end. The curtains opened and a beautiful horse entered and began to circle the ring. The ringmaster then asked was there any boy or girl who would like to learn how to ride bareback and perform some tricks. Nobody budged. Then Davy gave me a nudge and said, "now is your chance." I jumped over the barrier and said "I'll have a go." He put the harness on and hoisted me up on the horse. The horse began to move and so did I, I was sitting on his back. "Now stand up," came the order. "Now go head over heels and land on the horse." I went around and around for a long time. When I was lowered to the ground, I could hardly stand up. It was so exhilarating and wonderful.

4

Fun For All Seasons

Each season at the Copse brought its particular magic as Autumn changed to Winter, to Spring and Summer. Surrounded by forests, Autumn transforms the whole place into a wonderland of colour. Green leaves turn to orange and gold and every shade in between before they gentle float majestically to the earth to nourish it again for next year's growth. On Autumn evenings at dusk the bats come out to do their merry dance back and forth mysteriously catching flies on the way. My mother warned us that they can get entangled in your hair and give you a nasty bite. Luckily they never seemed to come down to our level. All the fruit and nuts had been collected and all was ready for the festivities of Halloween. I knew where the best hazel nuts were hidden in the forest and the chestnuts from the big tree by the tennis court bursting from their shells. There was an abundance of apples for the snap apple. We could still get witches masks but coconuts and monkey nuts were unavailable during the war, fireworks had also ceased to exist. I usually got the ring from the barm brack which everyone said was a sure sign that I would be first to be married. We ended the evening ducking in a bath of water to retrieve the threepenny and sixpenny coins. We always wished for snow for Christmas to match the scenery on the Christmas cards but it normally didn't come until January or February. We were thrilled when the first flakes began to fall and hoped that when we got up the next day everywhere would be covered with snow. The school was always closed when there was snow and in 1947 we had seven weeks of snow. There were drifts of over ten feet in places. Food had to be dropped from the air at isolated districts of Glendalough. We spent our days on our makeshift sleighs sliding down the hills opposite the house. The cold played havoc with the small birds and the red squirrels were wiped out. We rolled a snowball into large round slabs to make the biggest snowman ever. Over ten feet tall he looked life like with his carrot for a nose and pebbles for eyes and mouth. We put one of my father's old hats on his head. He lived on for ages after the rest of the snow was long gone.

With the arrival of spring everything came to life again. It seemed a miracle to see the green shoots push up from the hard earth. Soon the birds began to mate and slowly built their nests of every shape and size. I loved roaming the woods and seeking them out. Some were much more secretive in their locations than others. The blackbird and the song thrush were usually the easiest to find. The blackbird builds a solid nest in a bush or hedge with dry vegetation, lined with mud and dry leaves to cover the greenish spotted eggs. The song thrush constructs its nest with interwoven twigs and grasses. Its inside is smoothed out with mud or dung containing four blue spotted eggs. I used to take the blackbird and the thrush for granted and considered them very ordinary; now I find them most interesting. At an early age I began collecting birds eggs. I made a box with a sliding glass top, dividing it into sections with balsa wood. With two pin pricks I blew the liquid out and carefully placed the shell in its section, where it was named and numbered. You never took an egg from a nest if there were less than two. They say that the birds can count to two and if they discover that their nests have been discovered they abandon it. The robin can mate in December and build its nest in the crevice of a tree or in an old tin can. Each robin has a territory and defends it aggressively. There were hundreds of species of birds around the Copse and each had its own particular characteristics and ways of building their nests. The woodpigeon builds a flimsy nest of twigs in a tall tree. It lays two white eggs and the young stay in the nest until they are fully grown. The little wren is the smallest bird of all and builds a beautiful global nest with a side entrance. The family of tits are made up of coal tit, marsh tit, blue tit, great tit. Hearing a pecking noise you discover a woodpecker is hard at work and beside him a tree creeper running up and down the trunk collecting insects. A family of finches frequents the garden each with its distinctive colour, the goldfinch; greenfinch; hawfinch; chaffinch; bullfinch. As well as the song thrush there is a bigger species called the mistle thrush, and a jay thrush. One day I was attacked by a mistle thrush as he swooped down with beak open wide, only changing his direction at the last moment. I was unaware that I had probably disturbed its nest. With the coming of the swallows and swifts you knew that summer was here. The swallows usually returned to the same place every year. They built their nests with mud on the inside of the hay barn. They always amazed me with the speed with which they could enter the nest. The swift flies high in the sky and only comes to land in order to nest. They even mate on the wing. I was fascinated by all the different species of birds and loved to spend hours just observing them doing what comes naturally. I never wanted to domesticate them or try to make them do what I wanted. They were much more interesting just being themselves. Very often when we learn the names of birds we think we know them but there is much more to them than a name.

The war brought many disadvantages like rationing, no sweets, or chocolate, or oranges or bananas. But there were many advantages. England was crying out for food. Wood pigeons fetched 2/6 each and rabbits were 2 shillings. I soon became an expert at shooting pigeons. After the summer they formed large flocks and fed on the remains of the corn and the beech nuts. They always had a sentry on the tallest branch. When he moved they all moved. That solved the mystery of why they all rose in unison. As you approached them stealthily, you just had to observe the sentry. With the shotgun you could get five or six at a time. Another good time to get them was as they came in to roost at dusk. I would settle down under a tall beech tree and wait.

Sometimes it got too dark to see the sights on the rifle. They say that the pigeons were tinned and shipped to England as chicken. Often on my way out to school I would ask my father to get me a pigeon by the afternoon and usually he did. Rabbit meat was also very popular during the war. As well as shooting them I set snares, brass wire forming a loop attached to a peg hammered into the ground. The secret was to find a fresh track and place the loop at the proper height with a twig. Sometimes you would have two or three rabbits in the morning. Looking back now on snaring rabbits I get a shiver up my spine. How could I have done such a thing? The poor rabbits.

"I hear a sudden cry of pain,
There is a rabbit in a snare,
Now I hear the cry again,
But I cannot tell from where.

But I cannot tell from where,
He is calling out for aid,
Crying on the frightened air,
Making everything afraid.

All my summer holidays during the war were spent picking fraughans. I could pick a large bucketful every day. They were 2 shillings a pound and the bucket made up to a £1. There were fraughans in all the woods around the Copse but I knew where the best ones were across the river. I set off early with my bucket and lunch to Ballyhad, passing Tom Meegan's on the way. Kate was usually standing at the gate waiting for a chat. She would talk for an hour if you stayed but I was in a hurry. She always loved to tell me how she used to look after me as a baby when my mother had to go to Dublin. Past the dell and down through the pine forest to the river. The tall pines stood like sentries as they reached for the sky. I loved looking up at the green branches against the clear blue-sky. It was here that the wood pigeons liked to build their nests out of harm's way, impossible to reach. The workmen had built a wire bridge across the river. Two strands of steel cable attached to trees on either side. You held on for dear life with your hands as you inched your way across. As you reached the middle it began to wobble and if you were not careful you could somersault and end up gazing into the fast flowing river below. It wasn't too bad with an empty bucket but on the way back when it was full of fraughans it was a different story. The fraughan is a small blueish berry that grows on small green bushes underneath the trees. They thrive on swampy mossy ground. You picked as fast as you could, leaves and all until the bucket became heavier and heavier. Sometimes I lit a fire and made tea in my billycan to have with my sandwiches for lunch.

Bringing home the bird.
Each wood quest earned 2/6.

Wolahans in Rathdrum bought all the fraughans they could get. They had wonderful machine for separating the leaves and the twigs from the fruit and then they shipped them all to England where it was known as the Bilberry. It is a relative of the blueberry and the cranberry, both of which have noted health-promoting effects. The fraughan has long been regarded as having benefits for improved eyesight. It is claimed that R.A.F. pilots ate bilberry jam during the war to improve their night vision. Fraughans are used as a herbal remedy for a variety of vision impairment conditions including cataracts and an age related macular degeneration, a disease which damages central vision. For whatever reason, the R.A.F. could not get enough fraughans from Ireland.

5

The Joys Of Christmas

Christmas was beautiful at the Copse. In spite of the rationing and the threat of invasion there was no shortage of celebration. For months beforehand I had picked out a special pine sapling in the forest as a Christmas tree I also had to get one for Mr. Morrissey. Each of us had their own particular task. Davy decorated the tree with moss and leaves and of course twinkling fairy lights. I iced the cakes, adorned them with snowmen and Santa Claus, and a generous sprinkling of hundreds and thousands. I also helped Richie with the holly, balloons and coloured streamers. The Laughing Cavalier put on an extra smile for the occasion with sprigs of holly sticking out in all directions. I wanted to decorate the Sacred Heart but my mother wouldn't hear of it. "It just wouldn't be right," she said. "But I'm sure the Child Jesus wouldn't mind," I replied. "The Child Jesus has His own place in the Crib," she explained.

My mother spent the day preparing the dinner for the next day. I had collected the Turkey from Lil Jordan and it had to be plucked and the stuffing made. We also had a Turkey for New Year's Day. Nuala in Barry's had reserved a large smoked ham. My father provided all the vegetables from the garden. Eddie arrived from Baldonnel where he was training to be an aircraft electrician. As darkness fell an air of anticipation came over the whole house. My mother placed a large candle in the window to guide the Child Jesus on his way. Myself and Richie went to bed early to be asleep when Santa came, but not before my mother read the "Night before Christmas."

"Twas the night before Christmas, when all through the house
Not a creature was stirring, not even a mouse,
The stockings were hung by the chimney with care,
In hopes that St. Nicholas soon would be there.
The children were nestled all snug in their beds,
While visions of sugarplums danced in their heads;
And Mamma in her kerchief, and I in my cap,
Had just settled our brains for a long winter nap."

Each year this poem had a magical effect on us and transported us to a wonderful land of make believe. We had already placed our stockings at the end of the bed. I always made sure there was a big hole in mine so that Santa would not notice the presents falling out. In spite of all the excitement we were soon asleep. We awoke early as my parents went to the first Mass. We didn't let on we were awake, pretending we were fast asleep. Hearing the door closing we jumped out of bed and crept down the stairs in our pyjamas. We knew the presents were locked in the sitting room. We could hardly contain our excitement as we went outside and climbed up onto the windowsill and pressing our faces against the glass peered in to see the wonderful array of presents: boxes all covered with coloured paper, Christmas stockings stuffed with games and colouring books. "I see a cowboy hat with two six guns," exclaimed Richie, "I hope they are for me." There were tin soldiers and little search lights and tanks. By now we were freezing with the cold and went back to the warmth of the bed, only getting up when my parents returned from Mass. The sitting room door was opened and all our wishes were fulfilled. My father got a big lump of coal and a plug of tobacco in his stocking. After breakfast of sausages, black and white pudding and eggs, we went to second Mass. Christmas day was very special. There was something sacred about it. Christ was born as a little child in Bethlehem. All of nature reflected his coming. The trees and the woodland, the birds and the animals, even mammy's little pet robin seemed to know it was Christmas day. As we knelt at the crib at the back of the church it all seemed very real, the stable, the donkey, the shepherds, the cow, the sheep, Mary and Joseph, and the Child Jesus. We ran all the way home from Mass. The fire was lit in the sitting room and we played with our presents. Eddie got out the gramophone and began to play the large pile of records. The needle had to be changed after each one. He loved Nelson Eddie and Jeanette McDonald singing 'Rose Marie' while we laughed at Jimmie O'Dea and Harry O'Donovan singing 'Biddy Mulligan the Pride of the Coombe' and selling 'Fresh Fish' in Moore Street.

The real celebration of Christmas was sitting around the table for the dinner. There was a wonderful sense of joy and happiness as we joined together eating a lovely roast turkey and ham. Turkey was eaten just at Christmas time in those days. There were crackers with fancy hats and jokes all rounded off with the pouring of the whiskey on the pudding and setting it alight. After dinner we all gathered around the fire in the sitting room telling stories and playing games of Snakes and Ladders and Ludo. Late in the evening all we could manage was a cup of tea and a slice of Christmas Cake. Christmas day always seemed to be the shortest day in the year. On St. Stephen's Day we all went hunting deer in the forest. If there was snow it was easy to follow their tracks to their hiding place.

After Christmas every year we went to Dublin for the pantomime. We stayed with my aunt Mollie in Sandymount. My favorite was Jimmy O'Dea and Harry O'Donovan in the Royal. It seemed like magic to see Tommy Dando rising from the underground playing the organ. I followed in amazement the adventures of Cinderella and the ugly sisters, Little Red Riding Hood, Jack in the Beanstalk, Puss in Boots and Aladdin. We stayed for a week and saw two or three pantos as well as visiting the Zoo and the Botanic Gardens. I also went to many cowboy films at the Shack.

6

Communion and Confirmation

The master tapped on the desk with the tuning fork and we all began:

"Oro mo churaichin o
Oro mo braidin
O- o ro mo churaichin o
Oro mo braidin"

Just as we finished he tapped the desk again and said. "Someone is singing out of tune." Let's begin again. He came closer and cocked his ear. He stopped in front of me and said. "It's you, you are singing out of tune. Sing the scale." "Doha ray me," I began, but he had heard enough. "That's enough," he said. "You are tone deaf, just listen." From that day I was always excluded from choirs. I could hold the charts or ring the bell but not sing. I loved music and listened to the music charts on the radio all the time. I could sing notes but not in the right order. I always wanted to get a guitar and sing like Gene Autry or Roy Rodgers. All the songs we sang in school were in Irish. By now I had moved from Mr. Gordan's class to Mr. Morrissey's. There were three classes in the one room: 4th, 5th and 6th. While we were doing arithmetic, another class was doing Irish. It was like learning three subjects at the same time. Everything was taught through Irish except English. Mr. Morrissey was a fluent Irish speaker from Galway. All my Maths tables were learned off by heart in Irish. I still do mental arithmetic in my head in Irish. The same with the principal towns in each County. I still look at the road signs in Irish. We learned everything by rote, repeating it again and again until we could say it off by heart. Fr. Kennedy paid us a visit once a week. We all stood up as he entered the room and greeted him in Irish. In the Autumn he sent us up buckets of apples. He had a magnificent orchard. Fr. Kennedy came more often getting near to Confirmation. Confirmation was an anxious time for everyone especially those who were to receive the Sacrament. Confirmation would make us strong and perfect Christians. The Archbishop John Charles McQuaid came from Dublin to administer it. He asked each one of us a question from the Catechism and if we did not answer correctly we might not be confirmed. All other subjects took second place to the Catechism before Confirmation. We went over it again and again. We didn't understand what the questions meant but that didn't matter. With the coming of the Holy Ghost all would become clear.

On the day of the Confirmation we all arrived early in our new suits. We took our places in Church, boys on one side and girls on the other. The whole town was decked out with bunting for the arrival of the Archbishop.

The L.D.F. and L.S.F. formed a guard of honour outside the Church. The Archbishop inspected them with Fr. Kennedy trailing behind. The men were so excited that they didn't know whether to salute or not. I waited anxiously in my seat getting more nervous all the time. At last the Archbishop entered the church and the organ struck up a rousing tune. He went to the sacristy and put on his robes and arrived at the Altar preceded by the altar boys and Fr. Kennedy. Although the vestments were beautiful, the Archbishop looked gaunt and serious. Holy people never seemed to look happy. Now he came down to the seats to examine the Catechism. I was in the third seat, shivering with fear by this time. I knew all the questions he asked the others. Then he came to me. He was less than two feet away.

Archbishop John Charles McQuaid arriving for Confirmation at Rathdrum, 1944.

"How are we to love God above all?" he asked sternly.

"We are to love God above all, by loving Him more than ourselves and more than anything in the world and by being disposed to sacrifice everything that is most dear to us, even life, if necessary, rather than offend him by mortal sin."

That was it, I had passed the test and he moved quickly on. I took my place in the line approaching the Archbishop. He held out his hands over me and prayed that the Holy Ghost would descend upon me. Then he made the sign of the cross on my forehead with chrism. I had received the seven gifts of the Holy Ghost; Wisdom, Understanding, Counsel, Fortitude, Knowledge, Piety and the Fear of the Lord. I had nothing to fear, I could face anything. We didn't see the Archbishop afterwards. He had a quick lunch with Fr. Kennedy and was off to Roundwood for another Confirmation on his way back to Dublin.

A few years previously I had made my first Confession and Holy Communion. Again I was anxious about the Confession part. We learned all the sins that you could possibly commit and then took your pick. I decided that I was disobedient to my parents, told lies, and was unkind. These were the sins that I confessed for many years afterwards. Bless me Father for I have sinned, it's a month since my last Confession. You told your sins and received a penance usually three Hail Mary's We went to Confession in the Church from the school. My first Confession was a disaster. As I waited in line Johnny Mac decided he wanted to go next. The door opened , I made a dash to go in and collided with Johnny Mac crashing into the Confession box. I got in and quickly shut the door. Fr. Byrne the curate was hearing. When the little shutter opened he peered down at me and said. "Was it you who crashed into the Confession box? "Yes," I said. "Well go out and wait your turn," he said angrily. I had to come out without my confession having being heard and then wait until the end to go in again. The other lads must have thought I was a terrible sinner. It could have put me off going to Confession for life. My first Communion suit was very special. Mrs. Smyth had given my mother a beautiful little sailor's suit which she had specially made for her son. Nothing like it had ever been seen in Rathdrum. As I walked up the aisle of the Church dressed as a little sailor with my prayer book and rosary beads there were Oohs and Ahs from the congregation. It was the most wonderful day of my life.

First Communion 1939 in my sailor's suit very pious.

7

The Secret Garden

"Hurry home for school today" said my father one morning as I went out the door. "I'll be digging the spuds and I'll need a hand". I looked forward to it all day and ran all the way home only stopping for a drink from the stream at the end of Fr. Kennedy's field. My mother had my dinner on the table. I gulped it down quickly and made my way up the avenue to the big house. In springtime there were clumps of daffodils sown at intervals both sides of the avenue. I loved running along and jumping over them as I went. I ran around the back of the house past the duck pond to the garden. It was a big round walled garden which was the custom in all the big houses of the time. The house was completely self-sufficient in vegetables and fruit, eggs, poultry and milk. There was a long greenhouse against the wall where tomatoes, melons and cucumbers were grown. There were lots of apple trees and plums and cherries. Along the wall, pear trees had their branches trained on either side. We also had strawberries, raspberries, loganberries gooseberries and black currants. There was a big greengage tree that only gave fruit once in a blue moon.

Picking pears, in my secret garden.

In my secret garden.

I always thought of this garden as my secret garden. It had a garden house in the centre made from the huge yew trees that covered it like a giant canopy. It was dark inside, a perfect hiding place for playing hide and seek. From an early age I had my own flower plot in the garden. Each spring I anxiously waited for the seeds to sprout. I placed empty jam jars over the young shoots to help them on. "I thought you would never get here" said my father as I arrived. He had two plots of potatoes already dug, the Kerrs Pinks and British Queens. They were dry and ready for picking. There was another plot to be dug but it was covered with mare's tail, a wily weed with very long roots. They were impossible to eradicate. The potatoes were stored in a loft at one corner of the yard. There was a long wooden stairs leading up to the loft. The potatoes were carried up in buckets, laid out on the wooden floor and covered with straw to save them from the frost. We had potatoes for the year. When I had to collect them for the dinner I would gently open the door and rush in with a big stick to kill the mice as they scampered up the wall. I loved those afternoons with my father in the garden. He told me many stories and imparted words of wisdom from his experiences of life. I especially enjoyed his stories about the First World War where he served as a gunner on a 60 pound gun, over the battlegrounds of Ypres and Passchendaele. As a teenager he ran away from home with his cousin to join the British army. Before heading for the boat in Dun Laoghaire he went to Confession in Whitefriars St. where he met a kind Carmelite priest who gave him a special blessing. He also gave him two medals, one of Our Lady of Mt. Carmel and the other of St. Therese, the Little Flower. She was not yet a Saint and the inscription reads "Sister Teresa of the Child Jesus". These he wore in a leather pouch around his neck during the war together with his dog tag and the caul he was born with. It is considered a lucky charm.

On his enlistment at Catterick his training as a groom with Mrs. Philips at St. Anne's, Terenure was to be his saviour. Instead of being assigned to the infantry he was appointed to the Royal Artillery on a 60 pounder gun. He was in charge of the eight to twelve horses used in transporting this heavy gun. He fought in the bloodiest battle of the war, the third battle of Ypres, or Passchendaele as it was called. It is a tiny village on top of a hill about ten kilometres outside Ypres. Field Marshal Haig had planned the battle for months ahead to breakthrough to the Belgian coast where the German submarines were causing havoc to Allied shipping. He thought that capturing this hill would bring about the end of the war. My father's gun had been encamped outside Ypres for over a year. It took eight men to fire it. On the morning of 31st July the heavy preliminary bombardment began and it continued for ten days. Over three thousand guns fired over one and a quarter million shells. There were advances and retreats during the next few months. As well as this they were hampered by the heaviest rains for 30 years.

Dad in First World War, just after joining up at Catterick Garrison Barracks.

Dad with team at sixty pound gun in the Royal Garrison Artillery. He was assigned to this regiment because of his expertise with horses.

The fierce bombardment had made the infantry advance through no man's land almost impossible. The ground had become a muddy swamp. Even the newly invented tanks got stuck in the mud. The shell holes were filled with water and many fell into the mud and drowned. The Germans retaliated with mustard gas for the first time in the war. Previously they had used chorine. My father told me one day they heard the shells coming over and they just went plomp plomp. He thought they were firing dummies. Soon he could hardly breathe, his eyes became inflamed, and his skin began to blister. Passchendaele was obliterated on the 6th of November 1917, at the cost of 310,000 casualties. My father was shipped back to England to the Red Cross hospital at Ashbourne to recuperate.

Hospital ship on which Dad was transported back to England.

Dad in Red Cross Hospital in Ashbourne after an attack of mustard gas and a shrapnel wound to the shoulder. (bottom right)

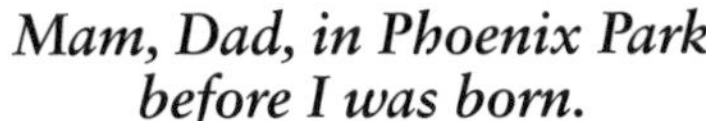

Mam, Dad, in Phoenix Park before I was born.

27th
H.A. BRIGADE.
No. AG 1764.
Date

S E C R E T and U R G E N T.

O.C.144 Heavy Battery R.G.A.

1. The C.R.A. 66th Division has offered the G.O.C. Advance Guard Force, Maj-Gen. BETHEL a section of 60-Pdrs. to engage masses of enemy transport seen and out of range for the 18-Pdrs with the advanced Guard.

2. An Ammunition supply of a 100 rounds perday if expended will be sent up by staging.
First Stage. from present wagon lines at AVESNES to a sub-section (B) of the ammunition column [illegible]
Second Stage. from E.14.central to SOIRE-le-CHATEAU by a sub-section (A) of the ammunition column.
As the advance continues further sections will have to be sent up. An Officer is to be detailed to be in charge of the ammunition column and ammunition supply.

3. These sub-sections would be rationed from the Battery Wagon Lines. The section of 60-Pdrs going forward will be rationed by the advance guard force.

4. O.C.144 H.B. will be prepared to detach one section complete as under, giving the name of the O.C. selected. This section is to be prepared to march to SOIRE-le-CHATEAU to-morrow taking the unexpended portion of the days ration and one day in hand.

Detail of Section.

Guns.	Wagons.	Officers.	Men.	Riders.	H.D.	L.D.
2		3	3 Batmen.	3		
			3 Grooms			
			24 Gunners	2		
			8 Drivers		16	
	4		1 N.C.O.	1		
	Ammo.		4½ Brakesmen.			
			8 Drivers		16	
	1		2 Drivers		4	
	Baggage.		1 Gunner			
	~~XXX~~ 1		2 Drivers		4	
	Technical.		1 Gunner			
	1		1 [illegible]			
	WaterCart.		1 Gunner			
			12 Mounted Orderlies & Signallers.	6		
			3 C.W. Wireless.			
			2 R.A.F. Wireless.			
			1 D.R.	1		
			1 Corpl. Shoeing Smith.		4 spare	
			2 Spare Drivers	13	44	2
TOTAL		3	79			

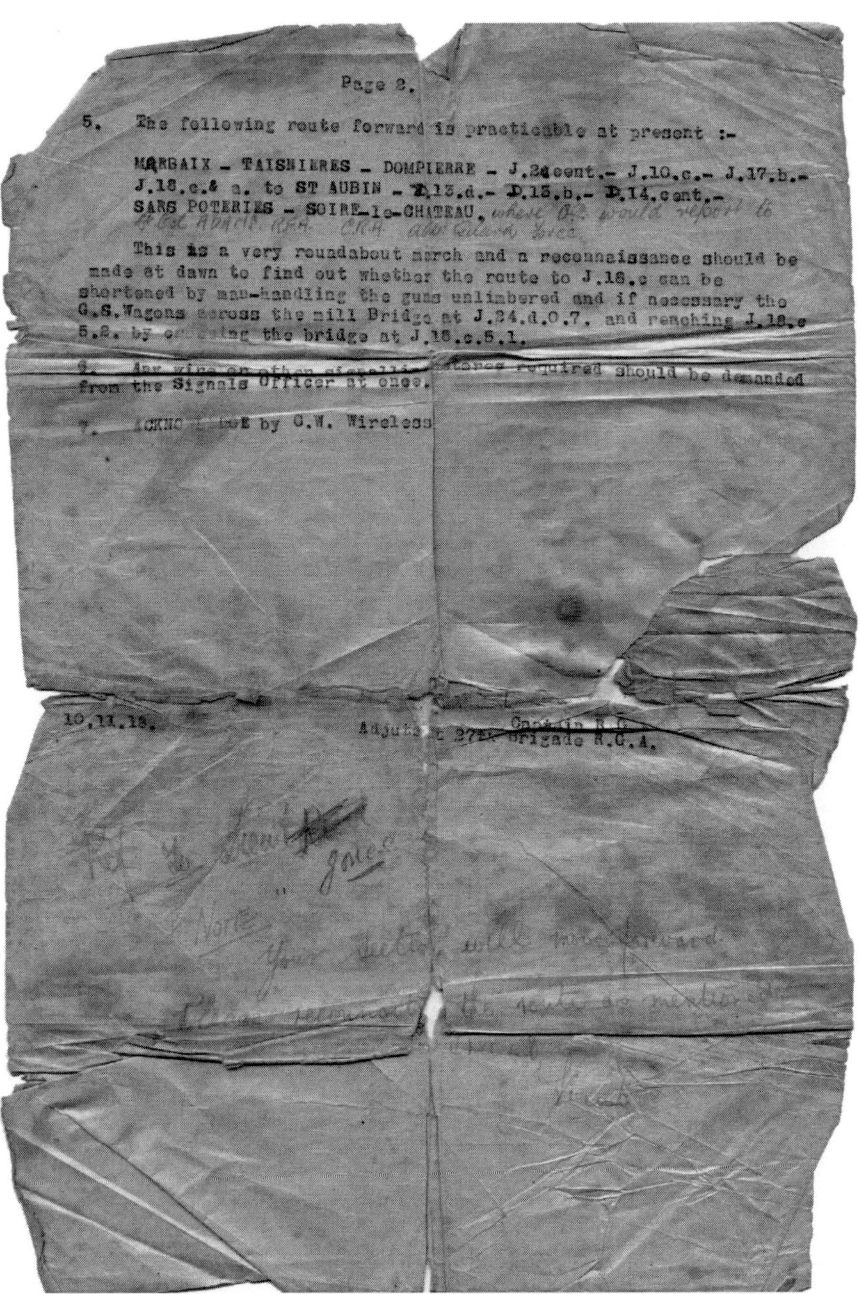

Page 2.

5. The following route forward is practicable at present :-

MARBAIX - TAISNIERES - DOMPIERRE - J.24 cent.- J.10.c.- J.17.b.- J.18.c.& a. to ST AUBIN - I.13.d.- D.15.b.- D.14.cent.- SARS POTERIES - SOIRE-le-CHATEAU, where O.C. would report to [illegible]

This is a very roundabout march and a reconnaissance should be made at dawn to find out whether the route to J.18.c can be shortened by man-handling the guns unlimbered and if necessary the G.S.Wagons across the mill Bridge at J.24.d.0.7. and reaching J.18.c 5.2. by [illegible] the bridge at J.18.c.5.1.

6. Any wire or other signalling stores required should be demanded from the Signals Officer at once.

7. ACKNOWLEDGE by C.W. Wireless

10.11.18. Adjutant 27th Brigade R.G.A.

Last orders of the First World War, dated 10.11.18 above

He returned to the battlefield in 1918 and again took up duty on the 60 pound gun. By now the war was heading for stalemate. The Russians had gone home and the Americans entered the war. Life on the battlefront hadn't got any easier. Food rations were meagre: 20oz of bread, 3oz of cheese, 20oz of tobacco, 6oz of tea, 4oz of jam, ½ oz of salt, $^1/_{30}$ oz of pepper, $^1/_{20}$ oz of mustard, 4oz of butter/margarine and 8oz of vegetables, a tot of rum each night to keep up the morale. The eight man gun team slept beside their gun whenever there was a lull in the fighting. Early one morning the Germans began shelling. My father awoke to find the others had gone and one of them had taken his boots by mistake. He left behind his, which were a few sizes smaller. My father cut the toe cap off and ran with his toes sticking out. They made tea with the water from a nearby shell hole. After a few weeks when the water dried up they discovered a dead German at the bottom of it. Towards the end of the year rumours began to circulate that the Germans were trying to negotiate an armistice. Late one evening my Father went back to the Command Post to get the orders for the next day. As he came near he heard loud shouting and singing coming from the tent. On entering he was offered a glass of beer by his Sergeant major and told to drink up, the war was over. After a while he moved over towards the desk and saw the printed page of the next days orders still in the typewriter. He quickly pulled them out and put them in his pocket. The first lines read his gun "was to accompany Maj. Gen. BETHEL to engage masses of enemy transport seen out of range for the 16 Pdrs.....etc." The date on the top of the page was 10.11.1918. Surely this was the last order of World War 1. My father gave it to me shortly before he died. It is my most treasured possession.

There could not have been a greater contrast from the horrors of war to the peace and tranquillity of those days picking potatoes at the Copse. My father had seen and experienced things that no young man should ever have to witness. Yet he lived to tell the tale and came home safely and unscathed. He had learned some great lessons in life and the importance of living in peace and happiness and not worrying about little things. I remember one day I arrived home to join him in the garden and I was worried about some trivial thing. He gave me a great piece of advice "Don't worry about little things, only big things. You will discover that most of the things you worry about never happen. Isn't today a lovely day, the sun is shining and the birds are singing. Why not just be happy today and let tomorrow look after itself." It was a piece of advice I never forgot.

8

The Farm Across The Hill

Jack Jordan cut a lonely figure as he followed the plough and two horses in the early morning mist. A screeching flock of gulls hovered overhead diving now and then as the overturned sod uncovered a juicy worm. They never appeared so far inland at any other time of year. I could not understand how they knew when the ploughing began and it was time to leave the choppy waters of Wicklow head or Brittas Bay. Not even the barking of Jack's sheepdog Blackie seemed to deter them. Jack waved in the distance as I passed on my way to the farm to collect the butter and a can of buttermilk from Lil his sister. Sometimes I collected a dozen eggs for hatching when we had eaten all our cocks. Each week I looked forward to my visit to the farm. Jack had two workmen, Christy Byrne and Paddy Mac. Christy was a jovial character like Friar Tuck always telling stories and having fun. Paddy Mac was much more serious and never seemed to smile. He had a sad look on his face and didn't say very much. Christy made up for him.

Christy Byrne asked me one day would I like to milk a cow. I was rather hesitant until he assured me that the black one at the end was very quiet and wouldn't hurt a fly. The cows come in in single file and quickly proceeded to their own stall in the cow byre. "How do they know where to go?" I wondered. Habit I suppose. I had noticed how some of the cows swished their tails at the flies while others tried to kick the bucket while being milked. "Don't worry" said Christy "the one at the end is very quiet." Paddy Mac and Lil agreed that I should have a go. Christy put the three legged stool in place as I sat down with the side of my face against the cow. I opened out my legs for the bucket but I was too small. Christy placed it underneath the cow. He also tied back his tail so that he couldn't swish. The cow turned its head to see what was going on. I don't think he liked what he saw. "Just catch a teat in each hand and pull" said Christy. By now Paddy Mac had almost a bucket of milk from his cow. I gently caught the teats and pulled but nothing happened. "Your hands are too dry" said Christy, "you want to wet them with a sup of milk." He brought over his bucket and told me to dip my hands in. "Now try" he said. I proceeded to squeeze the teats while pulling them up and down. Soon the milk began to squirt into the empty bucket making a hollow metallic sound. "Now you're thrashing," said Christy. Just as he said that the cow moved to one side, lifted its near leg gave a mighty kick sending me and the bucket flying into the centre channel. I was covered with milk, urine and fresh cow dung. Lil rushed over to pick me up. I was shaking but apart from my injured dignity I wasn't hurt. "Christy Byrne you should never have let the young lad near that cow," shouted Lil as she washed me down and cleaned me up. It was an incident like that could have put me off cows for life, but in fact it had the opposite effect. I love cows especially the smell of their hot sweat on a summer's day. I was to learn later how to stop a cow kicking the bucket. As soon as you feel the cow leaning to one side put your hand between his hind legs and block his kick. I never learned how to deal with the geese, though, when they came running at me with their long necks low down, beaks wide open and hissing ferociously. There was only one escape; run for your life, much to the amusement of everyone in the yard.

Lil was in charge of the dairy, a very cold room with its stone floor and little window. It was here that the milk was cooled before it was put in the separator which had to be turned at a particular speed. Then the cream was poured into the barrel churn to make the butter. Warm water was added from an iron kettle which had been boiled on the open fire. The lid was bolted down and the churning began. "Give me a hand with turning the churn" said Lil wiping the sweat from her brow. I turned and turned for what seemed like an eternity until I was exhausted. "Keep going it's not nearly done yet" she said checking the little glass spy hole in the lid. "You have to keep going until it's butter." At last the spy hole was clear and the butter was made. The churn was opened and she took out big lumps of lovely yellow butter. This she placed on the table and rolled it up and down until all the buttermilk was squeezed out. Salt was added and then further rolling. Next she shaped the butter into rectangular blocks using wooden paddles. These were then placed in greaseproof paper. She placed a couple of pounds in a bag and filled a large can of buttermilk which my mother used for making homemade bread. "Don't forget to collect the eggs before you go" said Christy as I came out of the dairy. This was my favourite job. It was like playing hide and seek with the hens. I went from one little outhouse to another. Each hen had its own particular place for laying. In the hay or high up on a ledge or in the window. When I returned with my little basket full and proudly presented them to Lil she took one glance and said, "I think you missed some, there should be more than that." So I had to go back again.

I was always fascinated seeing Lil making the homemade bread on the open fire. She patted the dough into a round iron pot, put a lid on it and placed it on a rail which swung in over the blazing fire. Then she placed red hot cinders on top of the lid until it baked. Meanwhile I turned the bellows at the side to keep the fire blazing. The result was the most beautiful bread I have ever tasted. In the summertime when everyone was out in the field making hay Lil would arrive with the afternoon tea. Lovely chunks of homemade brown bread covered with homemade butter and homemade jam. We each took a slice of bread and jam with a large mug of piping hot tea, lay back against a cock of hay and tucked in. That is one of my most wonderful memories of life on the farm.

Lil looked after the domestic side of the work on the farm while Jack took care of the fields and the livestock. I followed each cycle of the year with interest and as I grew up I presumed that everyone had the same experience but I soon realised that those who lived in the towns and cities knew nothing of these things, from the ploughing of the fields in the winter to the harrowing and sowing of the crops in the spring, seeing the green corn begin to grow and when it was about two inches high Jack came along with the roller to flatten it down again. This I could never understand, until later I realised it was to give the corn a firm foundation and prevent it from being lodged when the wind and rains came. What a wonderful sight to see a field of barley blowing in the wind as it ripened in the summer sunshine. I ran through it picking the hairy ears, rolling them in my tiny hands and eating the ripe grains. Years later, that scene always came into my mind when I heard Sting singing "Fields of Gold." Then came the cutting of the corn. Jack sat up on the reaper and binder with its great windmill arm, the machine dropping off sheaves as it went along. These were quickly put into stooks by Christy and Paddy who followed close behind. The machine began cutting on the outskirts of the field and gradually came closer and closer to the centre. Everyone gathered around with their pitch forks at the ready for the last little square. There were shouts and roars as the rats and mice and sometimes rabbits darted for cover. They had taken refuge in the middle of the field as the noise of the machine came nearer and nearer. Then there was nowhere to go. I can still see Christy with pitch fork ready to pounce running after a huge rat that had managed to make its escape. These were wonderful summer days as we moved from field to field from oats to wheat to barley. The stooks were later made into stacks in the field and eventually brought into the haggard to be built into reeks for the threshing in the autumn. This was the biggest event of the farm year and I looked forward to it like the coming of Christmas. It was for this that the ploughing was done, the seeds were sown, the corn was cut, the sheaves were stooked, stacked and reeked.

The preparation for the threshing began weeks before. The pig that had been fattened for the occasion had to be killed. This was one event that I never wanted to witness. I saw the table being prepared in the yard and the basins of boiling hot water. I hid in one of the outhouses as the pig was brought to the slaughter. Unlike the lamb, the pig never came quietly. He roared and squealed as Paddy and Christy wrestled with him, catching him by the ears as they dragged him along. It was as though he knew what was about to happen. When the roaring stopped I came out of my hiding place. Lil was pouring the blood from his slit throat into a bucket to be made into black pudding. The pig was washed and scraped and hung up in the shed. He was then cut down the middle and all his guts carefully washed and prepared. Nothing went to waste. Hazel sticks were put in his belly to keep the flesh apart for quick drying. Lil also made plenty of bread on the open fire. Extra butter was made and buckets of buttermilk kept for the thirst, together with a keg of beer.

Late in the evening the threshing engine made its way down the hill towed by a huge steam engine belching steam and smoke into the air. Slowly it was manoeuvred into place in the haggard between the ricks of corn. The driving belt was put on and all was ready for an early start the next day. I went to school with a heavy heart. I might as well not have been there because there was no way I could concentrate on algebra or history or geography. By the time I arrived home the threshing was in full swing. There were men busy at work all around the monstrous machine. Two men sat at the top while others pitched up the sheaves to them. They cut the binding twine and fed them evenly into the machine. The straw came out at the back where others quickly picked it away to be piled high in the barn (here I spent many hour jumping from the rafters of the barn into the straw). It was at the front of the engine that the real reward came. Jack Jordan stood by the sacks as the golden grain poured in. From time to time he put a handful of grain into his mouth to chew. He could almost tell by the taste what the flour would be like. As the grain reached the top of the sack it was removed and another put in its place. The full sacks were loaded onto a cart to be brought to the barn where the grain was poured out on the floor to dry. Once the engine was going there was no time to rest. Each man was like a cog in the great machine. When the engine spluttered its last gasp each man breathed a sigh of relief. They quickly helped themselves to a mug of cold buttermilk. Then they made their way to the house where Lil had prepared a feast. As the threshing machine moved from farm to farm, the farmers vied with one another to produce the best meal. They could never let it be said that the men went hungry. They talked about Lil's meal for months afterwards. She had long tables in the kitchen and the adjoining room. She boiled loads of spuds in three legged pots on the open fire. These were then emptied out onto the table where each man helped himself. Little pots of salt were also left on the table. There were bowls of cabbage, turnips, carrots and parsnips. Each man was given a large chunk of bacon. The meal began and the stories were told: characters they had known and funny incidents that had happened at other threshings down through the years. They drank from the keg of beer and sang songs and all agreed that Jack Jordan's was the best threshing ever. And so it was over for another year.

9

War Breaks Out

On the 3rd of September 1939 my father was listening to the one o'clock news from the B.B.C. It began with a solemn announcement. Prime Minister Chamberlain declares war on Germany:

> "I am speaking to you from the Cabinet Room at 10 Downing St. This morning the British Ambassador in Berlin handed the German Government a final note stating that unless we heard from them by 11 o'clock that they were prepared at once to withdraw their troops from Poland, a state of war would exist between us. I have to tell you now that no such undertaking has been received and that consequently this country is at war with Germany".

Mam, Eddie, Davy, Richie, Me.
Family just back from Sunday walk.

Germany had invaded Poland on the 1st Sept. 1939. De Valera declared Ireland as a small developing nation, neutral. We then entered what was known as the EMERGENCY. The English were furious. Churchill did not really accept our neutrality as being legal. Switzerland and Norway could be neutral but not Ireland. England restricted all trade with Ireland.

Churchill remarked "Let de Valera stew in his own juice". Soon we began to feel the pinch. Oranges and bananas disappeared from the shops. My weekly bar of chocolate was gone and sweets became very scarce. Lent was still a time of fast and abstinence but that was no bother because we gave up oranges and bananas and chocolate. Probably the most difficult thing was the black bread. Although this was better for us we longed for white bread. The shortages were felt much more severely in the city and towns than in the country. We had plenty of fruit and vegetables and Jack Jordan still supplied the extra butter and milk. The farmers were exhorted to grow more corn, wheat, oats, barley and potatoes. No coal could be imported but we had plenty of firewood. Everyone went to the bog to cut turf. Even soldiers were recruited and sent to cut turf much to the their disgust. One young recruit remarked "I joined the army to fight Hitler not to cut turf". Soon rationing was introduced. Everyone had a ration book and you needed coupons to purchase the very basic commodities: tea, sugar, butter, cocoa. Clothes and silk stockings could not be got for love or money except on the black market. Some women took to painting stockings on their legs. One woman arrived at an appointment with no stockings on, the rain had washed them off. There was also petrol rationing. Private cars were put on blocks in garages until after the war. The ordinary mode of transport became the bicycle. But within a short time tyres and tubes could not be got for love or money. The theft of bicycles was the majority of cases brought before the courts. One night all the tyres and tubes were stolen from our bicycles outside the front door. The bicycles were left neatly in a row minus their tyres and tubes. This meant walking everywhere for the next few weeks. But in spite of all the hardship, we did not lose our sense of humour and the music halls produced many songs about the situation, most blaming the Government for their plight.

"Bless them all, bless them all

The long and the short and the tall

Bless de Valera and Sean McEntee

Who gave us brown bread and a half ounce of tea

And they rationed the cocoa and all

And sure it needn't be rationed at all

They're bringing starvation, to our destination

So cheer up, me lads, bless them all".

There was also a spirit of defiance in the air. Churchill was threatening to take back the ports by force and Hitler was planning to invade Ireland as a stepping stone to England. How were we to defend ourselves? So the L.S.F. (Local Security Force) was born. Thousands flocked to Garda stations to join up. Within a week 44,870 had enrolled. Within a month the number had reached 148,306. Almost immediately there were problems. Bad organisation, lack of equipment and the manoeuvres were a joke. They didn't even have uniforms. This was our Dad's Army. Local lads stood at street corners and jeered as they paraded without uniforms. Soon the initial enthusiasm waned and many left. A letter appeared in the L.S.F Gasette. "Lately certain members have been airing their grouses to the Press. Our 'grumbles' do not concern non-members so why spread them abroad? There is no need to let the whole world know". The L.S.F. was later divided into two groups. The L.S.F. under the control of the Gardaí and the L.D.F as auxiliaries to the Army. The L.S.F were to assist the Gardaí. Their duties included traffic control, first aid and distributing ration books. They also went on night patrols in rural areas from 10pm to 6 am, to keep an eye out for enemy parachutists and spies. My father immediately joined up and as an ex-army man was assigned to the L.D.F. He was appointed District Transport Officer for the Wicklow area. He had to catalogue all vehicles in Wicklow that could be brought into service in an emergency. A group of L.D.F. men including Mr. Morrissey met two or three times a week in various towns. Notification of the meetings was spread by word of mouth. I brought the secret messages home from school from Mr. Morrissey. Their first uniforms were made of brown denim but these had the effect of dampening the enthusiasm of the new recruits. A section leader Thomas O'Keeffe wrote; "Strong men who had announced their desire to tackle tanks single handed, paled visibly when they saw how they were to be attired for the fray; many after a single glance stepped out into the night and were never seen again". The brown denims were replaced by green uniforms in 1942. I always enjoyed the first aid exercises which the L.S.F. carried out from time to time. I remember especially one occasion at the Burnt House near Clara. I was a stretcher case with little notes pinned all over me explaining the extent of my injuries. My wounds were almost fatal and I ended up being bandaged up like a mummy. Another function of the L.S.F. and L.D.F. was to take pride of place in the St. Patrick's Day Parade. They also marched to Mass on Sundays and formed a guard of honour for the Bishop when he came for Confirmation. Although they were a very motley group, "the long and the short and the tall", they inspired confidence in the people. After the fall of France in 1940 there were constant rumours of invasion. The army was on high alert and the soldiers were given General Absolution in several barracks.

Dad in bomb crater in the garden at the Copse.

On Friday the 25th of October 1940 myself and Davy went to a concert in Rathdrum market square. Everyone was enjoying the concert and it was nearing the end when suddenly at about ten o'clock some members of the L.S.F. burst in shouting "Extinguish all lights and make your way home as quickly as possible. Bombs have been heard exploding out the Copse road". There was a mad rush for the door. The town was in total darkness as we quickly made our way down the street and out the Copse road. People were running in all directions. At Ballygannon woods we met my mother with Ritchie in her arms running into the town. "The Germans are coming", she shouted, "there are bombs dropping everywhere." Just then my father arrived in a car with other members of the L.S.F. They were on their way to investigate. He brought us home and continued on his way. Tom Meegan came towards us on his bike, rushing in to collect his wife Kate from the concert. His bike was much too big for him and he always cycled from side to side. "I was sitting at the fire reading the paper waiting for the kettle to boil for the supper when the house shook. "The chaps were in bed" he said (he always referred to his daughters as 'chaps'). The 'chaps' screamed with terror.

The mountains are on fire". He kept going. The next day we discovered that four high explosive bombs and incendiary bombs had dropped in a straight line across the valley. The first one fell in the middle of the walled garden at the Copse breaking all the windows in the back of the house. It formed a crater several feet deep and 30 to 40 ft. wide and shattered all the glass in the glasshouse. There were pieces of shrapnel all over the place. The others fell at intervals down to the river. One was delayed action and exploded about two hours later. My most vivid memory was when I visited the craters in the wood; there were bits of rabbits hanging from the fir trees.

Mr. Gilbert said. "I heard the plane and I came out to look when I was blown off my feet with the blast. The windows shattered in the house and as I looked across the valley, the mountains were on fire and I would have thought that this was the safest place in the world". The plane took a sharp turn to the right at Clara Bridge and followed the river to the coast. It was believed to be a German plane that had gone off course. It just unloaded its bombs and headed for Germany. After the war Churchill suggested that Britain might have been responsible for German planes going off course by interfering with radio signals.

10

Hitler Is Dead

We talked about nothing else in school for months beforehand. The lads from the town claimed to know the time and the date but the days passed and nothing happened. Then the Ormonde Cinema opened in the Court house, the old Flannel Hall on the fair green in December 1944. A whole new world opened up to us. The Cinema was packed every night. It provided a great relief from the deprivations of the time. The older people liked the romantic films while we loved the cowboys. Gene Autry and Roy Rodgers were the singing cowboys. The theme of the cowboy films was always the same. Many involved bringing the Indians into submission and stealing their lands. The poor Indians were always the bad guys. The good guys always won. Other bad guys were the bandits or the rustlers who stole cattle or robbed banks and the good guys formed a posse and pursued them into the mountains cutting them off at the pass. We were glued to our seats and cheered them all the way. All through the shooting and killing Gene Autry and Roy Rodgers sang songs around the camp fires with their guitars and singing cowboys. Gene Autry had his faithful horse Champion, while Roy Rodgers had Trigger and he was accompanied by The Sons of the Pioneers. Dale Evans was Roy Rodger's girlfriend. She provided the romantic angle, riding her trusted horse, Buttermilk, she was known as the Queen of the West, while Roy Rodgers was the King of the Cowboys. Together they made over one hundred films and they eventually married in real life. Gene Autry was their great rival. He wrote most of his own songs and each film produced another hit. "The Yellow Rose of Texas", "San Fernando Valley", "Mexicali Rose", "You are my Sunshine", "South of the Border" and "Rudolf the Red Nosed Reindeer". This fantasy world was very real to us. Myself and Richie went to the Cinema on Friday nights and I sang the songs all the way home to the Copse. Although I sang out of tune there was no one to hear me except Richie and he didn't seem to mind. With our cowboy outfits, which we received from Santa, we had hours of fun playing Cowboys and Indians in the woods.

We were now entering the last year of the war. On the 6th of June 1944 Mr. Morrissey began class with a prayer. "Let us stand for a few minutes and say a prayer for all those brave soldiers who died this morning on the beaches of Normandy". I had not heard the news. From then on, each day I followed the arrows in the Paper as the allies got closer and closer to Germany. In the cinema too every week there were war films, some to boost the morale of the troops while others were newsreel of the actual battles. One film that made a great impression on me was "The 49th Parallel", the story of Nazi servicemen trying to reach neutral American land after their U-boat was sunk in the Gulf of the St. Laurence. The manhunt to try to capture them was tense and exciting. The mixture of films was such that one minute we were sad and almost in tears while the next we were howling with laughter. Charlie Chaplin with his funny walk and cane gave us hours of fun. He didn't have to say a word. Laurel and Hardy got into many a fine mess and as we laughed at their misfortunes it cheered us up for the night. Then there was the Marx Brothers and their unique blend of humour and Bud Abbot and Lou Costello. The world of fantasy was no less entertaining and we sat enthralled at such films as The Wizard of Oz and Walt Disney's Snow White and the Seven Dwarfs.

Then one Friday night the usual weekly newsreel, the March of Time showed the Allies liberating a concentration camp. These films were not censored because they wanted the whole world to see in every detail the terrible atrocities committed by the Nazis. Some people got physically sick, while others left the cinema in tears. It showed the British 11th Armoured Division liberating Belsen concentration camp on April 15th 1945. Sixty thousand prisoners were found inside, most of them seriously ill, and another 13,000 corpses lay around the camp unburied. The scenes were horrific. I had never even seen a dead person, now I was looking at bulldozers putting thousands of corpses into pits. Richard Dimbleby graphically describes the scene. "Here over an acre of ground lay dead and dying people. You could not see which was which .... the living lay with their heads against the corpses and around them moved the awful, ghostly procession of emaciated, aimless people. With nothing to do and with no hope of life, unable to move out of the way, unable to look at the terrible sights around them... Babies had been born here, tiny wizened things that could not live. A mother, driven mad, screamed at a British sentry to give her milk for her child, and thrust the tiny mite into his arms, then ran off, crying terribly. He opened the bundle and found the baby had been dead for days".

On Sunday April 30th 1945 Fr. J. O' Dea a Dominican began the yearly Retreat. He was a gentle kindly man and everyone was looking forward to the week. My parents and Davy went every night while myself and Richie stayed at home. I availed of the opportunity to listen to the radio. The eight o'clock News from the B.B.C began with a solemn announcement.

> "Hitler is Dead."
>
> "German radio announced last night that our Führer, Adolf Hitler has fallen this afternoon at his command post in the Reich Chancellery fighting to the last breath against Bolshevism and for Germany".

This was later discovered to be typical German propaganda. On the 30th April in the bunker underneath the Chancellery he had committed suicide with Eva Braun whom he had married the day before. Their bodies were partially burned in the Chancellery garden before the arrival of the Russians. The news travelled like wildfire throughout the world. I couldn't wait to tell everyone the good news. I ran in to Rathdrum to meet the people coming home from the Retreat. The first one I saw coming along on his bike swaying from side to side was Tom Meegan. He could hardly believe the news "And to think he nearly got me with that bomb" he said. Kate was walking behind with my parents. "That's the best sermon we heard tonight" said my father. As we walked home we discussed all the wonderful things we would soon be able to buy in the shops. Germany surrendered on the 8th of May; the war was over.

The death of Hitler was announced in the Irish papers on May 2nd De Valera in a very controversial move went to the German legation in Dublin to offer his condolences. He defended his right to do this as a neutral country, but to do so, when the images from the concentration camps were being shown in the Cinemas , disgusted many.

Churchill in his victory speech at the end of the war spoke very derogatorily about Mr. De Valera and Ireland. Every Irishman felt the insult personally and anxiously awaited De Valera's reply. I remember gathering around the radio on the night of the broadcast with great anticipation. De Valera spoke in a calm and measured tone after some days...

> "Mr. Churchill makes it clear that in certain circumstances he would have violated our neutrality and that he would justify his action by Britain's necessity. It seems strange to me that Mr. Churchill does not see that this, if accepted, would mean that Britain's necessity would become a moral code and that when this necessity become sufficiently great, other people's rights were not to count....this same code is precisely why we have the disastrous succession of wars."

This was De Valera's greatest hour.

11

Don't Mention Sex

Sex was never mentioned when I was growing up. At school or at home the subject never came up. Even when we learned the Catechism off by heart the Sixth and Ninth Commandments were never explained. The Ninth Commandment improper looks, idleness, bad company, all excess in eating and drinking and whatever tends to inflame the passions, may also be deemed immediate occasions of immodest thoughts and desires." None of these things would ever be considered when we were examining our conscience before Confession. When I reached puberty and my body began to change I wasn't aware of what was happening. I began to have erections at all times of the day and night and became very embarrassed and hoped no one would notice. Then there was the million dollar question of where did babies come from. But I was lucky that I lived in the country and saw sex taking place all around me.

One day when I went to collect the buttermilk and butter from Lil Jordan the cow was calving in the cow byre. As I entered Paddy Mac was holding the cow by the head while Christy Byrne had his arm up the cows backside as far as it would go. He had his head by the side of the cow and he was sweating profusely as he pulled as hard as he could. Eventually two little hooves began to appear. Slowly the rest of the calf came out and fell to the ground. The mother turned around and began to lick the calf until it sat up. Soon the little calf was standing on its spindly legs as it suckled milk from its mother's teats. Now at least I knew where calves came from, now I had to find out how it got there. This also happened in a casual way. Jack Jordan had a bull with a chain from its snout. There were many stories of how dangerous the bull was so I always avoided that field or ran quickly through it. One day Christy said "The cow is in heat, I have to bring her to the bull". I went along out of curiosity. As soon as Christy opened the gate the bull made a mad dash to meet her. We quickly shut the gate and observed from a safe distance. As soon as the bull reached the cow he jumped up on her back and made a connection. I had often seen the cows jumping up on other cows as they came in to be milked but this was different. Soon the whole operation was over and as Christy led the cow back to the farm he remarked. "We'll have a lovely little calf in a few months' time". From then on I became more aware of the drakes when they mounted the ducks. The dogs were always at it and of course the rabbits under the big oak trees around the Copse were constantly on top of one another. They were breeding like rabbits.

One Sunday afternoon I was out with the rifle looking for wood pigeons when I noticed something strange about Jack Jordan's horse in the middle of the field. As I came nearer I noticed two hooves sticking out of its backside. I ran across the fields to tell Jack. I hardly had the words out of my mouth when he shouted to Christy to get a rope and some sacking and come quickly. Speed wasn't Christy's strong point as he eventually arrived puffing and panting. While he held the horse's head, Jack tied the rope around the little hooves and with one foot against the horse he began to pull. Soon the little foal began to appear. Quickly a beautiful little foal was born and within minutes it was standing up and feeding from the mother.

When we had eaten all the cocks and my mother wanted a sitting of eggs she sent me to get them from Lil. "Haven't we got plenty of eggs of our own" I said. "They are no good without a cock" she replied. I didn't ask her why. I never saw the bees at it but I was very familiar with the birds. Then I discovered a book called the 'Home Doctor'. There was a couple of chapters on human anatomy. There were even diagrams of the male and female organs. It went on to explain how sexual intercourse takes place. How the male places the seed in the womb and after nine months a baby is born. I read the book secretly over and over again until I felt I understood where babies came from. It was a revelation to me and I couldn't understand why no-one ever told me. But in spite of all this I still couldn't understand the answers in the Catechism.

> "Unchaste thoughts are always very dangerous, and when they are entertained deliberately and with pleasure, they defile the soul like criminal actions."

What's that all about?

12

Cycling To School In Wicklow

I was in my final year at the Boys' National School in Rathdrum. Up to now I had not thought about what I would do when I finished school. One day a Brother Bernard, a De la Salle Brother , came to the school to talk to us about vocations. None of us had an idea what a vocation was. He pointed out what a wonderful thing it was to be called by God to be a De la Salle Brother. He said he would be in Barry's hotel after school if anyone would like to talk to him. The whole idea didn't appeal to me and I thought no more about it. That afternoon I was coming down the town with Johnny Mac and as I passed Barry's hotel I said "That's where your man said he would be after school". With that the door of the hotel opened and there was Brother Bernard beckoning me to come in. "No, I said, "I'm just passing on my way home". Johnny Mac ran down the street. "Just come in for a minute" he said "I won't keep you long".

He brought me in to the sitting room where there were two big arm chairs he sat in one and he put me in the other. I was trapped. How could I get out of this? As he began to talk I got a brainwave. "I was thinking of being a priest" I said. His eyes lit up when I said this and he said "That is wonderful, my young man, I'm sure you will make a great priest". "I won't detain you so" he continued and stood up to let me go. "I will pray for you" he said as he waved me goodbye. Johnny Mac was waiting for me at the bottom of the street laughing his head off. "How did you get on" he asked. "Are you going to be a Brother?" "Certainly not" I answered, "but I told him you would love to be a Brother but you hadn't the courage". "What did you tell him that for" he said. "What did he say?" "He said he would be back next week to see you". "I won't be around he said as he hurried home down the lower street with a worried look on his face I never mentioned anything about Bro. Bernard when I got home.

That summer I had to decide what I was going to do when I left school. The nearest secondary school was in Wicklow at the De la Salle College. The better off people sent their children to boarding school. One day when I was helping my father in the garden he wondered would I be able to cycle into Wicklow every day. I jumped at the suggestion and the following Saturday we both cycled into Wicklow to try it out. We went to the De la Salle College and met Bro. Francis the head master. He showed us around the College and said there were many pupils who cycled long distances from all around Wicklow every day. Looking at me he added that he didn't think it would be a problem for a strong lad like me.

I left home every morning about 7.30 am for the long journey. I flew down Lower Street in Rathdrum as far as the mill. Then there was a stiff climb up around the rock. There were no steep hills from there to Glenealy and from there on to Wicklow it was all downhill. It was a different story coming home especially if there was a wind in your face and it was raining. My cape and leggings acted as a buffer that almost blew me backwards. First year was a completely new experience for me. A separate classroom with a different teacher for every subject, the majority being Brothers. They wore long black robes with two little white bibs sticking down in front. I could never imagine myself being one of them. I was introduced to new subjects: Latin, Algebra, Geometry and accountancy. Discipline was strict but the Brothers administered corporal punishment sparingly, although they all carried a leather strap. The same could not be said for some of the lay teachers especially one who wielded a heavy stick. I was lucky he didn't teach first year. Religious Knowledge took pride of place where we moved beyond the Catechism to discussing Religious subjects. One day when Bro Cuthbert was busy at the blackboard explaining quadratic equations the door suddenly opened and there stood Bro. Bernard. He looked towards me and beckoned me to come out. "There is a Carmelite priest in the parlour who would like to talk to you" he said. I couldn't imagine what he wanted. As I entered the parlour there was a tall stout priest with a flushed complexion waiting for me.

First year at De la Salle College Wicklow 1947.

"This young man is thinking of becoming a priest" said Bro. Cuthbert as he introduced me. I sat down nervously beside him. "I'm a Wicklow man too" he said. "What part are you from?" "I live in Rathdrum" I answered, "near the meeting of the waters" he said. "Yes" I said, "but on the other side of the town on the way to Glendalough. "Have you ever heard of the Carmelites?" he asked. "No" I said.

"The Carmelites are the oldest order in the Church" he continued. "We are dedicated to Our Blessed Lady of Mr. Carmel. We have just sent three men on a new mission to Rhodesia in Africa". With the mention of Africa I began to get interested. The week before I had seen Spencer Tracey in "Stanley and Livingston". It looked to be a beautiful country with lovely scenery and many wild animals and birds. "The poor people are pagans" he continued "crying out for the faith but at the moment we haven't any more priests to send. We really need young men like you to carry on the work of spreading the Good News." He showed me pictures of the country and the people. After a while he looked at his watch and said, "I mustn't keep you from class any longer, think about it". With that he said "goodbye" and I returned to class. I never let on what I was called out for. I finished my first year in Wicklow in June and as I began my summer holidays I looked forward to returning in September.

13

Life Is Full Of Surprises

The Smyth's didn't come on their holidays that year. Their children had all grown up and they didn't come as often to the Copse. One day they suddenly announced that they would have to sell the Copse. After the war they had been compensated for the bombing and they also sold a small wood of pine trees for £10,000. This was more than they had paid for the Copse some years before. The news came as a bombshell to all of us as it made our future uncertain. Would the new owners want us to stay on.? At this stage of his life it would be difficult for my father to get another job. Day after day my parents showed prospective buyers around the place. They all seemed interested but weeks went by and nothing happened. Then one day a couple came from Cawnpore in India. They were Mr. and Mrs Horsman and they immediately fell in love with the place. They wanted to buy it there and then as it was with all the furniture. I was mowing the tennis court when Mrs Horsman came to talk to me. She was delighted to hear that I was part of the family. She said we would soon get to know each other better. They had already asked my father and mother to stay on and look after the place. But they had a major problem and asked my parents could they help. They would have to remain in India for another year to arrange everything but they would like their daughter Alicia to come immediately; "Would you be able to accept her into your family?

"You mean live with us?" asked my mother.

"Yes" they said "if you wouldn't mind".

"We would be honoured" said my mother, "if she wouldn't mind living in our humble home".

"She would be delighted and her governess will bring her over and leave her with you", Alicia's mother replied.

And so it was that one day a beautiful Indian girl dressed in a sari with black hair and a black spot painted on her forehead arrived with Alicia. We all fell in love with Alicia at first sight. She was about eight years of age and dressed in beautiful clothes. Her cases contained lovely fluffy towels from the cotton mill in Cawnpore. We gave her the best room in the house with the most comfortable bed. It was a wonderful experience to welcome a sister into the family and she was already eight years of age. She spoke with a pronounced English accent but she had no trouble understanding us. She thought we spoke quite funny. She was prepared to eat whatever was produced but we soon learned the things she liked. I read her bedtime stories before she went to sleep. She also loved to sit on my knee while I sang 'Delaney's Donkey' to her. She hopped up and down as if she was riding it. She loved the part where Riley was "pulling it and pushing it"

"There was Riley pushing it, shoving it shushing it

Hogan, Logan and everyone in town,

Lined up attacking it, shoving it and smacking it

They might as well have tried to push the town hall down.

The donkey was eyeing them, openly defying them

Winking, blinking, twisting out of place

Riley reversing it, everybody cursing it

The day Delany's donkey ran the half mile race."

***

Alicia on Delaney's Donkey which she loved

One day when I arrived back from hunting in the woods there was a priest at home talking to my parents. He was Fr. Meagher, a Carmelite from Wicklow. He was tired and sweating having cycled all the way from Wicklow. "I don't know how you do it every day" he said to me as I came in. My Mother made him a cup of tea. He said he was a teacher in Terenure College in Dublin and he had heard that I was thinking of becoming a Carmelite.

"I'm still thinking about it" I said, "I'm not sure yet."

"You have plenty of time" he said. "You have just finished first year and I believe you did very well in your exams".

"I just got my results the other day" I said. "I got a medal for excellence".

"Would you like to come to Terenure College as a boarder?" he asked. "It would mean you would have more time for study and you wouldn't have to cycle into Wicklow every day".

At this my father intervened. "That would be wonderful but I'm afraid I would not be able to afford the fees. I have four sons and I would like to treat them all the same".

"That would not be a problem" replied the priest. "We can help you out there; you would only have to pay what you can afford". At this point my mother turned to me and asked. "Would you like to go?". "Well it would save me cycling into Wicklow every day and I could get to know the Carmelites, I said. There was an expression of joy and sadness on my parents faces as they agreed that I could go to Terenure College.

14
Terenure College

It was a bright September morning when myself and my father took the bus from the market square in Rathdrum to Dublin. My neatly packed case was placed on top of the bus. The College had sent a list of all the things I would need including sheets and pillow cases. As we took the seat nearest the door I could already smell the stale smoke which filled the bus. I hated travelling by bus because I always got sick from the smoke. We had hardly reached the mill when I began to feel sick. I stood by the door for a while and I felt better. As we climbed the hill around the rock I remembered how I puffed and panted on the bike to reach the top. I knew every field and tree as we passed along. Passing the Church in Glenealy it was freewheel all the way to Rathnew. I was sad to leave the Copse with all its familiar memories: shooting the wood pigeon and the rabbits, hunting the deer and the pheasants, looking for birds' nests and trying to catch a squirrel. Alicia had told me that she wouldn't be around when I was leaving. She hated saying goodbye. She said she got butterflies in her stomach and she didn't like them. "I will hide in the wood until you are gone, and then I will cry," she said.

When we arrived in Dublin we went to the Pillar to get the number three bus to Sandymount where we would stay with my Aunt Molly for the night. We waited in the queue but the buses were full. Then one came along and as I went to follow my father on , the conductor put out his hand and shouted 'bus full' there will be another along in a minute." I was left standing at the front of the queue. I was lucky I had money for the ticket but I didn't know where to get off. I passed some very anxious moments as the bus sped along from stop to stop taking on more passengers all the time. As we came around a corner I saw The Star of the Sea Church and remembered that was where I was baptized and I got out at the next stop. My father was there. "I knew you would find your way" he said as calm as you like.

The next day we set out for Terenure College. We went back to the Pillar and took a tram to Terenure. I loved travelling on top of the tram and watching the world go by. My father was very familiar with Terenure village and its surrounding After leaving school he had worked as a groom just up the road. Every day he had passed Terenure College, little thinking that one day his son would go to school there. As we got off the tram he said "We'll get a taxi here so that we can arrive in style." We made our way to Thornton's garage and asked a mechanic who was working on a car, could we get a taxi.

"Certainly Sir" he said. "Where to?"

"Terenure College" replied my father.

"Sure that's just up the road" he said, "You don't need a taxi to get there."

"But we have a heavy case" explained my father.

"OK then, hop in"

Turning in the big gates off the Templeogue Road, we drove up the avenue past the football fields on either side to the main door of the old building. Ringing the bell, we were ushered into the hall where there were three or four Carmelites to greet us. To my amazement they were dressed in long brown habits with hoods. I could never see myself wearing one of these. How could I run or play football? They really looked elegant as they stood in this beautiful hall with tiled floor. There was a winding stairs to the left leading up to a long veranda. To the right a side board with a crucifix and some statues adorned with vases of flowers. What do you talk to priests in brown habits about? We were awestruck. We just answered questions yes or no. With that we were shown into a massive parlour adorned with antique furniture. We sat down at a magnificent mahogany table while Fr. Meagher sent for a boy to show me around. Soon the door opened and Conal Collier came in. He had been in the College for some years and would be happy to show me to the dormitory. I said goodbye to my father surrounded by the priests and he walked out the door alone. Conal carried my case up the winding stairs and into a vast dormitory. There were three rows of beds stretching the full length of the dormitory with little lockers between each one. There was no privacy. Most of the beds were already taken. Conal showed me my bed in the middle row near the door. Leading off the dormitory was a large wash hall with rows of washbasins and toilets at one end. As I looked out the window I saw my father walking down the avenue alone. He cut a very lonely figure as he walked slowly along. My aunt Molly told me that when he returned he cried his eyes out. "That's the beginning of the end" he sobbed.

We walked down a long corridor where the classrooms were. He showed me into an old classroom with old wooden desks and dusty blackboards. "This is where you will be," he said. "We have beautiful classrooms in the new wing." We passed into a big hall with large windows and ascended a terrazzo staircase to the new classrooms. There were very modern windows down one side, new desks and green blackboards. "I will have to leave you now" said Conal. "I'm going into the city to the pictures. Would you like to come?"

"No" I said, "I think I'll look around a bit more."

I didn't get much sleep that night and I was wide awake at 7.15am. The next morning when suddenly Fr. Keenan arrived clapping his hands and shouting "Everyone up, feet on the floor." Anyone who hesitated had their bed clothes pulled down. We gathered our towel and soap and there was a mad rush to the wash room where we washed in cold water. Then we made our way to the chapel for morning Mass. Masses were already being celebrated on the side altars. A boy was serving each one, ringing a little bell at the consecration as he held up the chasuble. There was a constant murmur of Latin all around as we waited for the priest to come out on the main altar. After Mass we marched to the refectory for breakfast: a bowl of porridge with tea and bread and a little pat of butter. I soon learned you could have extra food in your locker and bring it to the refectory as needed, jam, butter and cakes were the usual fare. We sat at long tables according to our year. Pat served the tea from a big pot as we each held up our cup. As I made my way up to the classrooms one of the prefects said Fr. O'Connor, the Dean of Studies wanted to see me in his office. Fr. O'Connor was a small man with a bald head and a rasping voice. He looked up over his glasses as I entered the office. "Sit down" he said. "I see you did very well in your first year exams, I'm sure you will do well with your studies here. I think you would be able to skip second year and go straight into third year. That would mean you would be doing your intermediate Certificate in June. I think you would be able for the A class. There are a lot of wasters in the B class and they would only hold you back. Your classroom is on the second floor."

The priests wore their brown habits while the lay teachers wore gowns. It appeared very formal. I soon learned that the teachers had nicknames, none very complimentary but very apt. There was Twiggy, Johnny Bear, Bunsen Burner, the Lib and the Huille. Mr Griffin was the latin teacher, he was the huille. He lived in the College and had been there for years. He made Virgil's Aeneid come alive as he walked back and forth across the room. He spoke so fast that he frothed at the mouth and sprayed spittle on the unfortunates in the front desks. There was a science laboratory where we did experiments with Bunsen Burner. We went to the Geography room for geography, that's where the maps were. Mr. Goddard took us for physical culture in the new concert hall. We did all kinds of physical jerks and practiced somersaults over the wooden horse.

Jumping in the lineout at cup match in Donnybrook on a very wet day 1951.

Sports day Terenure College, 1950.

Winning the long jump, 1950.

After class we all togged out for rugby. I was assigned to the second seniors. Nobody ever taught me the rules of the game. I soon learned you jumped high in the line out, passed the ball back and tried to score over the line. There was a half day on Wednesday and Saturday when we played matches against other schools. Our great rivals were Blackrock College. They had to be beaten at all costs. We also played St. Mary's, C.U.S. Castleknock, St Columba's, Wesley, Newbridge, Clongowes, Belvedere, and many more. Fr. Hegarty had a little cobbler shop underneath the stairs. He could put studs in your boots while you waited. We loved gathering around to watch him as he hammered away on the last. Whenever he hit his finger he would exclaim "Feck it" much to everyones amusement. We never heard a priest cursing before.

There was a great emphasis on religion in everything we did. It was just taken for granted. Apart from morning Mass there were confessions once a week.At break times many paid a visit to the Blessed Sacrament, but we soon learned that this was very dangerous if Bro. Franco had just polished the floor. He would chase you down the corridor for daring to walk on the shiny floor. Feast days were celebrated with a special Mass and then a half day with a film in the concert hall that night. Two weeks after arriving there was a three day Retreat with lectures in the chapel and total silence. It ended with a free day and "A night at the Opera" with the Marx Brothers.

It didn't take long to get into the routine of college life. It was like one big happy family with the older boys helping the younger ones. There was always the one that got homesick and couldn't settle down. There was a concert in the first term for all the newcomers to the College. Everyone was expected to do their party piece on the stage. As I couldn't sing, I did my recitation, "Albert and the Lion" and "Life gets tedious don't it." There was a lad from Cork called Denis O' Flynn who was immediately nick named 'Corky'. He was a great story teller and he had a fund of corny jokes, but his real forte was imitating Al Jolson. He blackened his face and gave a wonderful rendition of "Mammy". He really took the house down. The only problem was he didn't know when to stop. They almost had to haul him off the stage with a big hook.

Pope John XXIII was asked how he was feeling as he lay dying and he remarked. "Just like a schoolboy going home for the holidays." I know exactly what he meant. I didn't get sick on the bus home. As I approached the gate the first one to greet me was my dog Cane, closely followed by Alicia. She ran towards me and gave me a big hug. "Will you sing Delaney's Donkey?" she asked. My mother said. "The cakes are not iced yet, we were waiting for you." It was great to be back. The next day I went hunting with my gun and ended up in the farm across the hill. Everyone was delighted to see me. "How are you getting on with the high life in Dublin?" said Christy. "It's great to be back," I said. "I hear you are thinking of joining the Church" said Jack. "That's a long way off, if it ever happens," I replied. "Well, I'll be at your first Mass in Rathdrum" he said. "How could you go to Mass?" said Christy "and you a Protestant!" "That doesn't matter" said Jack, "I'll be there." "You will be very welcome, Jack" I said. Lil beckoned me to follow her out to the barn where there was a big fat turkey hanging from the rafters. "Take that home to your mother" she said "and have a lovely Christmas."

On a day out in the Wicklow Hills, 1950.

O' Connell Bridge 1949.

That was a wonderful Christmas with all the family together and especially Alicia. You only really appreciate home when you go away. As we sat around the table one evening my mother remarked "You must find the house very small after the big rooms in Terenure." "It's not the size of the house that matters" I said "its the people in it." Santa Claus brought some lovely presents that year. On Christmas morning I went into Alicia to wish her a happy Christmas. She sat up in the bed and wiping her eyes she said, "Today is the day that little Jesus was born. So before I wish you a Happy Christmas I would like to say. Happy Birthday Jesus."

My time in Terenure was very pleasant and I was very happy there.

***

By now the Horsmans had moved into the Copse and Alicia had gone to live in the big house. They followed the English custom of dressing for dinner at 8pm. Alicia had become accustomed to eating at six so she usually had her tea with us. By the time 8 o'clock came she was full and her parents were worried that she wasn't well when she didn't eat her supper. The Horsmans immediately accepted us as part of the family and we did everything together. Mrs Horsman was a lovely person. She loved coming down to us for dinner or to make toffee. At other times she asked me into the sitting room for a chat. One day she asked me what I was going to do when I left Terenure. "I am thinking of being a priest" I said. With a surprised look she said, "What a wasted life, after your parents working so hard to send you to college. "I hope to go on the Missions to Africa" I continued. "Your poor parents" she said. Some weeks after that I was playing tennis with Alicia, hitting the ball gently back and forth to her. The window opened and Mrs. Horsman beckoned for me to go in and join her. "I've been thinking about what you said and I think you would make a wonderful priest. Don't let anything stop you and I'm sure you will be very happy." With that she went over to a drawer and took out a miniature painting of The Nativity by a famous Italian artist. "This was my Mother's" she said, "and I would love you to have it".

15

Hitchhiking To Rome

On Christmas Eve, 1949, His Holiness Pope Pius XII lifted a gold encrusted hammer and struck it three times against the Holy Door of St. Peter's. As the door was pulled back into the Church's interior The Pope crossed the threshold and the Holy Year of 1950 solemnly began. I was determined to walk through that door before the year was over. I had no idea how I would do it but I was determined to try. My first problem was to get my parents to agree. I knew my father would not be a problem. When I mentioned I was thinking of hitch-hiking to Rome he thought it was a great idea. After all he had run away from home to join the British army and fight in France. What could be worse than that? "I think you will have a problem with your mother, though" he said. "She will be happy you are going to Rome but hitch-hiking is another matter." I broached the subject casually one day. "Wouldn't it be great to go on pilgrimage to Rome for the Holy Year," I said. "If you had the money" She said. "Maybe you could do it on the cheap," I continued. "I don't know of any cheap way" she said. "I could hitch-hike," I said quickly. "Hitch-hike!" she exclaimed, "That would be very dangerous. You would never know who you might meet on the way. There are some very strange characters in those foreign countries" she said. "I wouldn't go on my own," I continued, "I'd go with a couple of lads from the College." With that my father butted in and said. "That would be much safer; you could look out for one another." By now my mother was coming around, I was almost there.

One day I was chatting to Corky and I mentioned that I was thinking of hitch-hiking to Rome for the Holy Year, and would he like to join me. "You mean walk to Rome?" he said. "No," I said, hitch-hike, get lifts." You'll never get there" he continued. Hillaire Belloc did and he wrote a lovely book about his travels, giving a description of the people and places he encountered as he walked down through France , over the Alps and down to Rome. Hannibal also did it and he brought elephants." "If you are going, I'll come with you" he said. "Is it just the two of us?" "I was thinking of asking someone else" I said. "I thought three would be better, in case we had a row on the way." After a rugby match one day as we were having a shower I asked John O'Connor would he like to go to Rome. "Would I what" he said, "I'd love it, but where would I get the money?" "We could hitch-hike" I said, "and it wouldn't cost much." "Just the two of us?" he asked. "No," I said "Corky is thinking of coming." "That eejit?" he said laughing. "Sure we would never get there with him, he'd be singing all the time." "He'd be good for keeping our spirits up with his corny jokes." I said. The seeds were sown and from then on it was preparations all the way. John said we could rely on him for French, so we would have no trouble in France. Corky said he would study Italian, he bought Hugo's Italian in ten easy lessons. I planned the route and the bare essentials we would need for the journey. We would travel in shorts with a heavy haversack and large sun hat. One of the priests suggested we bring a supply of cigarettes, not to smoke, but as tips for the Italians. They loved Irish cigarettes.

Hitch-Hiking To Rome

From left: Masters John O'Connor, Christopher Conroy, and Denis O'Flynn, pupils of Terenure College, who are hitch-hiking to Rome.

Three students of Terenure College, Dublin, left Dun Laoghaire by mail boat last night on the first stage of a hitch-hiking journey to Rome.

They are Denis O'Flynn (16), Ballyvolane House, Cork; Christopher Conroy (17), The Copse, Rathdrum, Co. Wicklow; and John O'Connor (16), Lakelands Park, Terenure. The first two are boarders in the College and the third a day pupil.

The boys, who were interviewed by an *Irish Independent* representative before their departure, were enthusiastic about their trip. They will travel from Newhaven to Dieppe and thence to Paris, and from that stage onwards they will be "using their thumbs."

Continental residents will have no doubts about the nationality of these young men. Apart from a small Tricolour which they carry, one of the trio wears a green beret and the other pair straw hats adorned with green, white and orange. With the welcome which, by all acounts, Irish citizens are accorded on the Continent, the boys should have a reasonably easy passage. They are members of An Oige.

Irish Independent 1950.
The Three Musketeers off to Rome.

On the streets of Paris looking for a lift.

All hands on deck preparing a meal after a long days walk.

We set out on the 2nd of August 1950. We had our photos taken on top of Independent House with our big hats and waving the Irish flag. We were described as intrepid travellers setting out on a perilous journey to the Holy City. On arrival at Dieppe, Johnny asked a porter which was the train to Paris and he discovered that the porter expected a tip for just pointing to the train. In our carriage we met an American film star. He was a brother of the famous Jean Peters the star of many films. He talked about making cowboy films in the States and now he was on his way to Paris to make a film. He had made films with John Wayne and Gene Autry. When we told him we were hitch- hiking to Rome he thought it was a crazy idea but he wished us luck. In Paris he showed us the way to the Metro which would take us to the Youth Hostel, called Camp Volants. The Metro at this time of night was packed which meant that we were pushed out with our haversacks at each station and had to quickly scramble back before the train took off again. Arriving out of the Metro feeling lucky to be alive , we were in the middle of the hustle and bustle of Paris. Which way to the hostel?, Johnny tried asking a passer-by in his best French, but they didn't understand a word. "Wait until we get to Italy " said Corky, "we'll have no trouble with the language." Just then we were passing the 'Follies Bergeres with its bright lights and enticing photos. "I wonder would they let us in if I sang," said Corky. "Not a chance" I said "we are on a pilgrimage." When we did find the 'Camp Volants' it was full, we were turned away. We found a cheap hotel just around the corner . It wasn't the lap of luxury but we couldn't care less, we crashed out on the bed and fell fast asleep.

The next day our mission was to go to the fruit market at Les Halles where we hoped to find an empty fruit lorry returning to the south of France. The fruit market was an enormous place with sheds of fruit stacked sky high. "I was expecting something like Moore St.," said John as we walked around. John approached a man at one of the stalls and asked "Are there any lorries going to the South of France, the Riviera?" asked John. "Un moment" he replied as he went off to telephone. He came back all smiles and said "Oui, Oui, my friend, this evening at 5 o'clock," as he held up the fingers of one hand. There would be twelve other people with us. The lorry was enormous but when they opened up the back it was almost full of empty boxes. We all squeezed into a space that would hardly hold five. I sat down with my head between my knees. John and Corky sat on an old wooden box. There were Germans, Dutch, Belgian, two French lads and a large black lady with her son. She took up more space than the three of us. There was a German couple who appeared to be on their honeymoon. The Germans spoke angrily to Corky when he encroached on their space. He didn't understand a word but he knew what they meant. The covers were drawn and we started off on a nightmare journey. The driver said we were going to Orange and we would arrive tomorrow evening. We rattled along through the cobble stoned streets of Paris at a hectic speed. We were tired, hungry, cramped, as we tried to sleep in fits and starts. At one stage Corky said he might sing to cheer people up but we advised against it. In the middle of the night the two French lads started a fight. We realized it was serious when they drew knives. Two of the Germans intervened and disarmed them and they eventually calmed down. I recalled my mother saying "that would be very dangerous."

This was our abode for the night, beggars can't be choosers.

On the beach at Nice after a lovely swim

Taken on top of Independent House before setting out on our trip to Rome.

It was late in the evening when we reached our destination. We could hardly stand up with cramps but we decided we would walk outside the town and camp for the night. We bought some tomatoes which were very cheap together with two baguettes and some butter for supper. We later discovered we could collect tomatoes from the fields as we walked along. We decided to camp in a nearby field. We lit a fire to boil the water for the tea, put out our food on the ground sheet for our picnic. We were just about to start when suddenly a silvery snake wriggled across the groundsheet and scared the wits out of us. It disappeared as soon as it appeared. Corky was visibly shaken and he ran down the road to a caravan that we had noticed on the way up. The Dutch couple reassured him that the snake was harmless, and we had nothing to worry about. Nevertheless, discretion is the better part of valour, so we moved our camp to a nearby cluster of trees. We didn't feel like eating so we took out our sleeping bags and settled down for the night. Although we were exhausted we couldn't sleep. At every strange sound Corky jumped up thinking it was another snake. We had been warned to bring muslin to put around our faces in the open at night to keep off the mosquitoes. We looked like three ghosts in the dark.

The sun was blazing down on us as we set out on the road to Avignon. We soon realized that Sunday was not a good day for hitch-hiking. By now our water bottles were empty so we called at the next house for a refill. It was a German couple who had stayed in France after the war. They brought us in and gave us wine and more grapes. The Irish flag was a great advantage. Everyone seemed to love Ireland. It was night fall when we eventually reached Avignon. Corky burst into song as he danced across the bridge. "Sur le pont d'Avignon, on y danse, on y danse." In the distance the Palace of the Popes was beautifully illuminated against the starry sky. We prepared our supper in the hostel of tea, bagette, a tin of sardines, hard boiled eggs and some of the leftover tomatoes. Everything tasted the same. As usual we were very tired and just stretched out on our bunks and fell fast asleep. Early next morning we went on a tour of the city. Avignon is a beautiful renaissance city of museums, monuments, churches, chapels, magnificent buildings and restaurants. The later was out of our reach so we made our way to the Palace of the Popes. Clement V set up court here at the beginning of the fourteenth century. The sojourn of the Popes here wasn't the most illustrious in the history of the Catholic Church. "It's a pity the Pope is not still here" said Corky, as we left the city, "we wouldn't have to go any further."

We continued on to Aix-en- Provence. As we sat down in the shade of some trees for a rest, we heard a sudden screech of brakes. As we looked up, we saw the Irish flag and realized it was an Irish car. It was Eugene Davy, the famous rugby international, with a party of three others on their way to Rome. Although the car was already full he squeezed us in and brought us to Aix-en-Provence where he treated us to a lovely meal. After a long chat we waved goodbye and they continued on their way. We continued on foot to Brignoles. After about twenty kilometres as darkness fell near St. Maximim we began to look for a place to sleep. We were about to settle down in a farm outhouse when an angry farmer chased us away. We entered a field on the mountain side when the farmer returned apparently sorry for his hasty temper, and led us to an old bus where we could sleep for the night. At least we had a roof over our heads and we slept soundly through the night. The next day we continued to Brignoles but the going was tough. Many people cheered merrily at us but nobody stopped. As we had something to eat in Brignoles a Frenchman in a big car asked us would we like a lift to Nice. Would we what! He hardly had the words out of his mouth when we were in the back of the car. The man didn't speak any English so we had plenty of time to admire the wonderful scenery. Suddenly as we turned a corner we got our first glimpse of Cannes and the blue waters of the Mediterranean. Soon we were driving along this beautiful seaside resort.

Our friend left us at the outskirts of Nice and pointed to the trolley bus that would take us to the hostel. We booked in and had our first shower since we left Ireland. That evening we went for a walk along the Promenade des Anglais. This is the lovely walkway around the bay. It was built by the English visitors in the nineteenth Century. Queen Victoria first came here in 1882. She called it her "Paradise of Nature" and she returned year after year for her winter break. We were completely captivated by the magic of it all. It made up for all the hardship we had endured along the way. "I could stay here for ever" said Corky as he sang along to the music of the orchestras "Not a bad idea" said John. "I think we'll stay for two days at least." I added, "I'd love a swim in the sea in the morning." The motion was carried unanimously. For the next two days we just swam and sunbathed on the beach. We would have loved to stay longer but Rome was calling and we had to be on our way. As we left we understood how Queen Victoria felt when she was dying: " Oh, if only I were at Nice, I should recover."

We took a bus to Monte Carlo to see the Casino. The beauty of the Riviera continues to Monte Carlo. We didn't manage to see Prince Ranier but we did get a glimpse of his palace. We went to find the Casino, a beautiful building with a series of steps leading up to a great door with two guards standing at the entrance. As we took some photos Corky said "Let's go in and have a look around." We climbed the steps and headed for the door. The two guards blocked our way and we didn't have to know the language to realize that we couldn't go in. As we came away with our tails between our legs, Corky remarked, "Ah well, it was worth the gamble." We continued on to Mentone where we crossed the border into Italy. The scenery changed There were beautiful flower gardens on along the road. To our surprise most of the buildings were in ruins. They had not been repaired since the war. This was the legacy that Mussolini left his people by joining with Hitler in the war. Most of the country was left in ruins as the Allies advanced up the coast. The coastline was bombarded from air and sea.

We walked on to Bordighera. Here we stayed at the Don Bosco seminary. The next day we were on our way to San Remo arriving in the evening. We went to the parish priest's house but I think he thought we were beggars. "No room" he said sternly. Then John produced a letter in Italian which the Prior of Terenure College had given him. As he read it he mellowed and showed us to a room with two ping pong tables. "Beds" he said, as he left. The harder the bed the better we slept. We dozed off dreaming about a beautiful day. The next morning we were awoken by some boys coming to play ping pong. The parish priest arrived and asked us for our passports. It seemed he didn't believe we were pilgrims at all. We certainly didn't look very elegant. As he handed them back to us he said "goodbye". Our hope of breakfast was dashed.

As we walked out of San Remo we helped ourselves to some peaches from a garden. Eventually a lorry stopped and gave us a lift to Genoa. We went to the railway station to look for the Holy Year office. They directed us to the Franciscan seminary just up the road. We tried to explain to the Franciscan priest that we were very hungry but he didn't seem to understand. We pointed to our mouths and he led us to the refectory where he gave us hard boiled eggs and bread. Then he proceeded to lead us to the garret. Up and up we went and round and round on a flight of never ending stairs. "You sleep here" he said pointing to a stone floor. We imagined this must be the punishment cell for the misbehaving monks. We were so tired we could have slept on an iceberg. After breakfast next morning we left our haversacks at the monastery and went for a walk around the city. Looking out to sea is a magnificent statue of Christopher Columbus, who discovered America. Who was born here in 1451. He discovered America by accident. He set out from Spain with his three ships, the Pinta, the Nina and the Santa Maria to find a westward passage to the Orient. Ten weeks later he landed on an island called Hispaniola later to be called El Salvador. Believing he had reached the "Indies" the newcomers dubbed the natives "Indians". As I walked around I remembered that it was here that Daniel O 'Connell died in 1847 on his pilgrimage to Rome. He had requested that his heart be buried in the Irish College in Rome while his body lies in the O'Connell monument at Glasnevin.

The next day we met an American couple mending a puncture. We gave them a helping hand and in return they gave us a lift to Pisa. We stopped at a little village and they treated us to lunch. Again it was dark by the time we reached Pisa. Saying goodbye to our American friends we made our way down little streets looking for the priests house. Everyone stared at us as if we were spirits from another world. I didn't know whether it was the hats, or the shorts or our lean and hungry look. The priest gave us beds for the night and then gave us tickets for a nearby café. We looked over the door and read "La Populaire Café". We handed over our tickets and as we sat down we noticed we were the only ones there. We were really enjoying our meal when the door suddenly opened and about a dozen tramps entered: vagabonds, blackbeards, ruffians, all dressed much worse that we were if that was possible. Obviously they had just come from the parish priest. We finished up quickly and headed back to our beds. We were enjoying the luxury of a real bed when we discovered there was a catch. The place was full of mosquitoes and we hadn't put on the muslin. From time to time we woke up to discover them buzzing away about an inch from our noses. But it was only in the morning we discovered the damage mosquitoes can do. We were completely disfigured and itching all over. I was bitten in the most intimate places but John escaped with just a few bites. As Corky woke up he said "I wonder where the Leaning Tower is? It would be a pity to come to Pisa and miss it." We asked the parish priest but he looked puzzled. "Ah" he said, "Torre Pendente di Pisa!" He pulled back the curtain and there it was. How stupid can you get. We spent some time taking photos from all angles. Its a free standing bell tower of the Cathedral of Pisa. There was an ice cream seller nearby so we bought some. Italian ice cream is the most delicious in the world. He had been selling ice cream here for years and now he could speak seven languages. At least a few phrases from each. As we left Pisa we all agreed that if it wasn't for its leaning tower there was nothing in it.

We walked and walked all day without getting a lift of any kind. Towards evening we were helping ourselves to some fruit from a farmer's field when he caught us red handed. He could speak some English and he began to shout at us and wave a heavy stick. We calmly stared back at him and said "Ni thuigimid" We pretended not to understand English and waved the Irish flag at him. When he realized we weren't English he calmed down and told us we could sleep in his hay barn for the night. We fell asleep scratching our mosquito bites that become very itchy at night. The next day we faired no better with regard to lifts. The fact that we were getting nearer and nearer spurred us on. That night we were so tired and footsore we just crashed out in a field and fell asleep. Although the days were very hot the nights got very cold. John and Corky woke up in the middle of the night with their teeth chattering. Their nylon sleeping bags were as cold as fridges. The fellow in the shop said they would keep you as snug as a bug in a rug in all temperatures. "I'll be paying that fellow a visit when I get back" said Corky. I was lucky I had a woolen one. As we awoke next morning through the haze we could see an island out in the distance. "That's Elba where Napoleon was imprisoned" said John, reading from his tourist guide. We set off with renewed energy knowing that Rome was just a hundred kilometres away.

That evening we arrived at the outskirts of Rome. Corky asked a passer-by how to get to the Holy Year offices. He told us to take an MB bus which would leave us near St. Peter's Square. We turned towards one another and said. "We made it, we are here at last." The man behind a big desk welcomed us to Rome. He examined our passports and when we told him we had hitch-hiked from Ireland he gave us four free days' stay in Rome. It was like getting the freedom of the city. We had free lodgings, food, and travel for four days. He also gave us Holy Year medals and a booklet in English of places to see. We went immediately to our hostel to settle down for the night We had beds in a big dormitory like in Terenure College. There was an archbishop from the north of Italy in the bed next to me. He was here with a group from his diocese. We had a wonderful meal of spaghetti bolognese washed down with a big jug of wine. Bishops and clergy mixed freely with the riff raff recounting their adventures in a multitude of different languages. We decided to go our own ways while in Rome and meet each evening for supper to recount our experiences.

Rome at last, after a wonderful trip.

Basilica of St. Paul outside the walls.

Early next morning I made my way up the Via della Conciliazone towards St . Peter's Square. I went into the Carmelite Church, Santa Maria in Traspontina and knelt down before the altar of Our Blessed Lady of Mt. Carmel and thanked her for guiding us safely on our way to Rome. Transpontina means "across the Bridge" This was a last stopping place for pilgrims on their way to St. Peter's. I walked on to the centre of the Square and stood beside the giant Obelisk. It dates back to ancient Egypt and was brought to Rome in the first century to stand in Nero's circus.. It was later transferred here. Surrounded by the colonnade of Bernini, its open arms symbolically welcomed the world to Rome. On top of the Colonnade are 140 statues of the Saints. St. Peter and St Paul were silently looking down from on high as I entered the great Basilica of St. Peter's. It was a wonderful feeling walking through the Holy Door. My dream had come true, I had make it.

Massive pillar on way in through the Holy Door to St. Peters Rome. 1950.

Walking past the Pieta of Michael Angelo I touched the feet of Jesus in his Mother's arms and blessed myself. The magnificence of the interior is overwhelming. Every inch is a work of art. I walked up the centre aisle towards the baldacchino over the high altar. Painted above the massive pillars was the crests of all the religious orders in the Church. I searched for the Carmelite crest but couldn't find it. It didn't seem to be there. Then as I looked up over the high altar, there it was taking pride of place as the oldest order in the Church. I gazed up in amazement at the cupola of the dome created by Michael Angelo. But St. Peter's is not a museum or a work of art, it is a place of prayer. I knelt down to pray. In order to gain the Plenary Indulgence you had to visit the four Basilicas and pray for the Pope's intentions. From here I took the bus to the basilica of St. John Latern, the oldest basilica in Rome. It is the official ecclesiastical seat of the Pope. It contains the Papal throne. From here I went to St. Mary Major Basilica. This is the largest and most important place of prayer dedicated to the Blessed Virgen Mary. Lastly I went to St Paul's outside the Walls. This Basilica commemorates the martyrdom of St Paul. Each day I visited the four Basilicas to gain as many indulgences as possible.

The three of us paid a visit to St. Albert's, the Carmelite international College in Rome. There we met Fr. Devane who congratulated us on our great achievement and he entertained us to a beautiful meal. Before we left he said. "Don't forget to visit the Catacombs and Coloseum." The next day I went to the Catacombs of St. Callixtus. Dating back to the 2nd century, it is a vast complex over ninety acres and stretching over twelve miles long. It would be impossible to see it all.

My visit to the Colosseum was different. I found a quiet spot and just sat there imagining what it must have been like. The size of the structure was unbelievable. Although we are familiar with the size of modern buildings and skyscrapers I could not imagine how this great structure was built in the first century. It was the greatest amphitheatre in the Roman Empire, built as a symbol of Imperial Rome. It could hold over 50,000 people seated in tiers rising higher and higher. It was a monument to cruelty. How could people come to shout and cheer at the sight of Christians being mauled to death by fierce animals. The highlight of our visit to Rome was the Papal audience. We were in St. Peter's by 3.30pm for the audience at six. We took our place by the barrier where the Pope would pass by. The choirs from different countries sang hymns and everyone joined in. The Basilica was brilliantly illuminated with thousands of lights. The atmosphere was very tense as the singing reached a crescendo, with all eyes turned to the back of the Basilica for the arrival of Pope Pius XII. Suddenly the great doors opened, the trumpets sounded and the Pope entered carried high on the Sedea Gestatoria by the Swiss guards. The shouts of "Viva Il Papa" resounded throughout the Basilica. The Pope looked solemn and austere in his white garments, his Papal ring sparkling as he blessed the people. A woman fainted and had to be carried out. Now he was just beside me. I could have almost put out my hand to touch him. Here was the Vicar of Christ on earth passing by. He seemed to look straight towards me as he gave me the Papal Blessing It was a moment I will never forget. This is what I had come to Rome for. It was worth every minute. We just looked at one another and we didn't have to say a word.

The next day we left Rome. There was no way we could face hitch-hiking. We calculated our resources to see if we had enough for the train. We decided we could take the train to San Remo. Corky said he was low in funds and would only be able to manage a ticket to Genoa. "Don't worry" he said, "I'll take my chances after that." Everything went smoothly as far as Genoa. It was then that the excitement started. Corky didn't get out at Genoa. He said he had a plan. "I'll duck into the toilet when the inspector comes" he said. "One of you can stay at each end of the carriage and give me the signal when you see him coming." We were very sceptical and had visions of Corky being hauled off to jail. We stood at each end while Corky stood outside the toilet. In the middle of the night John must have dozed off because before he knew it, the inspector was nudging him for his ticket. As John searched for it he signalled frantically behind his back for Corky to disappear. Corky quickly entered the toilet but didn't pull the catch. Our hearts were in our mouths as the Inspector approached. He stopped outside the toilet for a moment but when he saw the 'vacant' sign he moved on. The first part of our plan had worked. But now we had another problem. "What are you going to do when they check your ticket on the way out of the station" asked John. "And there are always armed police at each station," I added. "Don't worry lads, I'll jump the train before the station." "You have been looking at too many cowboy films " said John "You will never get away with it." As the train approached San Remo , it began to slow down. "You look after my haversack lads " he said as he opened the door and lowered himself on to the step. The next minute he was gone and disappeared up a side street. When we met up around the corner we told him we had terrible trouble trying to explain to the police what we were doing with three haversacks. The next day we walked over the border to Mentone where we took a bus to Nice and then to Paris. As I looked out to sea, I saw the American fleet on its way to the war in Korea.

In Paris we made our way to the Camp Volants and were happy to find that this time they had vacancies. The next morning we spent our last francs at the train station in Paris. The hunger really hit us when we reached Euston station. We had a three hour wait for the train to Hollyhead. Corky decided there was nothing for it but to sing. Myself and John passed around our hats. I don't know whether it was pity or sympathy but people began to throw in coins. Soon we had enough for an English breakfast of rashers and eggs, coffee and cakes. This would keep us going until we reached Ireland.

We got our first glimpse of land early next morning as the sun rose over Dublin Bay.. It never looked so beautiful. Although we had a wonderful adventure it was wonderful to be safely home. I got a great welcome back at the Copse. My mother could not contain her joy. She ran to me, put her arms around me, gave me a big hug and kissed me. This was the first time she had ever kissed me. Alicia was also there to greet me, she wondered would I sing "Delaney's Donkey."

16

When Sorrows Come

Shortly after returning from Rome I was walking with my father on a Sunday afternoon in the woods around the Copse when a telegram arrived. "Davy in accident, Monkstown hospital." Immediately we got the jeep and headed for Dublin. It was a long and anxious journey, not knowing what to expect. Davy went to Dublin on his motorbike every Sunday to follow the Speedway racing that had just come to Shelbourne Park. A group of Wimbledon Dons came from London and set themselves up as the Shelbourne Tigers and took on all comers. It became very popular that summer but didn't last long after that. Eddie and Davy loved the speedway. Spilt Waterman and Aub Lawson were their favourites. He missed them that Sunday. Monkstown hospital was a small private hospital and we had difficulty finding it. Davy was in a ward with three others and he was awake when we arrived. Eddie was already with him. We were relieved to find that he was not in serious danger but he was in severe pain. His right leg had been crushed around the ankle and part of his heel had been shorn off. As he approached the traffic lights at the Punch Bowl Inn a car turning right from the opposite direction crashed into his side. His leg was crushed against the side of the bike. The doctor hoped he could save his leg but he would be in hospital for a long time. The bike was undamaged. As always he made light of his injuries and joked about being home for Christmas. In fact he was in hospital much longer and his injuries would eventually lead to his death when his leg turned cancerous many years later.

Eddie, aircraft electrician at Baldonnel, he dismantled any German planes that crashed during the war.

Eddie was an aircraft electrician and worked with Aer Lingus at Dublin airport, Collinstown as it was then called. After leaving the national school in Rathdrum , he studied at the technical school and from here he went to Baldonnel where he studied aircraft electrical maintenance. He loved his time there and played football and boxed for the Air Corps. During the war he dismantled the planes that crashed around Ireland. The R.A.F. planes were repaired and returned to England with their pilots, while the German ones were completely dismantled and the pilots interned until the end of the war. This was the way that Irish neutrality worked. Whenever he repaired an Irish plane it would have to be taken up to be tested. They were usually two seaters, just the pilot and himself. On these occasions he would swoop down over the Copse and wave to Daddy who was relieved that it wasn't another German bomber. In these two seater aeroplanes there was no communication with the pilot so he had to tip him on the shoulder and point to the Avonmore river and signal him to follow it. He then flew on to Rathdrum and Arklow before returning by Brittas Bay. Once after one of these flights he wrote home to say that he had a birds eye view of Fossets circus on the Fair green.

I was suddenly awoken in the middle of the night on the Friday after Christmas. Somebody was banging on the kitchen table and shouting "anyone home?" My mother jumped out of bed and ran down stairs. As soon as she saw the doctor she screamed. "Have you got a son?" he asked "Yes, yes, Eddie" she answered "what has happened?" "He has been in an accident " he replied, "and I'm sorry to have to tell you he is dead." My mother screamed again. By now my father had arrived. "I was called to an accident just outside Laragh, but when I got there, the young man was dead." explained the doctor. "His body has been taken to Laragh Inn." I felt a cold shiver up my spine. Myself and Richie jumped up, we were all in complete shock. My mother kept repeating "Holy Mary Mother of God have mercy on him." My father just sat there and sobbed away. My mother could not cry. I never saw her crying in my life, at least she didn't shed any tears on the outside but that night she cried a lot on the inside.

After a while my father decided to get the jeep and go to see what happened. I went with him. There was little said on the way. The body had been laid out on a couch in the front parlour of the Laragh Inn. There was a deep gash on his forehead. Otherwise he looked perfectly at peace, as if he was just sleeping. We knelt down beside him to pray. My father was very upset. Sergeant Wickam arrived from Glendalough. He sympathised with us and explained that he was called out at 3 o'clock to an accident. He reached the scene in about ten minutes. He found my brother dead underneath his motor bike on the side of the road. The doctor and priest had already been called and they arrived while he was there. The whole sequence of events came to light afterwards. He had gone to Glendalough at about 8.30pm to meet some friends. He had dinner at about 10 o'clock and at midnight he gave Christy Bolton a lift to Ballygannon in Rathdrum. Then he returned past the Copse to Glendalough for some unknown reason. At 2.30am he left the hotel. It was a cold and blustery night and it had begun to rain. Crossing over the small bridge the road was straight uphill for about 160 yards. There was a skid mark on the road leading to Derrybawn, the residence of Senator Sweetman. Apparently he hit his head on a coping stone which was protruding out from the wall. He continued on about another 30 yards up the road. He would have been killed instantly. Two lads who were playing cards in the house opposite found him a short time afterwards. They alerted the doctor, priest and the guards.

We continued on to Monkstown hospital to break the sad news to Davy. Naturally he was devastated and as we left he had plenty of time to grieve alone. I don't know what it must be like for parents to lose their eldest son. The joy and happiness of your first born. To see him grow up and take his first steps, go to school, First Communion, Confirmation, and then grow into a man. As the coffin was put into the hearse my father said "I thought I would be there long before You." The tragedy had a terrible affect on them. They were never the same again.

***

It was with a heavy heart that I returned to Terenure College after Christmas. Soon I became involved in College activities especially the rugby. Nothing could compare to the enthusiasm and enjoyment I had in playing on the senior cup team on two successive years. The highlight of the rugby season was the cup matches in Donnybrook. I moved from the first to the second row in the scrum. The rough and tumble of the lineouts and the scrums was very exhilarating. We had moulded together as a team and the team spirit was great. Karl Mullen, the Irish captain came to train us after winning the Triple Crown and the Grand Slam. He was a hooker and I held him up in the front row. This was every schoolboy's dream at the time. Fr. O'Connor, the trainer of the team had us up at 6 o'clock in the morning doing press-ups. He amazed us one morning by being able to do more than we could. The day of the cup match was very tense. As the bus reached the turn into Donnybrook the excitement grew and we began to get butterflies in our stomachs. Running out on to the pitch in the Terenure colours was an unforgettable experience. The crowded stands sang the Cup songs with great gusto. "Keep right on to the end of the game." We reached the semi-finals that year, narrowly beaten by Kings Hospital 6-3. The following year Terenure won the Senior Cup for the first time. There were only two changes from the year before. How I wished I was on that team.

Prefects at Terenure College with Fr. Clarke, a Wicklow man 1951

With the end of rugby season we moved on in the summer term to cricket, tennis and athletics. I never played cricket but I loved the tennis and the athletics Since the sports days in Rathdrum I was always keen on athletics. I practiced the high jump and the long jump in the field in front of the house. The first sports day in Terenure I surprised everyone by winning the high jump, long jump and coming second in the shot. I represented the College at the Leinster Sports each year. My parents always came up for the Sports day.

***

At the end of each year in Terenure I was asked by one of the priests if I still had a vocation. I was never quite sure what they meant. I hadn't thought about it much. I never heard voices or anything like that telling what I must do. To be a priest you had to be called by God. Not everyone is called. How do you know that you are being called by God? I never had any hesitation in answering yes. I knew that if I answered No I would be asked to leave. I was very happy there so I wanted to stay. Now at the end of my final year I had to be interviewed by the Provincial and two other priests. The interview was in the parlour, the same one that I was shown into on my first day. I hadn't been in it since. I sat down nervously in front of the table where the three sat.

"Why do you want to be a Carmelite priest?" asked the Provincial.

"I don't really know, I just feel I'd like to be a priest." I answered.

"A priest," he said "but you could be a Dominican or a Jesuit, or a Holy Ghost."

"I don't know anything about the Dominicans, the Jesuits, or the Holy Ghosts, except that when we played them in rugby we always wanted to win, especially against the Holy Ghosts." I replied.

" Why do you want to be a Carmelite?"

" I know the Carmelites, I have lived with them for the past three years" I said.

"Isn't it because we are dedicated to Our Blessed Lady of Mt Carmel" he said.

Oh, so that was the answer he was looking for. "Of course," I said.

"Is there anything you wish to ask us?" he enquired.

"No" I replied.

"Very good we'll see you in September then, enjoy your holidays." He said it in a tone which seemed to say it would be my last holiday. On my way out there were three other lads waiting to go in. They were as surprised to see me as I was to see them. We had lived together for the last three years and no one had mentioned joining the order.

After our trip to Rome we were bitten by the travel bug so we decided to do another exotic trip this year. Myself and John discussed going to the north or south pole, or to travel on the Tran Siberian railway behind the Iron Curtain into Russia. We also considered canoeing down the Amazon in South America or exploring the jungle. In the end we settled for a student exchange to Bavaria in Germany. This was to be the first student exchange since the war, eighteen Irish boys and girls spent the month of July in Bavaria with German families. They spent the month of August with us. I was paired with Norbert and his family and had a wonderful time exploring Germany in the aftermath of the war. From my window I could see the ruins of the Berghof, Hitler's Bavarian retreat. John stayed with Wolfgang and his family a short distance away. Wolfgang's father was in the Luftwaffe and kept his uniform and medals hidden in the attic. He ran the house in military style and John was awoken by a bugle every morning. When Wolfgang came to Ireland he embarrassed John by wearing lederhosen all the time. We had meetings with de Valera and the German ambassador with parties and celebrations everywhere we went. In the middle of it all I received a letter from the Provincial informing me to be in Kinsale by the 7th of Sept. It also had a list of the things I had to bring.

1. Black suit (also an old suit would be useful.)

2. Black raincoat.

3 Black pullover

4 Black hat.

5 Good supply of shirts (winter and summer)

6 Underwear

7. Two sets of pyjamas.

8. Supply of socks. (black)

9. Football outfit and swimming costume.

10. Handkerchiefs, white collars, black tie.

11. 4 towels, 2 serviettes, 2 sets of bed linen , boot brushes and clothes brush.

12. 1 Dressing gown, and toilet requisites .

13. Footwear, pair of boots and shoes, football boots, house shoes.

14. Mass. Daily Roman Missal, Crucifix, 4 and a half yds of linen. Liber Usualis.

15 Brown habit and White Cloak will be supplied in Kinsale.

16 Financial arrangements for the Novitiate year will be made with the Provincial.

Very Rev. Fr. Provincial O Carm.

My mother ticked off the list and when she came to the end she said "What's a liber usualis?" My father took a look and admitted he never heard of it. "Wouldn't you think they would tell you what it was," said my mother.

"I suppose they thought you would know" I said.

"Well, if you don't know how are we supposed to know?" said my father," it must be something that priests use. Anyway you can write and tell us what it is and we will send it on."

"But I can't write" I said.

"You'll have to do without it so," he said.

Alicia was delighted to have me back again but she knew I would be going away soon. She loved going for walks in the woods and playing tennis. Sometimes we spent the day in Brittas Bay, building sand castles in the dunes. She didn't like talking about me going away but she did say she would be very sad.

17

KINSALE

Alicia had warned me that she would not be around the day I left. She said she got butterflies in her stomach and she didn't like it. She had one last request. Would I sing the 'Red River Valley' one more time. She sat on my knee and put her arms around me.

"From this valley they say you are going

I will miss your bright eyes and sweet smile

For they say you are taking the sunshine

That has brightened our path for a while"

***

Won't you think of the valley you're leaving

Oh, how lonely, how sad it will be

Oh, think of the fond heart you're breaking

And the grief you are causing to me."

"I will really miss you" she sobbed with tears streaming down her face. She then kissed me goodbye The next day she hid in the woods.

My father drove me in the jeep to Kingsbridge station. to catch the train to Cork. He blessed himself as he passed the spot where Eddie was killed. He never said a word but I'm sure he was thinking that this was the third son he was losing within a year. Conversation doesn't come easy at times like this. "The first year will be the worst," he said as we passed through Roundwood. "If you don't like it you can always come home" he continued. "I know" I said, knowing the stigma that a failed priest would bring on the family. Its the finality of everything that hits you.. Things will never be the same again. You will never live at home again. The leaves will never be as green, the flowers will never be as beautiful. You will return dressed in black with a collar around your neck and that's what separates you from everyone. You will be loved or despised because of that collar. We made our way to Monkstown hospital to say goodbye to Davy. He was sitting out the back with some of the nurses. I hoped he would be back home when I came back. There were three other lads waiting at the station. They had already said their goodbyes. I wished I could just get on the train and disappear. I got in the carriage and settled down with the others. Just before the train pulled away my father appeared at the door. He wanted to say goodbye. I went out and he gave me a big hug and said. “Good luck I hope all goes well.” There were tears in his eyes. “Look after the pigeons and the rabbits” I said, not knowing what to say. The train pulled out and we were on our way. We talked for a while about the Summer holidays and then I just wanted to be left alone with my thoughts.

From Cork we took the bus to Kinsale. It was a mad rush to get all our cases on top of the bus. Kinsale is by the sea and it had seen better days. It was here that the history of Ireland changed for ever. Over 3,000 Spaniards were besieged in the town by the English while the battle raged against O‘Neill and O’Donnell all around. The Carmelite church is on top of the hill overlooking the harbour. We made our way up the narrow streets where you could almost shake hands across them. I would not have been surprised to see Spanish soldiers standing at the corner. The road leading up to the church is very steep and lined on each side with leafy trees. We had to stop every few yards to catch our breath. There were two old women in long black cloaks on the way down from the church. They looked to be from another world and another age. Their hoods were pulled up over their heads so that they could observe us without being seen.

“Fine young lads,” they thought, “I wonder how many will last the course.” They had seen the Novices coming and going for years. As we reached the top there was a lovely grotto to Our Lady. We knelt to say a prayer. “So far, so good.” We climbed the last few steps to the Friary where we were met by the Novice master Fr. Declan Sugrue. He was a tall man with a commanding presence. His hair was short growing up straight and turning grey. He was a Kerryman and had a loud hearty laugh. “Welcome to Kinsale” he said, “I hope you will all be very happy here.” “Some of the other Novices have already arrived, they are in the common room.” There were ten Novices altogether from all over the country. This was to be the biggest Novitiate ever. After the introductions the first task was to allot the rooms or cells as they would be called from now on. But there was a problem. There wasn’t enough cells for everyone, so someone would have to sleep in the box room in the middle of the house. It was just a big cupboard with no windows and no air. “The cells rotate every month” he said. “The friar must not get attached to his cell.” “The cells are all numbered so you just draw the numbers out of a hat.” Luckily I missed the dungeon, at least for the first month.

The cells were cold and sparse. A bare wooden floor , a bed in the corner with a crucifix over it. A small wardrobe , a table and chair and a hand basin. There were no curtains on the windows but at least we had windows not like the fellow in the box room. Bro. Norbert who was just finishing his Novitiate showed us around. There was a garden out the back which would keep us occupied for many an hour. A path led to the farmyard where Fr. O’Malley, the prior was in charge. From here we visited the church. The Carmelites first came to Kinsale in the fourteenth. Century. They were invited by an Earl who had probably met them on one of the Crusades to the Holy Land. The present church was built in the middle of the nineteenth century. Just outside the passage to the church stood the bell which pealed out the Angelus twice a day.

The following day we began a week's Retreat. Seven days of silence, with three lectures a day in the Oratory. This was in preparation for our reception into the Order by receiving the habit and white cloak. Then came the real test. We received the tonsure. This meant cutting a round patch on the crown of our heads. As we all had fine heads of hair this was very humiliating. It was a bit like branding cattle or shaving the prisoners . We were marked men. From now on the Novice Master would mould us into a perfect religious. We must follow his every directive without question. It was quite simple. God had spoken in the Bible, Christ commissioned the Church to transmit and interpret truth for all time. The truth was transmitted through the Superior whose every whim and prejudice carried Divine approval. This system of religious life had been in existence for centuries. It had been Divinely sanctioned and ensured eternal rewards. Superiors were never tempted to change or innovate anything All they had to do was fuel and oil the system. As we began the Retreat we were spurred on by a spirit of first fervour, each striving to outdo the other in holiness. We had left the world. We were on our way to Paradise. Silence was part of this, we could make all the signs we liked but don't open your mouth. The Provincial received us into the Order after the Retreat. Now at least we looked like Carmelites in our habit and white cloak. This was a symbol of the fact that we had left the world. We were also given religious names. I chose Bro. Colman as the best of a bad lot. When I looked up who St. Colman was I found there were hundreds , so I could take my pick. This symbolized that we had also left our families. The daily routine soon became second nature to us. From the call at six o'clock to lights out at ten our day was regulated. The lector shouted 'Bendicamus Domino' (Let us bless the Lord) as he knocked on our door in the morning. When he heard 'Deo Gratias' (Thanks be to God) he moved on. We had ten minutes to be down in the church. We formed two lines in the passageway to the Church and waited for the Novice Master to arrive. As he arrived , in a high pitched voice he intoned the 'Laetatus sum' (I rejoice). How we were meant to rejoice at that time of the morning I will never know. We continued the psalm as we processed into the church and took our places in the choir stalls around the sanctuary. We knelt down and the lector began to read the Meditation. Describing a scene from the gospel we were invited to put ourselves in the scene. Mentally we were to listen to Jesus talking just to us. We contemplated, we prayed, we made resolutions and examined our conscience. It was considered an act of charity if you gave the fellow beside you a nudge if he began to snore. The temptation to sleep was great at that time of the morning. After the Meditation we recited the Divine Office in Latin. We didn't understand a word but we proceeded to belt it out in a high pitched tone. It was difficult to keep up with the older Novices who were already familiar with it. Then came Mass. Many of the people from the town came to morning Mass. It was strictly forbidden for the Novices to look down the Church, but we soon became expert at seeing people out of the side of our eye. One of our year ,Bro Maurice, was from Kinsale so he could tell us afterwards who everyone was. But even he, didn't know who the women in the black cloaks were. After Mass, we ate breakfast in silence. There were two forms of silence, Major silence which lasted from night prayers until after breakfast. and Minor silence the rest of the time apart from recreation. After breakfast there was housework. The whole house had to be cleaned every day. First the priests' bedrooms , beds made, floors swept and polished, washbasin cleaned, We were all assigned a different area which changed around every month. The corridors had to be polished and the showers cleaned. Two were assigned to the washing up in the kitchen. Maggie was the cook and she had a great weakness for letting out snippets of news that she had read in the paper or heard on the news. Newspapers magazines were forbidden to the Novices as was the radio. The stairs was the most difficult. to clean. On one occasion when I had just reached the bottom, the Novice Master came along and said it wasn't done properly. I was to do it again, this time with a tooth brush. There was no answering back , you just did it. On another occasion when the shower wasn't cleaned properly, I was given the penance of washing the centre aisle of the church between 3am and 4am This meant getting up at 2.45am and boiling a bucket of water, opening the church, putting on the lights and scrubbing the tiles in the centre aisle. There was an eerie sound throughout the church as I scrubbed away. When I was finished I felt that I deserved a cup of tea. I was just enjoying it when the Novice master appeared at the door. " I said nothing about having tea" he said, "repeat the washing tomorrow without the tea."

Each morning we had two hours of instruction from the Novice Master. We learned the history and charism of the Carmelite Order. Carmelite spirituality had a special place in the history of the church. It is based on two people in Particular: the prophet Elijah and the Blessed Virgin Mary Elijah; The spiritual life of Carmel is completely impregnated with the spirit of Elijah. Although Elijah did not give the rule in writing, never the less he is the example and model of a Carmelite. Mary: The first Carmelite hermits assembled around a chapel on Mt. Carmel dedicated themselves to "St Mary of Mt Carmel" and later the "Brothers of Our Blessed Lady of Mt Carmel." The double ideal of Elijah and Mary is the first article of the oldest constitutions in the Order from the General Chapter of Barcelona (1324). "From the times of the Holy Prophets, Elijah, and Elisha, devout hermits lived continuously on Mt Carmel, sought this Holy mountain and loved its solitude in order to give their minds over to the contemplation of heavenly things, they built a Chapel here in honour of the Virgin and thus deserved to be called the Brothers of Our Lady of Mt Carmel, a name recognised by Popes. St. Albert gave them a Rule which was approved by the Church. Even when the Carmelites came to Europe and took their place among the Mendicant Orders, they still retained their Contemplative Spirit. Each particular Order is renowned for one particular aspect of religion. The Dominicans are known for their preaching, the Jesuits for their teaching, the Carmelites for prayer and contemplation. We were gradually initiated into the system. We became completely dependent on the novice master. He was controlling our emotions and our free will. He told us how we should think. We accepted everything he said. We learned to deny ourselves in order to bring us closer to God. We became independent of material things, our bare cells appeared luxurious. We practised penance. We ate with moderation what was put before us. We kept control of our ears, eyes, and tongue. We slept to maintain our strength and health. We endured cold and heat with patience. Mediocrity became a virtue. Any expression of our talents or other sign of excellence was a sign of pride and temptation of the Devil. We were always to be on our guard because "the devil went around like a roaring lion seeking whom he may devour." We were so indoctrinated that by the end of the year we felt privileged to be accepted into the Order. Our day consisted of Meditation, Mass, recital of the Divine Office. Reading of spiritual books. Devotions such as the Rosary, Way of the Cross, visits to the Blessed Sacrament and examination of conscience. On Wednesday evening there was 'Culpa'. This was a public declaration of our faults. You knelt in front of the Brothers and confessed. "I looked down the Church, I didn't answer the bell, I spoke during minor silence, and other silly misdemeanours, all of which was geared to make us feel humble and embarrassed. One Bro, when he could think of nothing else confessed that he had eaten some candles in the sacristy. This caused a general titter all round. On another occasion he said "This week I have no faults." That got a bigger titter. The novice master gave us a penance at the end.

Friday night was discipline night. In the past this meant self-flagellation, now we prostrated ourselves in the centre aisle of the church, held our arms out in the form of a cross while we chanted the psalm " Miserere." This was in memory of Christ's scourging at the Pillar and death on the cross.

There was a lectern in the refectory in the form of a pulpit. From here the Lector read during meals from the lives of the Saints or other spiritual book. On Wednesdays a chapter of the Constitutions was read and on Friday a chapter of the rule. The Rule of St Albert has twenty chapters in latin and these must be learned off by heart and recited in the Refectory at the end of the Novitiate year. We didn't understand a word but we spent hours learning it by heart and then the ordeal of reciting it in the Refectory. We decided that we would have a little competition among ourselves to see who could recite it the fastest. Bro. Fergus with his Cork accent won hands down, seven minutes flat. Bro. Fergus also caused some excitement during the year when he decided to go on hunger strike. He felt he had been dealt with unjustly so he would fight for his rights by going on hunger strike. This was unheard of, and considered by most as a very dangerous move. You could be immediately dismissed. He would come to meals but not take any food. Soon this was observed from the priests table but no action was taken. But Bro Fergus didn't starve. Some of us smuggled food from the kitchen to his room every day. After a week he called it off. Fergus turned out to be a wonderful Carmelite. He became superior in Rhodesia during the war of Independence. This necessitated him travelling around the Mission stations where the roads were mined and the guerrillas shooting on sight. His strong will and determination carried him through.

Each afternoon we did a couple of hours' manual work in the garden or on the farm. The Prior supervised this and he couldn't believe his luck in having ten strong men at his disposal. He had no trouble in finding work for us. We spent months chopping up an old tree stump. Bro. Donal was in his element. He was an expert with an axe. The only problem was that he broke the handle of the axe almost every week. This meant he had to report to the Prior with the broken handle and confess his lack of care. After four weeks of broken handles he couldn't face it any more. "Good God lads, I can't take it. Someone else will have to take the blame" he said. We decided to draw lots and the winner took the rap. At Christmas we could receive letters and parcels from home. This was considered a great privilege. Like little children we received our presents in the common room after breakfast on Christmas morning. Our real test came in February when Terenure was playing the Senior Cup matches. How were we to get the results? Maggie in the kitchen was our saviour I'm sure she didn't know what a rugby ball looked like but she said she would look up the result in the newspaper. We agreed on a sign language so that she wouldn't have to break the rule. She just gave thumbs up if we won and thumbs down if we lost. It was thumbs up all the way. Terenure won the Senior Cup for the first time. How we wished we were there, but in the circumstances we couldn't even celebrate. The novice master asked us one day did we know the result. We looked innocent and shook our heads. When he told us the great news we had to pretend we were excited. A few days afterwards one of the Terenure lads got a guilty conscience. He came to us and said. "I can't keep it up and longer, I am going to the novice master to tell him we knew all along." This is what first fervour does. It changes your personality. One day the Novice master said we would practise Gregorian chant, so we should bring our books. Everyone arrived with a big red book under their arm. I didn't have one. "What's that ?" I asked "That's our liber usualis " they said in unison. Mystery solved, so that's what a liber usualis is, wasn't I lucky I didn't bring one. I couldn't sing anyway.

A very important part of the Novitiate was looking after Fr. Magannity. He was an invalid, partly paralysed but his mind was perfect. He could walk if you held on to him at the shoulder. Coming down the stairs as you held on to the banister for dear life he swung out into mid air. He was fearless. He had to be washed, shaved and dressed, shoes and socks put on, false teeth which soaked in a glass overnight put carefully into his mouth. Each month a different Novice was assigned to looking after him. He was very set in his ways and didn't take to everyone. His first test was to ask you to write a letter to his sister. He began, "My dear E," then he asked to see it. If you had written "My Dearie " you were dismissed immediately, his false teeth flying across the room. I passed the test and afterwards got on very well with him. He loved going out for a drive in the pony and trap in the afternoon. First of all you had to catch the pony and then harness it to the trap and bring it from the farm to the front of the house. There was a steep hill down from the farm and at the bottom you had to negotiate a sharp left turn. The pony was so frisky that he would gallop down the hill taking the corner on one wheel. Every time I pictured myself going to the Prior and confessing. "I crashed the trap and the pony had to be put down." Luckily it never happened. Fr. Megannity had to be lifted into the trap, a warm rug put around his legs and off we went. He gave the orders where to go: Bandon road, Cork Road, Old Head, Compass hill. The pony knew all the roads perfectly but he had certain preferences. You had to hold a tight rein until you got him on the right road. Fr. Magannity gave a running commentary as we went along and admonished you for going too near the ditch or too far out on the road. There were very few cars on the roads then and whenever we met someone walking or on a bike he stopped to have a chat. When he was in bad humour you could do nothing right. Coming across a stream on the side of the road the pony stopped for a drink. "What did you let him stop for" he grunted. "keep going ,you don't let a pony drink where he likes." The next time when I kept going, he shouted "Why didn't you let him have a drink, he might be thirsty." He loved going out to the old Head. Pointing out to sea he always repeated the same story. "That's where the Lusitania was sunk by a German U-boat on the 7th of May 1915. The immediate effect of this was that the Americans entered the First World War. He believed the theory that Churchill knew of the danger from U-boats and did nothing about it so that the Americans would enter the War. Over one thousand lives were lost, many of whom are buried in Kinsale. My father often spoke of the delight in the trenches when they heard the Americans were coming.

Every Sunday we went on long walks around the roads of Kinsale. Dressed in our black suits, black tie and hat we set out 'bini et bini' (two by two)

First Profession, Kinsale, at the end of my Noviciate year 1952.

Reception into Carmelite Order 1952.

Mam and Dad at Kinsale after my profession 1952.

Particular friendships were forbidden so you had to change your partner each time. The senior student was in charge. He choose the route. Bro. Maurice was very helpful in showing us the best places to go. We marched for hours out the Bandon Rd., or up Compas hill, of down to Pier head or up Breakheart Hill, There was also the high road and the low road out to Summercove. The people of the town were familiar with the Novices out on exercise from their enclosed cloisters. They knew we couldn't talk to them. Even Bro Maurice when he saw his brother who had a butcher's shop in the town could not speak to him. During the summer all the walks led in one direction, Charles Fort, for a swim. We set out at a fast pace past Scilly along the low road to Summercove and on to the fort. There was a beautiful bathing place just beyond the fort. Charles Fort had been abandoned at this time and we spent many hours exploring its dungeons and fortifications.

The year in the Novitiate passed by quickly. By the end of the year we felt moulded, some of us more than others. We had learned to accept whatever we were told to do without question. If we wanted to be Carmelites this is what we had to do. Reason or common sense didn't come into it. We had left the world and entered another level of religion. We were gaining more merit and coming closer to God. We were superior to ordinary lay people and we would show them a more perfect way by our teaching and example. People would look up to us because we wore a collar and not only a collar but a habit. I am reminded of the story of the little girl waiting at the bus stop with her mother when a Nun comes along in her habit. The little girl nudges her mother and asks "What's that?" "That's a nun" whispered her mother. "Yes, but what's underneath?" asked the girl puzzled. What was underneath was important.

One good effect of the Novitiate was that it bonded the ten of us together. We remained good friends for the rest of our lives. We had been through the difficult times together. Of the ten three have died, three left the Order and the other four are still Carmelites.

We made our Simple Profession and took the vows of Poverty, Chastity and Obedience before the Provincial after the Retreat in September. Poverty meant we couldn't call anything our own." Chastity was never mentioned in the Novitiate. The rule says "Your loins are to be girt with Chastity." Obedience was blind obedience. Do what the superior says without question. These vows were temporary for three years after which we can make them permanent by Solemn vows. Our parents were invited to Kinsale for the ceremony. My parents arrived from Rathdrum in the jeep. It was wonderful to see them again. This for them was the beginning of a dream come true, the first stage of their son becoming a priest. They were overawed by the ceremony and seeing me in the brown habit for the first time. After the celebrations the Provincial announced that we could spend two days at home with our families. Coming home in the jeep was like being released from prison after a life sentence. It is impossible to describe the joy and exhilaration of arriving home to the Copse. Alicia was there to greet me. The fact that I was dressed in black with a white collar didn't deter her from sitting on my knee and asking. "Would you sing Delaney's Donkey." I was back in the real world.

18

Student Years At Gort Muire

"This would remind you of home" remarked my father as we drove up the tree-lined avenue at Gort Muire past the chapel and stopped outside the old house. Fr. Burke welcomed us into a beautiful parlour which he said was the ballroom in the original house. The floor was sprung underneath to facilitate the waltzing. The house was built in the middle of the nineteenth century when waltzing was all the rage. There was no waltzing these days. The Carmelites came here from Ardavon (now Mt. Carmel hospital) on the 20th of March 1944, the feast of St. Joseph. The Carmelites changed the name to Gort Muire and immediately began to build a student wing and Community chapel. Having said my goodbyes I made my way up the big terrazzo stairs to the Philosophers corridor with its polished linoleum floors where I found my room. The new wing was built of solid concrete at the end of the war to withstand earthquakes and air raids. The rest of the lads from the Novitiate had already arrived. The bell sounded for night prayers, we quickly put on our habits and made our way to the chapel. We took our place in the wooden choir stalls in order of seniority. There were about fifty students altogether from philosophers, to theologians to student priests. The chapel was very modern with its block wooden floor and marble altar . Over the altar was a large painting of Our Lady of Mt Carmel by the artist Sean Keating. He depicted the figure of Elias as himself and his wife represented Our Lady. Each night at the end of night prayers we turned towards this painting and sang;

Flos Carmeli *(Flower of Carmel)*
Vitis florigera *(Blossoming vine)*
Splender Coeli *(Splendour of Heaven)*
Virgo Puerpera *(Child bearing maiden)*
Singularis *(None equals Thee)*
Mater mitis *(Mother so tender)*
Sed viri nescia *(who no man didst know)*
Carmelites *(on Carmels children)*
Esto propitia *(Thy favours bestow)*
Stella Maris *(Star of the sea)*

Chapel at Gort Muire 1958 with Sean Keating's painting.

Every Carmelite remembers this hymn and whenever it is sung they are back in spirit in Gort Muire. The next morning the "Benedicamus Domino" resounded around the building at six o'clock.. We waited outside the chapel for the "Laetatus sum" and took our places in the stalls for meditation. followed by the Divine Office, then Mass and afterwards breakfast. Then housework, washing the terrazzo stairs, or blocking long linoleum corridors. The blocking consisted of heavy leaden blocks on cloths pulled back and forth until the corridor was shining. Shortly after arriving in Gort Muire we had a seven day retreat and then we prepared for the University. The whole system of preparing students for the priesthood had been laid down by the Church and it varied little from Order to Congregation. The Carmelites just adopted the system with emphasis on the Carmelite charism. The most important ingredient was discipline. There was just one way of doing things, that was the way the superior decided. So the regime of the Novitiate was carried on in the student house. A student master was appointed to enforce the rules. No radio, no newspapers, no contact with the outside world . We could write letters but all letters, outgoing and incoming were censored . Although we were to attend the University we were not to take part in any of its activities. We set off on our bicycles each morning, dressed in black with white collar and hat. Past Dundrum down by the asylum to Windy Arbour, through Milltown to Earlsfort Terrace. On wet and windy mornings we wore capes and leggings over the black. But there were also privileges. At coffee break we went down to the canteen past all the other lay students forming a long queue to our reserved tables where we were served our coffee and buns before everyone else . We passed some of our old school friends much to our embarrassment. They were mere second class citizens The canteen ladies loved serving the clerics first. God help them they deserve it. Each year as students went up for the student council, they declared that this was the first thing they would abolish. It took years to abolish it.

It was forbidden to speak to girls. During the Sunday morning lecture the student master referred to this rule. "Girls are not evil in themselves," he said "but they can lead us into temptation." We could sit beside them during lectures and smell the perfume but we couldn't say a word. One of the brothers became friendly with a girl he met in the library. She made the fatal mistake of writing to him at Gort Muire. The student master opened the letter, interrogated him and reprimanded him. He proceeded to Solemn Profession where he received a black bean. Each priest member of the community had to vote on the suitability of each student. They were given a little bag with black and white beans. They secretly placed a black or white bean into a separate bag. A black bean meant you had been rejected. No explanation was ever given, you just had to leave. No one ever knew who had put the black bean in the bag. The secrecy of the Vatican permeated every corner of the Church.

Dad and Mam down by the lake at Gort Muire.

Every master of students seemed to have a particular aptitude for the task. Following the rules became more important than love, or kindness, or common sense, or even Christian charity. What does the rule say? That was all that mattered. That's how you gained merit. There were two kinds of students. The ones who kept all the rules without question and the ones who tried to get around them, without being caught. I was part of the latter group. The result of the strict regime in Gort Muire was that the students stuck together and became a very united group. They were 'agin the government' as it were.

Thursday morning was shop. You queued up for toiletries, copy books. etc. "Could I have a razor blade please?" "Ah like, you got a blade recently, how many shaves did you get out of it?" asked the student master. "I'm not sure but it's gone rusty." said the student. "I got fifty shaves out of my last blade, you must be more careful." he said, reluctantly handing over a blade. On another occasion a student brought up his shoes to be mended. After close examination the student master declared. "Ah like, that one has a lot of wear in it yet, the other you can have repaired."

The senior student was the intermediary between the students and authority. One day he went to the Prior to ask if the students could play a football match in the afternoon. "Why , of course," said the Prior, "I'll meet you all down in the changing room at 3 o'clock." We all got into our togs, picked the teams and waited for the Prior. Eventually he came and with a loud laugh he said. "Now we'll all go down to the field to pick the potatoes." Nobody uttered a word (out loud). The students helped out with manual work on the farm and in the fields. We grew most of our own vegetables and kept cows which supplied most of our own milk. We had a professional cook in the kitchen helped out by lay brothers and students. Two students were detailed to do the washing up after each meal. The food was frugal but wholesome . Very often we went hungry especially on Wednesdays, Fridays and Saturdays, these were the fish days. You could smell the "Liffey wanderers" as we called them as they arrived at the gate. The smell of fish permeated the whole house. I hated fish in those days as did a lot of the students. We tried to have a little supplement in our rooms. a bar of chocolate, sweets, an apple or maybe a chicken if we were lucky to have a kind friend. A group gathered in a room and secretly devoured it. It was like Stalig 29. Things got worse when the cook was sick or on holidays. It was then that Bro. Joseph , a lay brother took over. He knew nothing about cooking but when he was told to do it he just said 'yes'. He always kept his habit on in the kitchen in spite of the heat. As he stood sweating over a big pot of soup, drops of sweat fell in and occasionally part of his dirty habit. He just picked it out, squeezed it back into the soup and carried on. "What harm could the Holy Scapular do to the soup." he said.

The lector read during meals except on feast days and birthdays when the Prior rang the little bell and proclaimed a 'prosit' which meant we could talk. The books usually consisted of the lives of the Saints or books on spirituality, like "The Imitation of Christ" by Thomas a Kempis. We spent months listening to the autobiography of Bishop William Bernard Ullathorne, a Benedictine monk who became the first Bishop of Birmingham,. He recounted his many experiences on the missions in Australia. The lector had to prepare his reading beforehand, because if he pronounced a word wrong the Prior tapped on his glass and corrected him, much to his embarrassment. Bro. Donal had a theory that when he came across a difficult word he just called it "Manchester" and continued on hoping no one would notice. He usually got away with it. Once while Bro Fergus was reading he came across the word "subtle" and pronounced it "sub till." There was a tap on the glass and the Prior said "Bro, that word is pronounced suttle" Fergus looked down on the word and said "No, Fr. Prior it's spelt s-u-b-t-l-e " Everyone just laughed. On another occasion Bro Norbert was reading from the old Testament when he came out with "her brassiere was full of fire" instead of brazier. The whole refectory erupted with laughter.

One Friday afternoon Bro. Terence and Bro Joe were on their way into town with the horse and cart to collect a load of the by-product of barley and hops from Guinness's Brewery at St. James Gate. This was a wonderful feed for the pigs and cows. The fish had been particularly bad that day so they were really hungry. As they reached Windy Arbour they put their hands in their pockets to see how much money they could muster. Between them they only had two shillings. This would have done nothing for their hunger so they decided to go into the bookies and gamble it on a horse. Then they proceeded into town to collect the grain. On the way back they called into the bookies to see how their horse had got on. To their amazement it had won at 8 to 1. Now they had enough for a good meal. They tied the horse and cart to a tree and went to the chipper and had a wonderful meal of fish and chips and all the trimmings. The following Saturday as they queued up for Confession Bro Joe got qualms of conscience. The 'Doc' Taylor was hearing, a renowned theologian, and a stickler for detail. He confessed the episode in every detail as the Doc listened intently. Then he waited for the verdict. He noticed the Doc turn towards him behind the grille and with a smile on his face he blurted out "Ingenious my young man, ingenious."

An Order of nuns rang the Student master one day and said they were just concluding a wonderful sale of work in the Mansion House. Could he let them have some students to dismantle the stalls? A group was detailed to be in the Mansion house by 9 o'clock. Myself and Bro Leonard decided we would make a detour and visit a family in Terenure where we had something to eat. We had a lovely evening and then proceeded on our bikes into the Mansion House for 9 o'clock. As we arrived one of the lads was at the door warning us that the Student master had arrived and was looking for us. We dodged into the toilets to change into our working clothes . Bro Frederick smuggled in a plank when the Master wasn't looking.. After a while we nonchalantly walked out with Bro Leonard at one end of the plank and I at the other. We walked past the Student master without a word. The next day I was summoned to the student masters office. As I sat down he asked. "Where were you last night when you should have been in the Mansion house.?" I knew the game was up so I admitted everything. Lucky that I did because he had already spoken to Bro Leonard "This is very serious" he continued in a solemn voice. "After all the years of preparation and formation" Bro. Leonard said, "it was all your idea." He had probably told him that I said it was his idea. This is a serious breaking of the rules and we will have to consider your remaining in the Order. As far as I am concerned you will have to leave." I knew I was in for a long lecture, so I immediately interrupted. "Alright" I said, "if you think I should leave the Order you can arrange it with the Provincial and let me know when to go." "Ah, like," he said. "Don't act too hastily." "You said I should leave" I replied, "just let me know when." That put a sudden end to the lecture. As I left the office, I knew I had called his bluff.

A student at Gort Muire 1954.

A few days later Fr. Bonaventure, the Provincial came to visit me. "What's this I hear about you leaving?" he asked. "There is no way you are leaving" he said.

"It's the Student master who said I must leave" I replied. "There is no question of that," he continued. "Your penance is to offer up your Easter Communion and I'll talk to the student master," he said with a smile. Some years later the student Master was heard to remark "Ah like, the Provincial handled that situation all wrong."

On the 21st of July, 1955, the President of Ireland, Mr. Sean T. O'Kelly was invited for dinner to Gort Muire. Mr. O Kelly was a life long friend of the Carmelites, especially Fr. Peter Magennis the first Irish General of the Order. Fr. Magennis married Sean T. O'Kelly in Whitefriar St. on the 1st of September 1936. The priests formed a guard of honour in their white cloaks. Shortly before he arrived the Provincial Fr. Bonaventure asked me to go down to the gate to guide him in. After a while he appeared in his beautiful presidential Rolls Royce. As I beckoned him in he stopped , rolled down the window, and asked me to sit in and accompany him up the avenue. I sat in beside him in the back and he chatted away until we reached the guard of honour. The Provincial stepped forward to open the door for the President and I stepped out much to his disgust. He brushed me aside with a scowl as he welcomed the President. After a magnificent meal the President arose to speak. "My connection with the Carmelites go back a long number of years. I will be seventy three years of age next week and I can say that I was friendly with and known to the Carmelites for sixty of these, ever since the time I used to take my holidays on the south side of the river. It was then that I made my first visits to Whitefriar St. and it was there that I befriended Fr. Peter Magennis, whom I was later to meet in Rome. Some years later I was in Rome on important business. I was not an official representative of Ireland to the Vatican. I made myself representative and this was later officially confirmed. While in Rome I met Fr. Magennis and another defender of Irish independence, Mgr. O' Hagan, rector of the Irish College. Fr. Peter was to my mind, the greatest Irish Republican of his time. We got word of a document that was being sought by England from the Vatican, condemning the Irish Government and the fight for Independence. Something had to be done to prevent the issue of that document, which would have been very prejudicial to Ireland and to the Church in Ireland. So Fr. Peter Magennis and Mgr.

O'Hagan told me that I must get an audience with the Pope (Benedict XV), give him the true picture and thus prevent the issue of the document. I protested that I was unequal to the task, but they insisted all the more. They said, "We cannot do it - we are clerics. It will be much better if it is done by a layman." So there was I with this extraordinary task of getting an audience with the Pope, even though I was not an official representative or an envoy. They told me that I was Speaker in the Government and that I must go as representative of the people. How was I to get an audience with the Pope?. Well, I knew Mgr. Cerretti, who held the position Tardini now has. So I set out to see him. I told him that I wanted to arrange a Papal audience for me. "What for ?" he asked. I then told him about the document and our fight for independence. "How do you know about this document?" he asked. I told him that I had it from reliable sources. He then cross-examined me very thoroughly, much to my embarrassment. He asked me some very exciting questions. When this was over he promised to arrange an audience. "But," he said "there is one thing I want you to do. I want you to prepare a written statement to give to the Pope. Write out briefly all the claims of the Irish to their independence. The Pope will ask you a lot of questions. But before you leave him make sure that you give him the written account and get a promise from him that he will read it." A nice job for me.

Well, I came home to the Irish College and when Fr Magennis and Mgr. Hagan heard the news they were absolutely thrilled. "But," I said, "I have to prepare a written statement." "That will be alright," said O'Hagan, I'll do that for you." They came to my bedroom and between them they banged it out on a typewriter. When the paper was handed to me I was stunned. I said I couldn't give it to the Pope ... everything in it was a dig at the Pope. I had my audience and was received most cordially by Benedict XV. He also questioned me very severely. He asked me every question which Mgr. Cerretti had already asked me. It looked as if he had prepared a list of questions for His Holiness and had already primed me for the answers. I was now very glad that I had such a severe examination from Mgr. Cerretti. I was with the Pope for a very long time --45 minutes -- during which he asked me, for example. "What do you mean by ambush". I tried to explain as best I could that a very good method of warfare was to take the enemy by surprise. It was also quite a good idea when short of arms to acquire them. The Pope could not see the reason for this. He couldn't see why an Irish army was not able to appear in uniform and fight the English on the battlefield. Nor could I persuade him of the necessity or explain adequately to him the meaning of ambush. At the end of the audience he said to me "The Irish have every right to their independence, and every right to fight for their independence, but be careful of the means you use," I asked him what he meant by this remark about methods and again he got back to the "ambush". I told the Pope that this was the first time in 350 years that we had got such a declaration in favour of our fight for freedom. We fought and we freed seven-eighths of our country and, please God, we'll free the other eighth.

I'll tell you another incident. Cardinal Logue and Fr. Magennis were guests at a dinner once in Rome. When the Cardinal was speaking he said he had a word for "this little boy" (Fr. Magennis). "My boy," he said addressing him as one of the youngest, "I'm an old man with one foot in the grave (he was 83), and I want to say this much. I have heard talk now for a good many years about an independent Ireland but it hasn't come yet. It won't come in my lifetime. I will be dead when it comes (if it does come), I may be dead a long time when it does come, but I say this-that the day Ireland declares herself an independent country no soul will rise in joy more than that of Michael Logue" (Cardinal of Armagh and Primate of all Ireland). I've had a lot of associations with the Carmelites in my lifetime in Dublin, Rome, and elsewhere. Since I have been made President I have not had the same opportunities as I used have of coming in contact with you, so that on my visits now I am all the more endeared to you. And if I have achieved anything in my public capacity I attribute it to the influence of the Carmelites of Dublin and Ireland."

***

BA at U.C.D. after three long years. 1955.
Then the H.Dip. the following year.

I had one great friend in Gort Muire which made life more bearable. Although some priests when they were in positions of authority became tyrants there were others who were never in authority and were the finest men I have ever known. One such was Fr. Michael Carroll, fondly known as Mick. He was the kindest, most gentle and human person you could ever meet. Although he was many years my senior we became great friends from the moment we met. He never kept a rule in his life. This may have been one of the reasons I was attracted to him. He was a past pupil of Terenure college and , being from Kilkenny, a keen hurler. He was sent to Rome to do his theology. One of the very strict rules at the time was the No Smoking rule. Within a short time Mick was caught smoking and promptly sent home. This caused a dilemma for the Irish Provincial because there was no place for him to continue his theology. The Jesuits at Milltown Park came to our rescue and accepted the Carmelite students to join them for Theology, an arrangement that continues to the present day. Mick was a genius and took to theology like a fish to water. For all his intelligence he often acted like the absent minded professor. Sometimes he would forget to put on the chasuble on his way out to say Mass. He only realized it as he bowed down to say the Confiteor. Embarrassed he side-stepped back into the sacristy to put it on. Afterwards he would laugh and say "I bet nobody noticed." Mick was fond of a drink. I suppose you would say he was an alcoholic but I never saw him in a state of intoxication. He held his drink very well and became jolly and brave and full of fun especially after a day out. Opening the door wide on his return he would stick out his chest and say." Where is he now and I'll talk to him. Where is he?" (the Prior). A student would gently lead him up to his room and put him to bed. Some of the students availed of this opportunity to go to confession hoping he would be lenient, but Mick heard everything clearly and let them away with nothing.

Mick was not long in one place before he dirtied his bib and was transferred to another house. He spent many years in Moate where he endeared himself to everyone except the superior. He was put on the 'quest'. This is a custom dating back to penal days where members of religious orders go around the countryside collecting money. Mick had a pony and trap and set off each day to visit all the farms around Moate. He had to contend with dogs and bulls and wild geese but Mick was in his element. He loved talking to people. He never had to mention money, everyone knew what he was there for. He also blessed the baby and the cows and horses and pigs. One day after a good collection he dropped into a pub on the way home for a drink. He tied the pony outside to a telegraph pole as in the cowboy films. There was a sharp east wind blowing and the pony resented this treatment. After a while he pulled on the reins and managed to free himself and find his own way home. When Mick came out much later there was no pony and trap. There was nothing for it but to walk home. Luckily there was no accident, apart from the trap being wrecked as the pony dashed in through the narrow entrance to the farmyard. The Prior was waiting for Mick when he returned.

Shortly after this Mick was transferred to Gort Muire hoping that the strict regime would keep him under control. He was a godsend to the students and provided an enormous amount of light relief. A few weeks before I sat for the B.A. the Prior called me one day and assigned me to the farm. This meant helping Bro Ignatius with the farm work. Arriving at the farm shortly after six o clock in the morning, I had to mangle the turnips and feed the pigs. The cows had to be milked and the byre cleaned out. One day Bro Luke arrived on the farm. He was a late vocation having already qualified as a medical doctor. He also represented Ireland at tennis in Wimbleton The Prior decided his obedience should be tested. He arrived with a bucket and brush. His task was to wash the cows backsides. I will never forget seeing him gently lifting up the cow's tail and scrubbing it's backside.

Having completed my B.A. I was sent to Terenure College to study for the Higher Diploma in education. I taught in the Junior school and enjoyed every minute of it. I could see the inspector coming up the long avenue on his surprise visits and always had a special class prepared for him. Of course the students thought he was examining them. In the evening we attended lectures at the University. By now I had taken Solemn vows, Poverty, Chastity and Obedience, for life. Now there was no going back.

***

The following year I began Theology in Milltown park. We joined a group of Jesuits who were much older than us, having completed some years teaching before studying theology. All the professors were learned Jesuits who gave all the lectures in Latin. This was a complete shock to us who didn't understand a word. At least the Jesuit students had studied Philosophy through Latin so they were familiar with the language. For the first three months we just sat in class dumbfounded. We cycled in to Milltown every day, sat through three or four classes and then cycled home, having learned nothing. Everyone said we would be alright after Christmas but we didn't believe it. But believe it or not they were right. By the second term we began to understand more and more.

Carmelite students on holiday at Tinakilly house.

*Carmelite football team playing Wicklow County.
We won every year.*

The main objective of our study seemed to be to decry the beliefs of other religions, such as Jewish, Islamic and Oriental. We were still years away from the Second Vatican Council's examination of the spiritual values enshrined in all the world's religions. Our concern was to point out how we were right and they were wrong. Years afterwards as I rode a mule up the narrow stony tracks of the Andes looking down on a vast abyss below, and praying that the mule wouldn't stumble, I looked back on the wasted years of studying theology in Milltown Park. How I wished there were courses in mule riding, or cooking or car mechanics. How grateful I was for the education I received at the Copse. My mother taught me how to cook and I have been cooking for myself for the past thirty years. My father taught me everything he knew about servicing a car. How often did we dismantle the engine of the Armstrong Siddley and put it back together again?

An important part of Theology is Canon Law, all of its ten thousand canons. We studied each one in detail and had to defend it in an examination before three professors in Latin. We became lawyers and barristers able to defend every canon as it applied to the life of the Church. We accepted everything as perfectly normal and divinely dictated. It appeared perfectly normal that the Church was structured in such a way to ensure Rome had total control over all its parts. The Pope over bishops, bishops over priests, priests over lay people with women, including nuns reduced to second class citizens. Many years later as I lived among the poor Indians of Peru I realized that it represented the triumph of law over love. It had lost the true message of Jesus Christ. The poor Indians were asked by the Church to observe Lenten fast when they had little to eat at any time. I adopted the principle that canon law did not apply above ten thousand feet. In a recent court case when canon law was quoted, the Judge said it had no more relevance than the rules of a golf club.

Moral theology covers a multitude of sins. It deals with the broad question of what from the point of view of moral action it means to be a Christian. 'Good must be done and evil avoided.' Everything must be examined and analysed. We must define good and evil, right and wrong, sin and virtue. It also deals with specific issues such as justice, sexuality, truth telling, and the sanctity of life. All this in Latin could be very dull and boring if it wasn't for the personality and expertise of the professor. We were very fortunate to have a wonderful Jesuit, Fr. Eddie Coyne. "Wait until you come to sex and the sixth and nineth Commandments," was the constant remark from the older students. We couldn't wait. After all this would be the first time that sex was even mentioned, never mind discussed. At last the big day came. Eddie began in his usual good humour by saying. "now the first thing I want you all to do the next time you are having a bath is to examine every part of your body thoroughly." The next day he brought a whole series of charts of the human body. He began to give a class in anatomy. He had a large chart of the penis and gave us all the medical terms in Latin for each part. He went on to describe the function of each part and what happens when it is aroused and becomes erect. This was all done in the best of taste and in a way that didn't cause any embarrassment. We then moved on to the female charts. These would have come as a surprise to many of the students. I had already seen most of them in the home doctor book that I studied at home. But these were much larger and left nothing to the imagination. He explained the function of each part and what happens when the female is sexually aroused. Next he told us how intercourse takes place and the importance of foreplay to prepare the body for it. He enumerated the many positions that could be adopted during intercourse. He then went on to explain how babies are conceived and born. And during all this there was never a mention of the birds and the bees. This was reality laid bare at last. Eddie encouraged us to ask questions about anything that wasn't clear. The Jesuit students were quick to avail of the opportunity to ask all kinds of questions. The Carmelites were too shy and bashful.

Having studied the background we then moved on to the reason why we went into so much detail about human sexuality. We moved on to right and wrong. Moral theology was the study of all the possible sins a person could possibly commit. An evaluation of the gravity of each and an analysis of the circumstances that might increase or lessen the guilt of the sinner. One day we would be sitting in a confession box hearing people's confessions. We would have to identify, classify, cross-reference and evaluate the seriousness of the sin. We must understand the nature of the sin, make a judgement as to its gravity and give an appropriate penance. In this way the lay people did not have to make any moral decisions. They simply abdicated that function to the priest who disposed of one complicated situation after another.

The Jesuit system of education involves a revision of the whole programme at the end of the year. A student takes over the class and the professor bombards them with questions for an hour, all in Latin. The Carmelites were usually excused because of their lack of expertise in Latin. I was unfortunate to be chosen two years in succession. Fr. Hannigan was really giving me a grilling when he suddenly stopped and asked; "Are you reading from your book?" I just held up my closed book and he continued on. The exams consisted of appearing before three professors and defending a thesis. Each one in turn acted as the devil's advocate and put forward objections.

Having passed our exams we presented ourselves before John Charles McQuaid, together with hundreds of others to receive first of all Minor Orders, two at a time. Porter, Reader, and afterwards Exorcist and Acolyte. These were duties connected with the care of the Church and the Celebration of the Mass. The minor orders were abolished in 1972 by Pope Paul VI after the Second Vatican Council. Most of these duties are now carried out by lay people. Although we were conferred with the power of exorcism we were never asked to perform one. Usually the Bishop in each diocese appoints one priest to carry out an exorcism. Then came the Major Orders of Sub-

Deacon, Deacon, and Priest. I received the Sub-Deaconate about a year before ordination. This meant I cycled into Whitefriar St. on Sunday to take part in the High Mass at twelve o'clock. The high mass consisted of the Celebrant, Deacon and Sub-Deacon. It was sung in Latin to accompaniment of the organ and Gregorian chant sung by the choir.

The night before I received the Deaconate the Master of Students summoned me to his room. "Please sit down " he said. "Do you realize the importance of what the Deaconate means?" he continued., "Yes, it is the last step to the priesthood." I answered. "It means much more than that " he said. "It means you can never get married." "I hadn't any plans in that direction." I said. with a smile on my face. "This is a serious matter " he said "I have the duty to tell you that the Deaconate means you can never get married," "I understand" I said, trying not to smile. That was the only time he ever mentioned marriage.

Ordained Deacon 1958, marriage was out after that.

The Deaconate meant I could baptize, witness marriages, and preach. As theologians we had to prepare a sermon and preach before the rest of the priests and students. It was a real ordeal. You were given a subject and a couple of months to prepare it. On one occasion my subject was "Our Lady." I spent hours studying every book in the library. Its not a subject that you could tell stories or invent things I decided to stick to the gospel. On a cold afternoon I arrived down in the chapel in my white cloak, ascended the altar and began to preach to a group of bored looking students and priests. I felt like Robert Emmet speaking from the dock. Then came the dissection. Each one offered their advice and criticism. I was praised for my preaching voice. Mick Carroll wondered what book I had cogged it out of. One of the lads admitted afterwards he slept through it.

***

I was ordained on the morning of Sunday July 12th 1959 with four other Carmelites and many others in Clonliffe College by Archbishop John Charles McQuaid, the same man that had confirmed me many years before. It is impossible to describe the feelings and emotions as I prostrated myself before the altar, put on the sacred vestments and the placing of the hands of the Archbishop on my head as he ordained me as a priest. Jesus Christ ordained the Apostles at the Last Supper. They in turn had ordained others down through the centuries to the present day. Now I had become another Christ. The Cure of Ars puts it very well when he says. "The Sacrament of ordination raises man up to God. What is a priest? A man who holds the place of God.....a man who is invested with all the powers of God." "Go" said Our Lord to the priest.; as my Father sent Me I send you. All power has been given me in Heaven and on earth. Go, then teach all nations..... he who listens to you listens to Me. He who despises you despises me. When the priest remits sins he does not say. "God pardons you," he says "I absolve you." At the Consecration, he does not say, "This is the Body of Our Lord." he says, "This is my Body", Oh how great is the priest. The priest will not understand the greatness of his office till he is in Heaven. If he understood it on earth, he would die, not out of fear, but of LOVE."

Ordination at Clonliffe 12th. July 1959
when there was an abundance of priests.

My mother, Davy and Ritchie knelt down for my first blessing. My father was in Loughlinstown hospital with pleurisy . He had just gone in the week before and I cant imagine how he must have felt missing the one day he had looked forward to all his life. I had my ordination breakfast at Jury's hotel with a small group of very close friends. Then I made my way to Loughlinstown hospital to give my father my first blessing. Tears of joy ran down his face as he sat up in the bed looking pale and gaunt. He could hardly speak. "A priest at last," he said, amid the tears, "and I missed it." He was overcome with joy and happiness. I gave everyone in the ward my blessing including the doctors and nurses. I then went back to Gort Muire to give everyone my blessing and to sit down to a "pranzoni" (feast) with the other four newly ordained.

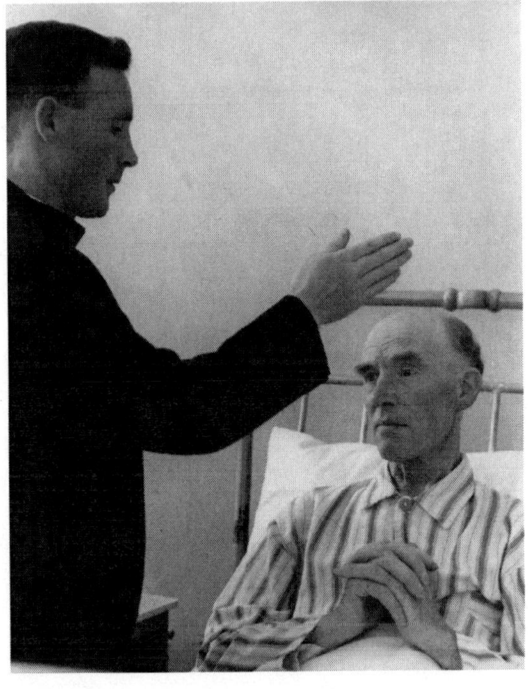

Dad receiving my First Blessing at Loughlinstown Hospital.

Afterwards we drove home to the Copse, through Enniskerry, up past the Sugarloaf mountain where they say the sun dances on Easter Sunday morning. The sun seemed to be dancing that day. Through Roundwood, the highest village in Ireland, on to Laragh and Senator Sweetman's gate where my brother met his death. A brief pause for a prayer and a promise that I would remember him in my first Mass the next day. Past Clara with its ancient bridge and beautiful Church nestled in the valley below. Over the switch-back undulating winding road and at last I was home. There was no Alicia there to greet me. The Horsmans had left a short time before. Mrs Horsman had died and the family decided to move to Jersey. Once more the beautiful big house was vacant.

With news of my arrival home the neighbours began to arrive for my blessing. Mick and Kate Meegan and the chaps. Jack and Lil Jordan together with Christy Byrne and Paddy Mac. I said my first Mass the following morning in the Church in Rathdrum, the same church where I had made my First Communion in my little sailor's suit and my Confirmation, sitting in fear and trembling waiting for the Bishop to ask me a question. With my back to the people I began;

"Introibo as altare Dei,

Ad Deum qui Laetificat juventutem meum.

My First Mass, Rathdrum 13th July 1959
a wonderful day with all my family and friends.

The Church was packed, the choir sang beautifully, and everyone came for my first blessing at the end. The reception was held at the Vale View hotel overlooking the Meeting of the Waters. It was a beautiful setting on the side of a hill.

"There is not in this wide world a valley so sweet

As the Vale in whose bosom the bright waters meet."

Cutting the Cake with mam, Avoca.

All my relations were there, uncles, aunts, cousins as well as all my friends from down through the years. Mr. Morrissey and Mr. Gordon, my old teachers. Mr. Gordon had already begun training for the priesthood in England. John O'Connor and Corky were there and our photo was in the Independent the next day. By now John O'Connor was engaged to be married to Sheila Lemass, the youngest daughter of An Taoiseach, Mr. Sean Lemass, while Corky was making a name for himself as a playwright. It was wonderful to be able to share such a happy occasion with so many of my family and friends. There was also a touch of sadness that my father was not present. My mother helped me to cut the big cake and it was distributed among the guests while the many speeches took place. Now I was a priest forever and I began my priestly life not knowing what lay ahead.

Rome To Rathdrum : Story With A Happy Ending :

HITCH-HIKING TRIO

Same trio on top in 1950 and below on ordination day. Left to right—Mr. John O'Connor, Rev. Father Christopher Conroy, O.Carm., and Mr. Denis O'Flynn.

A SCHOOLBOY friendship between three hitch-hiking students of Terenure College was renewed under very happy circumstances. The three students who, nine years ago, hitch-hiked to Rome for the Holy Year, met at the Parish Church in Rathdrum where one of the friends, Christopher Conroy, now **Rev. Father Conroy, O.Carm.**, celebrated his first Mass in his native parish.

Reliving Their Tour

THE other two members of the hitch-hiking trio were **Mr. John O'Connor**, a commercial traveller of Lakelands Park, Terenure, who has recently become engaged to **Miss Sheila Lemass**, youngest daughter of An Taoiseach, Mr. Sean Lemass, and **Mr. Denis O'Flynn**, Ballyvolane House, Cork, who is making a name for himself as an amateur playwright. At last year's Cork Festival he was highly commended for one of his plays.

After their adventure across Europe, the three students remained firm friends, and when they met after Father Conroy's first Mass following his ordination in Clonliffe College they enjoyed recounting incidents of their tour., during their school careers and afterwards.

Through The Iron Curtain

FATHER CONROY, a native of The Copse, Rathdrum, Co. Wicklow, entered the Carmelite Novitiate in Kinsale and continued his studies for the priesthood in Gort Muire, Dundrum, and taught for a year in his old school, Terenure College.

John O'Connor was captain of the Terenure team which won the Leinster Schools Senior Rugby Cup for the first time in 1952. In the same year he was captain of the Leinster Schools Interprovincial team. Since then he has had a successful career in business circles in Dublin.

Denis O'Flynn, member of a prominent Cork business family, since his first experience of touring has been an intrepid hitch-hiker and has visited nearly every country in Europe—and has even penetrated the Iron Curtain.

Before leaving on their Holy Year journey to Rome, the three boys, then all aged about 16, were interviewed by an *Irish Independent* reporter and now their happy reunion has forged another link in a strong bond of friendship.

On Wednesday next, Father Conroy will celebrate the Nuptial Mass at the marriage of Mr O'Connor and Miss Lemass at the Church of The Good Shepherd, Churchtown.

Report in the Independent on the reunion of the three musketeers.

The three Musketeers reunite after my first Mass Avoca 1959.

John and Sheila were to be married on the following Wednesday. They arranged it especially so that I could perform the ceremony. I called to see Sheila's family beforehand in Churchtown. Sean and Kathleen knelt down humbly before me for my blessing. Just then Charlie Haughey arrived in a bubble car. "Will you look at what he is driving now" remarked Sean as he came in. He too knelt down for my blessing. He had been elected to the Dail two years before. He was Sean Lemass's son in law, being married to his daughter Maureen. My first marriage couldn't have been more important or spectacular. Most of the Government of the day was present. The President Eamon De Valera and his wife Sinéad came into the sacristy and promptly knelt down for my blessing. In my wildest dreams I could never have imagined that I would give my first blessing to the President and Taoiseach of Ireland. The reception was in the Royal Marine Hotel in Dun Laoghaire. My second wedding was my brother Davy who married Margaret in Monkstown Church in September. This was to be my first family wedding but there were to be many more.

Wedding of John O Connor and Sheila Lemass,my first wedding.

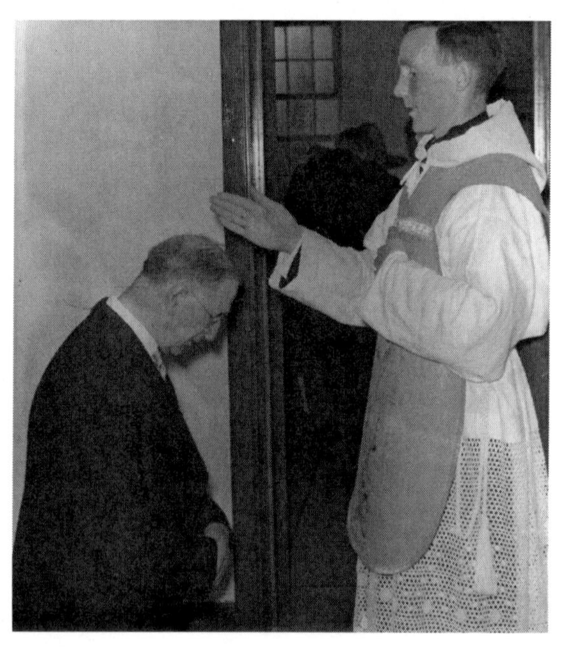

Eamon de Valera receiving my first Blessing.

Chatting with Eamon de Valera and Sean Lemass.

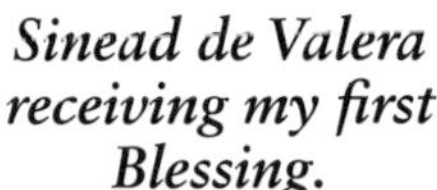

Sinead de Valera receiving my first Blessing.

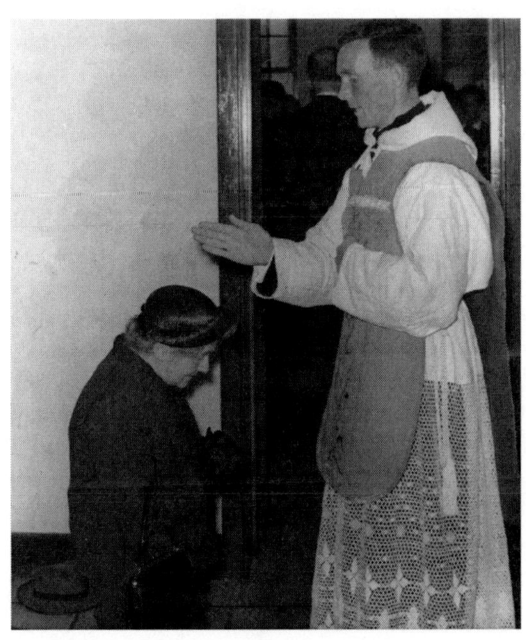

I was happy one day when the Prior asked me would I do research in the National Library on the history of Terenure College that was celebrating its Centenary the following year 1960. It was with great foresight that Fr. Bennet, the Provincial at the time bought Terenure house in 1859 with the intention of opening a boarding school there. The College of Our Blessed Lady of Mount Carmel was formally opened on January 10th 1860. It is a strange coincidence that it was also Fr. Bennet who invited the first Holy Ghost fathers to Ireland. When Father Holley CSSp came in search of a suitable house he stayed with the Carmelites in Whitefriar St. It was the Carmelites that helped him to discover Castle Dawson House at Williamstown where the "French College" and now known as Blackrock College was established in the same year 1860 as Fr. Bennet established Terenure College. The two Colleges have been great rivals on the rugby field ever since. The College passed through troubled times from 1917 to 1922 when it was regularly used by "rebels on the run". Michael Collins spent long periods here and he introduced this hiding place to many others. I wrote to Dan Breen to ask him for his memories. He wrote back.

Dear Fr. Conroy

"Your letter to hand. I can recall my stay in Terenure College after 40 yrs and our meeting Fr. Gerhard, Fr. Lynch and many others. I went out there sometime in January 1920. I was recovering from wounds received in Ashtown when we attacked Lord French and his convoy. It was the late Michael Collins that took me out to the College and I feel I stayed over a week in the place.

The old memory is fading but I'll call on W. T. Cosgrave and he will help me to revive it.

Wishing you all the best,

Sincerely yours,

Dan Breen."

Sean Treacy also took refuge there as did William T. Cosgrave. Fr. Gerhard, a native Australian who had done his studies in Ireland was Prior from 1916 to 1922. He was an active and open supporter of the Irish Republicans. He narrowly escaped death on one occasion when the Black and Tans raided the College immediately after a lightening departure of Michael Collins. Terenure College has the distinction of being the first Secondary School to be affiliated to the G.A.A.

"United Ireland" for October 31st 1885 carries the following notice.

"The professors and students of the Carmelite College held a meeting on the 24th of October, with the Very Rev. T Bartley O.C.C., President, in the chair, at which the following resolutions were passed unanimously:

Firstly: That we hail with delight the efforts of the Gaelic Association under the patronage of Most Rev. Dr. Croke, Charles Stewart Parnell, M.P. and Michael Davitt, to revive the ancient and historic pastimes of our country.

Secondly: That believing it to be one of the functions of educational establishments to provide for the physical no less than the moral and intellectual training of the rising generation of Irishmen in accordance with the instinct and traditions of their
ancient race, we hereby form ourselves into a branch of the G.A.A."

The Gaelic games of football and hurling were played in Terenure with distinction in the early days and were the only games allowed at that time.

***

Towards the end of the year the Provincial, Fr. O Shea came to Gort Muire to see me. He informed me that I had been appointed to the mission team and I would be stationed in Whitefriar street. He added that I would be joining Fr. McGrath, Fr. Bulbert, and Fr. Griffin on a parish mission in the Cathedral in Ballina in September. I was flabbergasted. Not only was I not going on the foreign missions to Rhodesia, but I was being thrown in at the deep end of parish missions.

19

Parish Missions

I took the Saturday morning train to Ballina for the two week mission. As I placed my heavy case on the overhead rack I wondered had I remembered everything and my brown habit and white cloak which Carmelites wear while preaching. I also had the two evening sermons and four morning instructions which Fr. McGrath had given me to prepare a couple of months before. The Carmelites were new to parish missions. We had less than half a dozen priests on our mission team. The Dominicans and the Redemptorists were well known preachers, the Redemptorists for their hell fire and brimstone. They raised their voices and thumped the pulpit as they harangued the people into repentance. Everyone attended the mission, the women the first week and the men the second. The women had the reputation of being more religious and easier to deal with. The men were considered hard and stubborn, and more set in their ways, standing at the back of the church. often talking during the sermon.

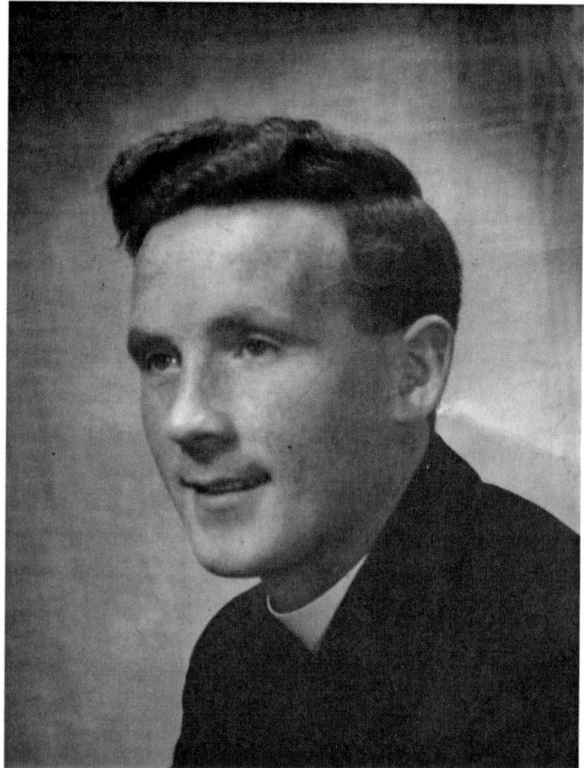

A priest at last

The Carmelites led by Fr. McGrath adopted a different style of parish mission. We didn't raise our voices but spoke gently and kindly encouraging the people to change their ways. Fr. McGrath always preached with his eyes closed. He told me how this came about. He ascended the pulpit in Dundrum parish church to preach his first sermon and as he looked down on the congregation, there in the front seat was Frank Aiken, the minister for external affairs, looking up at him. He quickly closed his eyes and never opened them again.

By now I was half way to Ballina. The carriage had filled with people on the way home for the weekend. Apart from a quick nod and salute they left me to myself by the window. I took out my breviary and began to say the Divine office. It was still in Latin. It worked as a 'don't disturb' sign. I had learned my sermons off by heart so I went through them again. By the time we reached Ballina there was just one woman left in the carriage. "Are you on holiday's father?" she asked. "No" I said hesitantly, "I'm one of the missioners." "Oh," she said, "We are all looking forward to the mission, we never had the Carmelites before. "I'm one of four" I said, "the others came on Wednesday for the children's mission." "You are very young to be a missioner," she said. "We usually have old men." "It's my first time," I said. "Oh, the young people will love you," she continued, "They need someone young these days." I blushed and smiled. "Good luck with the mission" she said as she waved me goodbye.

As I stepped onto the platform there was a band to meet me. Someone took my case and I marched up to the Administrator's house to the sound of music. The others were at the door to meet me. Fr. Bulbert had been a chaplain with the British forces during the second world war. He had seen action in the desert in Tobruck and El Alamein. He had some great stories about Montgomery and Rommel which went down very well during the men's week. Fr. Griffin was a few years older than me. He had a wonderful preaching voice and the women loved him. I was to do many missions with him and he was very kind to me. Fr. McGrath welcomed me to my first mission and after supper called me up to his room. "We preach at all the Masses tomorrow morning encouraging the people to attend the mission," he said. "I'll put you on the ten and twelve. "The bishop is saying the 11 o'clock, so I'll do that one." "But I haven't anything prepared," I said surprised, "I don't know what to say." "Don't worry" he said, "I'll write down a few notes." He took an envelope from his pocket and began to write on the back of it. "A mission is a time of great grace. It's a time to take stock of our lives and to see where we are going. The mission takes place each evening at 8 o'clock and each morning at 10 o'clock. There will be a short instruction during the Mass at 10 o'clock. Confessions will be heard each night after the Sermon and Benediction." He handed me the envelope and told me to learn it off by heart before I went to bed. I spent an uneasy night tossing and turning. The next morning I arrived down at the Cathedral at about a quarter to ten. Fr. McGrath was coming out of the sacristy. "There's been a slight change" he said, "The Bishop is saying your Mass." I was completely taken aback. I was sure he would say he would do it, but no, "Go ahead as usual" he said, as he went back for his breakfast. After the gospel the Bishop sat on his throne while I made my way up into the pulpit. I had never been in a pulpit before in my life. My knees were knocking beneath my habit and white cloak. I looked down on a sea of faces with all eyes on me. Once I began I was alright. It was strange hearing your voice resounding around the Cathedral through the microphones. After the sermon I had to read out the notices, these included names of the dead and the place names from around the parish. I'm sure I pronounced them all wrong. What a terrible start. This indeed had been a real baptism of fire. It was probably the best thing that ever happened to me. From now on I could face anything.

I went for long walks with Fr.McGrath every afternoon on the by-roads of Ballina. As soon as we reached the outskirts of the town he would say "Now you can begin." I had to preach my sermon to him as we walked along. He listened attentively to every word and made suggestions from time to time. The following day if I changed anything he would say. "You didn't say that yesterday." It was a wonderful training but one that I would not like to repeat. We formed a friendship that would last for the rest of his life. St. Paul tells us that he learned everything from the Rabbi Gamaliel in Jerusalem. Fr. McGrath was my Gamaliel and I will be eternally grateful to him.

This was the heyday of parish missions. Each parish priest considered it his duty to have a mission every year. The lost souls had to be rounded up and brought back to the fold. The parish priests also looked forward to the Missioners coming from Dublin to be brought up to date with what was happening in the Dublin Archdiocese and to exchange stories and jokes. One parish priest wrote to the provincial and said he was thinking of having a mission He would appreciate it if he could send him two wits. The provincial wrote. "I'm sorry I haven't two wits but I am sending you two half wits." All parish priests did their best to make the missioner welcome. One built a little hut at the bottom of the garden as there was no inside loo. On the first morning of the mission as the Missioner was in it, the door suddenly opened and a woman knelt down and said. "Bless me father for I have sinned, it's a month since my last confession." (This actually happened to me years later when I had to go in a hole in the ground in Peru.) The mission also gave the people the opportunity to hear different sermons. By now they knew all the parish priests sermons off by heart. The story is told of Fr. Philbin, a parish priest in a country parish outside Westport. One Sunday morning two lads went out early to shoot pheasants and woodcock and decided to get Mass in Fr. Philbin's church. They joined the men standing at the back of the church. Fr. Philbin began to preach. After twenty minutes he was still going strong. The lads could see pheasants rising all over the place. They turned to one of the men and whispered. "? Will he be long more?" Without batting an eyelid he replied. "The hawk didn't swoop yet." And on he went. Suddenly in a loud voice he shouted. "And the hawk of death swooped." The man turned towards the two lads and said. "ten minutes more."

During the next few years I went on missions all over the country but especially in the North. This was before the troubles in 1969 and I saw at first hand the discrimination between the two communities. The tension was simmering underneath. I made a big mistake during a mission in the Waterside in Derry. I was reading out the notices during Mass and there was a letter from the Council. I read out exactly what was written......Londonderry. Fr. McGrath was waiting for me when I arrived back into the sacristy. "You never say 'Londonderry', always refer to it as Derry." One evening I met a girl coming into the church. "What's on" she asked as she approached. "A mission" I said. "What's a mission?" she said. " A sermon, with Benediction" I said. "Will there be music" she asked "You see I'm a Protestant, but I never go to Church." She told me afterwards she loved it and returned for the week. On another occasion in Armagh I was reading my breviary, walking up and down on the road outside the church. The parish priest called me "You don't do that up here" he said. In the afternoon I went for a long walk in the countryside. I met some children coming home from school. I stopped to have a chat with them about school. That evening at supper I mentioned it to the parish priest. "Where did you meet them?" I explained as best I could. "They are Protestants" he said. "You don't talk to them." I also went on missions to London, Manchester, Liverpool and Birmingham. I remember especially a mission in Romford in Essex. We watched the beginning of the Second Vatican Council from Rome. Everyone was amazed when Pope John XXIII called a Council. Little did we realise the changes it would bring about in the church.

The mission took the form of Rosary, notices, sermon and Benediction. The notices usually contained a little story to cheer the people up. Like the one about the parish priest who preached a stupendous sermon on the miracle that Our Lord performed when he fed five people with five thousand loaves. When he realized his mistake he decided to keep going and hoped no-one would notice. There were two lads underneath the pulpit and one nudged the other and said "Sure anyone could do that." The parish priest overheard them and during the week he wondered how to rectify his mistake. The following Sunday he began with the stupendous miracle that Our Lord did when he fed five thousand people with five loaves. He paused, looked down at the two lads and said. "Could you do that?" "Sure we could father, with what we had left over from last week."

A MISSION

AT

St. Mary's Catholic Church, Evesham
Sunday, March 15th to
Sunday, March 22nd, 1970

SUNDAY, MARCH 15th:
MISSION OPENS WITH MASSES AT 8 a.m. 10 a.m.
EVENING MASS 6.30 p.m.

WEEKDAYS:
MORNING MASS 9.15 a.m.
EVENING MASS 7.30 p.m.

SUNDAY, MARCH 22nd:
CLOSE OF MISSION AND RENEWAL OF BAPTISMAL VOWS.

VISITATION OF THE HOMES OF THE PARISH BY THE MISSIONER: MARCH 8th to MARCH 22nd.

CHILDREN'S MISSION: MARCH 18th, 19th, 20th.

MISSIONER

REV. CHRISTOPHER CONROY O. CARM.

Confessions each evening after Mission.

A MISSION IS A VERY IMPORTANT EVENT IN EVERY PARISH. IT IS A CALLING TOGETHER TO RENEW OURSELVES IN THE LIGHT OF GOD'S GRACE.
DON'T LET THIS OPPORTUNITY PASS YOU BY.
BRING YOUR FRIENDS, **CATHOLIC** AND **NON-CATHOLIC.**

ALL ARE WELCOME

This Notice should be placed where it may be seen by all members of the family. If any of your friends or relatives are neglecting their religious duties, take care to **tell them about the Mission at once:** give them a copy of this bill, and do all you can to bring them with you to Church. Read the above carefully every night, and pray to obtain for yourself and the whole Parish the grace to make a good Mission.

ALL NON-CATHOLICS
are cordially invited to attend the Mission, and will be welcome to all the Services. Catholics should bring their non-Catholic relatives and friends regularly to the Mission.

Sharp Bros. (Printers) Ltd., Evesham, Worcs.

Mission in Evesham. 1970.
I gave missions throughout Ireland, England, Scotland and Wales.

The most important part of an English mission was the visitation. Every Catholic family in the parish had to be visited the week before the mission. This was very difficult when there was no parish registrar. Where do you start? Wolverhampton was particularly difficult. There were a large number of West Indians and black people. Most of the people had never seen a priest before. Some of the streets on the list didn't even exist anymore. They had been bombed during the war. We went to the Catholic school and got all the children to write down their names and addresses. Then we began. I called to see an Irishman one Friday evening. This was still the time of 'No meat on Friday.' As he opened the door there was a beautiful smell of rashers and sausages coming from the kitchen. He invited me in to have supper with him. I said I would just have a cup of tea. We chatted away about old Ireland while he tucked into his rashers and sausages. I called to another house where only the children were home. The older girl immediately recognised me and asked me in. We were talking when the door suddenly opened and the Father came in. He was stocious and as soon as he saw me he came towards me, picked me up and physically threw me out the door. I will never forget the look of consternation on the young girl's face. Dusting myself down I continued on. I noticed the picture of the Sacred Heart and Our Lady through the window of a house. I looked at my list but they weren't on it. I knocked on the door and a young West Indian man answered. "What can I do for you, Sir." he said. "I'm the missioner, and I'm just visiting the Catholics. I said. "We ain't Catholics," he said in a jovial manner. "But you have the picture of the Sacred Heart and Our Lady," I said. "We got the pictures" he said laughing, "but we ain't Catholic. The parish priest in Gillingham had a particular problem. An Irish woman in the Parish had died and asked to be cremated. There were no cremations in Ireland at the time. Then her wish was that the ashes would be sent back to Ireland and scattered around the farm in Mayo. The urn was sitting on the mantelpiece in the parish priest's sitting room. He had written to the parish priest in Ireland, who had written back saying "I'm not familiar with that situation." He decided to post the urn to him anyway. I can just imagine the parish priest's face when he opened the package. They never said anything about that in Maynooth.

An important part of the mission was confession. There were long queues outside each box and the last one didn't leave the church until after midnight. Some had returned to the fold after twenty or thirty years in the wilderness. It was like throwing out a net to catch the big fish and was considered the most important result of the mission. There are many jokes told about confession. Two women went to confession, one on each side. As they entered they didn't notice the priest leaving. One of the women put her head down and began telling her sins. After a long list of all kinds of sins she looked up and saw the woman opposite looking at her. "Where's the priest?" she asked "I don't know" said her friend, but if he heard half of what I have just heard he is probably gone for the guards." Hearing confessions can be very boring. Sitting for hours in a confined space with very little fresh air is exhausting. Christmas Eve was especially difficult. The queues stretched around the church and it could take up to two hours to reach the box. On one occasion a young girl came in and said: "Father, I have being waiting for a long time, and I wanted to go somewhere. I'm afraid I've just gone." There was no mistaking the sound. I asked the person on the other side to go into the office and ask Paul to come and clean things up. After a while I heard scrubbing and mopping next door. When I thought he was finished I gently opened the slide to get a burst of disinfectant in my eye. On another occasion a girl fainted as she finished her confession and fell out of the box. I can just imagine what it must have looked like seeing the door open and a girl falling out. When I looked out everyone had gone. I am not surprised that this old style ritualistic confession has gone.

Another important part was visiting the sick. The curate drove me out into the most remote regions of the parish. In the middle of nowhere he stopped the car, opened up the boot, gave me a pair of Wellingtons and pointed me to a farmhouse in the distance across a number of fields. "Don't forget to close the gates" he said "there might be a bull." As I approached the farm the dogs came out barking to greet me. In the farmyard it was difficult to know which was the dwelling and which was the outhouses. All had been freshly whitewashed for the arrival of the missioner. An old woman appeared at the door and blessed herself as she led me in. There was a big open fire blazing away with a table laden with food. She brought me down to the bedroom to her husband who was sitting up in the bed to greet me. "He's been laid up now for a number of years Father," she said as she left me. I heard his confession and then he said. "They wanted me to go to hospital, Father, but I wouldn't go." "Did you not think they could do anything for you" I said. "It wasn't that Father," he replied "they say the first thing they do when they get you in there is give you a bath. I wasn't going to risk that." I gave him communion and anointed him. "Do you think I'll get better" he asked. "If it's Gods will" I said. "Just say Thy Holy Will be done." He looked at me and said "Thy Holy will be done, and I hope to God that I'm not done." Before I left he told me to open the little drawer and find five pounds for a Mass for the family. His wife had the tea made when I arrived back in the kitchen. "Sit yourself, down, Father and have something to eat." she said pouring out the tea. There was a roast chicken in the centre of the table and lovely brown bread and scones with country butter. "I'm afraid I can't stay long" I said, "Fr O Reilly is waiting for me on the road." She knelt down for my blessing and asked me to bless the house before I left. As I made my way back through the fields I felt humbled and privileged to have met such people of great faith and generosity. How much time and effort they had spent preparing for the arrival of the missioner. As we drove back in the car I remembered that my father had asked me to get him a bottle of Poitín. I asked Fr. O'Reilly was it possible. The next day he presented me with a bottle of Poitín, one hundred per cent proof.

The mission always concluded with a flourish. Religious objects had been bought during the week and all these had to be blessed; Rosaries, medals, statues, pictures of the Sacred Heart, scapulars and of course candles. Every house had blessed candles, in case the priest had to be called. Some were kept in reserve, while others lit continuously before the picture of the Sacred Heart. These were replaced by a little red bulb when the electricity arrived. The candles were also used for the renewing of Baptismal vows. Holding up their lighted candles, amid a sea of light the missioner shouted. "Do you renounce Satan"? The response was shouted back with great enthusiasm. "We do." "And all his works" "We do" "And all his pomps" "We do" No one ever knew what pomps were. There was also a special collection for the missioners to which the people were asked to give generously.

20

Whitefriar Street

The Carmelites came to Whitefriar St. in 1279 not long after they had arrived in England from the Holy Land. They were dispossessed during the Reformation in 1539 and weren't re-established until after Catholic Emancipation in 1829. It was after this that the present church and monastery were built. It is a magnificent building with long corridors and large spacious rooms. The church one of the largest in Dublin was renowned for Mass and confessions. People came from far and wide and it was said that the Carmelites heard half the confessions of Dublin. Each priest had his own clientele and long queues could be seen outside for Fr. Devlin, Fr. Haughey and Fr. Smith. I was given a box beside Fr. McGrath near Our Lady of Dublin. Shortly after arriving I was given the position of Sacristan. This meant I was in charge of all the Masses and the altar boys as well as the Shrines The Church is renowned for its Shrines. There are nineteen altogether. As you enter the church from Aungier St., there is a large Calvary in front of you with St Albert's well to the right. On entering the church Our Lady of Dublin is on the right with Our Lady of Lourdes on the left. Our Lady of Dublin had been rescued from a farm where its hollowed back was being used as a pig trough. It ended up in a second hand shop in Capel St. Fr Spratt discovered it and bought it for a pittance . It now takes pride of place among the Shrines of Whitefriar St. Up near the sanctuary there was a little cluster of Shrines which were very popular. In the centre was St Therese of Lisieux. There was a Novena for her feast day. Mrs. Byrne from the flower shop in Grafton St. presented us with hundreds of red roses for her feast. A blessed rose was worth its weight in gold on St. Therese's feast day. Beside St Therese is St. Jude, the patron of hopeless cases. The devotions to St. Jude took place every Tuesday evening. The church was packed. Sometimes the congregation overflowed on to Aungier St. and stopped the traffic. Once a year on the 14th of February St Valentine was the centre of attention. His remains had been given to a famous Carmelite Fr. John Spratt by Pope Gregory XVI in 1835. Young engaged couples visited the church all day to place flowers on his Shrine. I had the privilege once of seeing inside the casket containing his remains. All that was left was a few bones. Around each Shrine were large candelabras which were continuously ablaze with candles. Once as I was coming home on the bus to Whitefriar St. there were two elderly women in the seat in front of me. As we neared the church one turned to the other and said. "Daisy are you going into Whitefriar St to say a prayer.?" "No Philomena, I gave up praying in there. If you stayed longer than five minutes they would put a Shrine around you."

Shortly after arriving in Whitefriar St. Fr. McGreevy took ill. He was teaching religion in Crumlin Road Technical School. The Prior asked me if I would fill in until he got better. So I found myself going up on the bus every day for nine o'clock to teach teenage girls. The Principal Miss O'Carroll arranged the timetable so that I would always have first and last class. She said she liked having me in the school in case anything happened. I don't know what she expected might happen.

The teaching of religion was a continuation of what I had learned in the National School: an explanation of the commandments and the Sacraments as well as parables and stories from Bible. The girls were very well behaved so I had no discipline problems. Some of the other teachers did but they seemed to respect the priest. On Thursday we had a half day and went to the recreational grounds in Terenure, just below the college for sports. I took the Camogie team. Some of the girls were very good and we won most of our matches. There was one girl who used to mark me in training and she was as tough as nails as strong and talented as any boy. I was only meant to be there for a few weeks, but the weeks went into months and I was there until the end of the year. On the way home on the bus there was a big crowd of the girls who got off at their various stops. But there was one girl that lived near Whitefriar St. and she got off at the same stop as me. One day the Prior was looking out the window and saw the two of us getting off the bus together. He was waiting for me at the top of the stairs. "Who was that girl you got off the bus with?" he asked sternly. "She's from the school," I said "she lives down the road." "Well from now on you are to take a different bus home."

***

My camogie team at Crumlin Rd. A winning team.

Whitefriar St. took care of the nearby hospitals, Mercers, the Adelaide, Cork St., Meath St. and the South Dublin Union known as St. Kevin's. I spent some time in each one but I spent months in St. Kevin's, which is the present day St. James's Hospital. The South Dublin Union was originally built on the site of an older hospital in the middle of the 19th century. It was built as a workhouse for the poor and the elderly. The first Carmelite entry in the baptismal registry was Fr. John Carr in 1861. The Carmelites had been chaplains to the hospital since that date. In my time they were Fr. Coffey and Fr. Tyndall, Fr. Coffey trained me in. I went up with him on the bus after breakfast and he showed me around the different hospitals which were known by a number. He introduced me to the nurses, and the doctors and especially the Matron. She ruled with an iron hand and everyone was afraid of her. Once she caught me having a cup of tea in the tea-room with a group of nurses. Some were sitting on the table when she came in. She gave them one look and they jumped to attention. She greeted me with a smile and said "Good morning ,Father." They told me afterwards that she read the riot act to them about giving me bad example by showing their legs. My first duty was to attend to the emergencies, the people in the various wards who had to be anointed. Then I distributed Holy Communion to a number of wards. Then there were confessions to be heard. Once Fr. Coffey asked me to hear confessions in the old women's ward. They were in their 80's and 90's. I bent down beside each one for confession, some hugged me, others kissed me, I did my best to get them to tell me their sins, and give them absolution. When I met Fr. Coffey afterwards he asked; "Did you hear all the confessions." "I did," I said. "All except the Jewish lady" he said. "I heard hers as well" I said. "No-one told me about a Jewish lady." He smiled and said. "I don't suppose it will do her any harm." We always heard the confession of those going for an operation. Sometimes there was resistance. I remember a man in Mercers who refused to have anything to do with me. I went back three or four times but he just cursed at me. During dinner there was an urgent phone call from Mercers. The man wanted to see me. I heard his confession as he was being wheeled into the theatre. An operation is wonderful for concentrating the mind. Being on duty meant you attended all emergencies during the day or night. You could be called three or four times a night. The phone rang, you jumped out of bed, put on your habit and by the time you reached the door the taxi was waiting. You rushed to the ward anointed the person and consoled the relatives. Often the person died so you had to share the pain of the bereaved. This could happen more than once a night. It was difficult to go back to sleep as if nothing happened. Fr. Coffey was chaplain at the South Dublin Union for many years. He was very kind and understanding with all the patients. He had a special place for the old men. There was a press in the office full of plug tobacco which he always carried in his pockets for those who had none. He always encouraged me to make sure I had some. The South Dublin Union was a wonderful pastoral training ground and I couldn't have had a better teacher than Fr. Coffey. I learned listening skills and counseling at the bedsides of the sick and the dying which have remained with me to the present day.

A Carmelite

A little girl came home late from school one day. Her mother was annoyed and scolded her. "Your dinner is burnt" she said, "what kept you?" "I couldn't help it," she said, "I was helping my friend. Her doll fell and got broken." "Oh," said her mother, "you were helping her to put it back together again." "No" said her daughter. "It was too badly broken. I was helping her to cry." I helped many people to cry.

***

We all assembled in the oratory at 9.30 pm for night prayer. After about ten minutes there would be an unmerciful racket just outside the door on the back stairs. It was the boys from the club on their way home. All eyes turned towards me. No words were necessary to get the message. "Why can't you control these scoundrels and teach them to walk down the stairs quietly. Do they not know that the priests are saying their prayers." I quickly exited the back door and stopped the pandemonium. There were over one hundred boys between the ages of 12 and 18 in the Carmelite Boys Club. Whitefriar St. was surrounded by old Georgian houses, once the homes of the wealthy, which had been converted to flats and tenements. York St and Digges St were the worst: large families living in one or two rooms. Although the people were poor they were loyal to the Church. Their children went to St Peter's school beside the church and they attended Mass on Sundays. For the children of these families, the Club was their only place of refuge. It kept them off the street and out of mischief. The Legion of Mary provided the leaders for the club. We took over the old unused part of the house and converted it into a miniature boys town There was a television room, lounge, billiard room, we even had our own shop. We had our own gazette, produced, edited and illustrated by the boys themselves.

There were also classes in shoe repairing, carpentry and arts and crafts. We also had three football teams with games most week-ends. The club nurtured many future well known players. I got to know all the boys very well and helped them through all their problems and difficulties, visiting their homes and often providing financial help when needed. The boys themselves were responsible for the upkeep of the club, doing all the painting and decorating. The club had no income so I had to run a bingo session every Friday night. This brought together most of the mothers and many others from the area. I did the shopping every week for the variety of prizes The boys went hiking with the leaders up the Dublin mountains most week-ends in the winter and camping week-ends in the Summer. It was difficult for me to get away on week-ends but I never missed the Summer holidays by the sea side. We usually went to Balbriggan or Skerries. This took a lot of organisation. We had to bring almost everything we needed as well as food and a cook. To see the joy and excitement on the faces of the boys made it all worthwhile. These were the only holidays they had. I also saw the lads in a different light swimming in the sea and on the rides at the Carnival in Skerries. There were no strict rules and regulations in the Club. The older ones looked after the younger and if anyone stepped out of line they were usually taken care of by the boys themselves. During my time with the Boys Club there was little teenage crime around Whitefriar St. And drugs had not yet arrived. Most of my work in the Boys Club had to be done in my spare time as there was no allowance made on the list for playing with boys.

***

It was during a mission in Dundalk that one of the major decrees of the Second Vatican Council came into force. The Mass was said in English for the first time at all the Masses. The altars had not being turned around yet but now at least the people could understand what was being said. Part of the mystery and mystique had been taken away. When John Charles McQuaid arrived home at the end of the Council he assured everyone at the airport that nothing had changed. The motto seemed to be ‘Don’t disturb the poor lay people in their Faith. It soon became evident that the laity were much more acceptable to change than many of the Bishops and priests. While the Carmelites didn’t come under the jurisdiction of Archbishop McQuaid as religious , his influence extended to every corner of the diocese. The Catholic Church in Dublin saw a massive expansion during his term of thirty two years. Many new parishes were founded and new churches built. He built up a wide range of social services for the poor in the city. While the people applauded this, it was his influence in every aspect of church life that annoyed a lot of people. A letter from the Archbishop to the Provincial could remove a religious from his office discreetly without any consultation. Ministers of the Government were influenced behind the scenes and legislation was withdrawn or modified. His Lenten pastorals were read in all churches during Lent. The prohibition on Catholics attending Trinity College was repeated every year. He influenced the Theatre protests against Orson Welles, Danny Kaye, Larry Adler and Arthur Miller. He tried to prevent the Republic of Ireland soccer team from playing Yugoslavia in Dublin although most of the team were Catholics. He did succeed in preventing the President from attending the match and the No 1 army band from playing. Little wonder then that he did not welcome the changes of the Second Vatican Council. He resisted them as long as possible. An image commission was set up to report on the 'image' of the Catholic Church in Dublin. The term 'public image' originated in commercial and advertising circles. It is based on the fact that a person sees what he wants to see and his reaction to a statement may not be the statement but his personal interpretation of it. Every priest is familiar with the situation where someone comes to him after a sermon and accuses him of saying something he never said. The 'image' of the bishop was examined in great detail. The Archbishop was considered too aloof from the people, living in a palace and being wheeled out every now and then to perform ceremonies or make statements. A leader must lead as well as rule. Get out of his fancy dress and take a walk down O'Connell St. and talk to the people. Full use must be made of the mass media., press, radio, and television. Society in Ireland was rapidly changing especially in education. People's education is now on a par with the clergy. Before the Vatican Council the people took it for granted that there was an official line in the church on most problems and that Bishops more or less held the same views without having to arrive at them by discussion. The News of the Vatican Council came from popular reporting in the newspapers rather than the church. In this light the Irish Hierarchy appeared conservative. The public image of the Church depends to a great extent on the image of the Bishop.

***

The image of the Church has changed many times down through the years. The Church of fifty years ago is not recognisable now The church is a living thing, it is constantly changing . As Cardinal Newman said 'to live is to change and to be perfect is to have changed a lot.' . No place is this more evident than in the hearing of Confession. There were sixteen confession boxes in Whitefriar St. and they were constantly in use. On Saturdays and on the Eve of holy days confessions began with the 10 o'clock Mass and continued all day until 10 o'clock at night. There was a confession bell in the church which could be rung for the priest on duty at any time. Confession was very frightening for the penitent and often very boring for the priest. No one liked going to Confession. The same list of sins was always trotted out. A person could be away for a year and rattle off "I was disobedient, told lies, and cursed, that's all father." Men never liked to talk. Women were more ready for a chat, not necessarily about their sins. You entered the confession box with a certain amount of fear and anxiety and came away relieved and with your soul as white as snow. Individual confession in a box did not exist in the early church. If you committed a public sin against the community, you were expelled from the community until you made a public act of repentance. This might happen once in a lifetime. It began in the monasteries of Irish monks. The people went to individual monks to discuss their problems. The monks gave them a blessing and they went away happy. When the Irish monks spread the gospel throughout Europe they brought the tradition of individual confession with them and put confession boxes in the churches. The Council of Trent put it into a ritualistic formula and confirmed it as a Sacrament. It was an outward sign of inward Grace. Frightening sermons of Hell fire and brimstone were all the rage. If you died in mortal sin you went straight to Hell for all eternity. The priest was battling with the devil for the salvation of souls. Going to confession became legalistic, frightening, and solemn. It soon became a ritual which had little relation to reality. The main difficulty about going to confession was sex. Anything to do with sex was considered a mortal sin. People who were struggling with their own sexuality did not know how to talk about it in confession. They tried to cover it up with less important sins, hoping the priest would not hear and if he did that he wouldn't ask any questions. "I told lies, I didn't say my prayers, I had bad thoughts." Then came the all important question; "Did you take pleasure in them." I must say I never delved into the details of any sexual matters. I gave forgiveness for whatever had occurred. Another way of getting around the subject was to say. "I committed bad actions." That covered a multitude as it could mean anything. "Company keeping" was another phrase that covered everything.

The story goes that a student in the University put his head around the priests door and asked. "How far can you go with a girl, Father, without committing a mortal sin?" (He wanted a quick answer.) "It all depends," said the priest. "If you are walking you can go so far; if you are on a bike you could go a bit further, if you were in a car you can go to hell altogether." There are many jokes told about confession.

***

One day I was coming out of my room when who was coming up the stairs carrying two heavy cases but my old friend Fr. Mick Carroll. He was on the move again. His eyes lit up as he came towards me and said. "Thanks be to God there is someone I can talk to." He came into my room for a chat. "I'm free at last " he said, "there is nothing else they can do to me, I've been everywhere. This is the last roundup." I recalled the words of the song "Freedom is another word for nothing left to lose." I helped him with his cases up the next flight of stairs to his room directly over me. Most of the priests in Whitefriar St. were much older than me and were there to end their days. Many were in their 70's and 80's. They had borne the heat of the day, they had fought the good fight, they had finished the race. Some had been on the missions in Australia and America as well as England and Wales. Fr. Haughey had served with the Australian forces in the Second World War. Fr. Bulbert was with the British. They both met on the battlefield in the desert in North Africa. Here we all came together to form a Carmelite community. In Kinsale we frequently sang "Ecce quam bonum, et quam jucundum habitare fratres in unum." (How good it is and how joyful for the brothers to live together in common). I'm afraid it didn't always turn out that way. Everything depended on the Prior. He was there to make sure you kept the rule and laws and regulations. The keeping of petty rules was linked to a progress in sanctity. You earned a lot of merit by promptly answering the bell... As the superior was appointed by God you were doing God's will. In my time we had a few sergeant majors who would not have been out of place on the parade ground. As soon as you entered the house you could cut the atmosphere with a knife. Once when we had a celebration for the helpers at Christmas there was a sing song afterwards. The Prior looked towards Fr. Bulbert and shouted "sing Bulbert sing." There was a long refectory on the ground floor for meals. Everyone sat in seniority from the Prior down to me at the end. The Bursar sat in the centre at the bottom to cut the meat. Grace before meals was said in Latin. The Lector read from the rule and constitutions. By the time I was served everyone else was finished and the Prior was staring at me waiting to ring the bell We all then processed to the Oratory saying the 'Miserere ' There was coffee afterwards in the common room. All the fathers must be back for night prayer at 9.30pm on Sundays and on your half day. Not that you could be up to any mischief because clerics were forbidden to attend the theatre or to go to race meetings. After night prayer the older fathers went to the refectory for their tot of whiskey which had been carefully measured out by the bursar. I often wondered what the driver from Jameson's thought as he delivered the keg of whiskey every week. It was only natural that in a large community you would get on with some better than others There were many petty jealousies and disagreements . Some of these went very deep. One of the things that shocked me was the fact that there were three priests who never spoke or communicated with one another. This became very difficult when I was in their presence and they spoke to me but not to each other. I thought it very sad that three men who had dedicated their lives to the Order could end their lives like this. I made a resolution then that I would never end my days in Whitefriar St. in such a situation. While the shrines were being constructed in the church, the workmen could not begin work until after the 10 o clock Mass. One day when Fr. Tommy was saying the ten he went on a bit. The workmen began before he was finished. He stopped the Mass and asked them to wait until he concluded. On his way down the church to get some breakfast he met an irate Provincial. "Fr. pack your bags and get the one o'clock bus to Knocktopher. You are being transferred there until further notice," he said. Fr. Tommy proceeded to his room to pack. As he came down the stairs the Provincial was waiting for him. "I've changed my mind " he said, "Get the train to Moate instead."

Some years later when the former Provincial was transferred to England, Fr. Tommy was coming up the stairs from the refectory. As he reached the landing he met the former Provincial. "Do you remember the time you gave me the long kick" said Tommy. "Oh, now father we won't talk about that," said the former Provincial. "Well," said Tommy, "now you have got the long kick yourself and I hope you enjoy it." I must say I really enjoyed my time in Whitefriar St. Those years were the happiest of my life. The priests were among the finest I have ever met. Each of them by their different personalities made the Carmelite Church the most popular in Dublin. It was into this community that Fr Mick arrived one September day. He was a breath of fresh air. You wouldn't describe him as pious but you would say he was devout, a man of deep and abiding faith. There were so many different aspects to his personality. He had a very attractive personality. He had a touch of genius. He was simple yet profound, gentle yet rugged, he was very tolerant, but he was always his own man. He never trimmed his sails to suit the company. He loved his friends but never adapted to their whims and humours. "Take me as I am" was his motto. He offered his friendship and how fortunate you were to accept it. He was the greatest friend I ever had. He was always true to himself, a great priest who helped so many in his own particular way. He had a great love for the Carmelite Order. If he did any harm , he only did it to himself. Where ever you met him he was ready for a chat. Sometimes I would meet him on his way down to the ten Mass at a quarter past ten He would be all on for a chat. I gently reminded him of the time. "I'll be finished at the same time as the rest of them" he would say as he rushed on his way. And so he would. One afternoon he rushed into my room in a terrible state. He had been visiting his friends. He always carried a briefcase and he had left it on the bus. Everyone knew what he had in briefcase but he never let on. "Get me the G.P.O. quick," he said The phone was outside my door in the corridor. "Hello, is that the G.P.O.," he asked in an urgent tone. "Who might I be speaking to," he continued. "Mary, would you be so kind as to do me a favour? There'll be a number 22 bus passing by the G.P.O. in a couple of minutes, would you go down and on the top deck in the second seat you'll find a briefcase. No I can't, go to the lost property office. You can't do it, you can't do it. Would you ever put someone on who would be a little bit obliging?".......

A major problem arose coming up to Christmas. We all received about twenty Christmas cards each but of course this wasn't nearly enough for Mick. He arrived down to know had I any left over. I gave him what I had. He used them up quickly and was down again. "What am I going to do?" I asked him if he had last year's cards. "I have" he said, "but what good are they, they are used." "You could cut the bottom off them and no-one would know." I said. "Ah God you couldn't do that, they'd notice." he said. "Not if you wrote a poem and put it in the card. They would be so busy reading the poem they wouldn't notice the card." He didn't seem convinced but he went off to think about it. He had a wonderful gift for writing poetry. He came down in the middle of the night at about 3 o'clock and woke me up. "Ah, God, you're asleep" he said as he sat on the end of the bed. "Don't you go to sleep very early?" "It's 3 o'clock" I said. "I wrote a poem" he said "and I wanted to see what you thought of it."

He began.

"How happy those of us who see the star,
And follow in its wake to Bethlehem,
Where Majesty itself hath welcome there
For all who come to him.
His infant finger, friend to you be guide
The Manger ever light your troubled way
His presence give you peace and all beside
The love of Christ be yours this Christmas day."

"Wonderful" I said as I fell back to sleep.

***

The Carmelites, like most religious Orders hold Chapters every three years to elect Provincials and Councils. In those early days all the Province elected a number of delegates who had a vote at the Chapter. Now everyone has a vote. There are three rounds of votes. All voting is done in secret. Whoever comes out on top after the third round is elected. As in all elections, even for the Pope, there is a lot of activity behind the scenes. Various groups were promoting their own man. I had been elected a delegate to the Chapter in Whitefriar St. and observed for the first time all the intrigue and canvassing that went on. On the day of the voting there were two men in contention. In my opinion one would be worse than the other. I voted for Fr. McGrath who was not promoting himself for anything. After the first round one man was leading by a couple of votes. I let out an audible gasp of disbelief. After the second round the other man was leading by one vote. We had reached stalemate. In the third round all the people who did not belong to either faction switched their vote for Fr. McGrath. Everyone was dumbfounded when Fr. McGrath was elected Provincial. I'm sure there was never a more reluctant Provincial in the history of the Order. The story is told of when Pope John XIII went to heaven. No one recognised him. St. Peter sent for the Holy Ghost to find out who he was. "Who?" said the Holy Ghost. "Pope John," said St. Peter, the Pope who called the Second Vatican Council." "Good God, said the Holy Ghost, I was supposed to go to that." This was one Chapter where the Holy Ghost was definitely present.

It should not have come as a surprise that Fr. McGrath was elected Provincial when we realise that he was a nephew of the famous Fr. Peter Elias Magennis, the first Irish Carmelite General of the Order of whom we have already spoken. The members of the Order trebled during his time as General. One particular incident will indicate what kind of man he was. The English Bishops were imploring the Pope to excommunicate the I.R.A. Fr. Magennis repeatedly asked for an audience with the Pope, but the Pope always declined to see him when he found out it was about events in Ireland. Each year the Generals of all the Religious Orders have a half hour audience with the Pope and they brought with them a generous contribution from the Order. The practice was that you would have the audience, and when leaving place the envelope with a cheque on a side table which the Cardinals who were with the Holy Father would take. On the appointed day he was received by the Pope, discussions ensued about the Order and the progress it was making throughout the world and he again raised the Irish question. He said that this was causing the Order considerable concern, particularly in Ireland because the Whitefriar St. Carmelites had always been closely linked with the national movement. (Funerals took place at four or five in the morning to avoid police activity.) Again he got the cold shoulder from the Pope who coldly remarked that he had already expressed his views on this. He was given to understand that the church was not anxious to take any action which could be regarded as inimical to Great Britain at the time. Fr. Magennis took his leave without leaving the envelope containing the cheque which was the contribution of the Carmelite Order. He said some prayers in the Vatican and then walked around the city, visiting some nuns who were ill in hospital. He wandered around all day and only arrived back at St. Albert's at about nine o clock. There were three Cardinals waiting for him. They had been waiting for hours. "Where have you been?" "We have been waiting here all day." "Oh," he said, "I went to see Sister in the hospital. What is the matter?" The Cardinals told him he had forgotten to leave the cheque when he left the audience. "I know," he said. "I thought the Pope wasn't interested in what I had to say, so I kept the cheque." The Cardinals were very annoyed and suggested he give them the cheque. "Oh no, if the

Holy Father wants to see me again, I'll certainly go to see him. Then I'll consider the cheque.

An appointment was made for the next day. Fr. Magennis saw the Pope discussed the Irish question. The Pope agreed to send a Papal legate to Ireland. In those days there was no Nuncio in Ireland. Ireland was still regarded as being under the jurisdiction of the Papal legate in England. The Irish Hierarchy weren't keen on a representative of the Pope sitting in Dublin. The Pope sent Monsignor Luzio to Ireland. He had to stay at the Shelbourne Hotel. This had caused considerable shock in the Vatican. Normally a papal nuncio would be received and put up by the Archbishop or Cardinal. In his report back he said there were twenty six Popes in Ireland. One important result of his visit was that more priests were sent as chaplains to prisons. They could give absolution without requiring any undertaking. Each priest was to follow his own conscience. They had no right to refuse absolution.

Fr McGrath inherited many of the qualities of his famous uncle. His first duty was to appoint the Priors and Bursars of the various houses. These were considered the plum jobs and were usually reserved for those who supported and voted for you. Someone once remarked that Prior and Bursar were the only jobs worth having. Why do you say that? "Money is the answer, just money." Fr. McGrath didn't drive, so the first thing he did was asked me would I be his chauffeur. I drove him everywhere. The car was parked in Fanagans yard across from Whitefriar St. They are the funeral directors and every time you collected the car you observed the making of coffins. It was a good meditation to drive carefully. Fr McGrath had a week to appoint the Priors and bursars. As we drove along one day he casually remarked "I'm making you Prior of Whitefriar St." "You're what?" I said. "You are the best for the job," he continued. This was the last thing I wanted to do. It would be like going into the lion's den. But how could I refuse. I suddenly thought of suggesting someone else. "How about Fr. Arthur in Terenure," I said, "he would do a better job." He said nothing, but a couple of days later he said Fr. Arthur had accepted. During the next couple of years as we drove around the country he shared all his worries and problems with me. He hated having to reprimand anyone or to remove a Prior from his position. He soon developed an ulcer. He came into my room at night and talked for hours. One day he had a very difficult job to do. Fr. Tyndall who had been very ill for some time had developed cancer. He was convalescing with his family in Kildare. The next day we must go down and break the bad news. Fr Tyndall was a very saintly man and a wonderful Carmelite. He had been the Dean of Studies in Terenure and replaced Fr. Sugrue, as Novice master in Kinsale. Fr. McGrath did not foresee any problem in telling him he hadn't long to live. No one knew how they would react to such news. In fact Fr. Tyndall took the news very badly and Fr McGrath spent some time with him in prayer.

Fr. McGrath had friends all over the country and whenever we were in the vicinity we always paid them a visit. Often they were farmers or rich old ladies who lived in big houses with winding avenues leading up to them. He was welcomed with open arms into the parlor and immediately introduced me to his friend. He then proceeded to remain silent as I had to do all the talking while the tea was being served. He was a very shy man. He had spent years in our monastery in Kildare. He was famous for his blessings, both of animals and of humans. The story is told of the woman who couldn't become pregnant and after years of trying came to Fr. McGrath for a blessing. Within a short time she found herself expecting a baby. She returned to Fr. McGrath to thank him "Father," she said, "it was your holy hand that did it." "Ah now," he said. "I don't think I can take all the credit." On another occasion he was faced with a delicate situation. He had received a letter from the Archbishop of Tuam. He had been informed that a priest was seen, under the cover of darkness removing a stone from the ruins of the Carmelite Abbey in Ballinasmalla in Mayo. He had reason to believe that this priest might be a Carmelite. If this was the case he would be happy if the stone was returned immediately. Some years previously myself and Fr. McGrath had visited the Archbishop after a mission. He had proudly showed us chalices and other religious artefacts which had been recovered from the ruins of Carmelite monasteries in Mayo. I felt that these belonged to the Carmelites and should be returned to us. There was no way the Archbishop was going to give them back. Now he wanted a stone. Fr. McGrath came to me and asked would I have any idea who took the stone. At this time Fr. Peter, the prior of Gort Muire was building a new extension. Peter was the Province historian and there was nothing he didn't know about Carmelite Monasteries in Ireland. I suggested that our first stop should be Gort Muire. The foundations had just been laid and there in the corner was a big corner stone. We just looked at each other and laughed. I don't know what he said to Peter but shortly afterwards the stone mysteriously reappeared in the Carmelite Abbey in Ballinasmalla.

One day Fr. Flanagan arrived in Whitefriar St. on holidays from New York. He was a great friend of President Eamon de Valera having being at school with him in Blackrock college. Fr. Flanagan was on night duty at Belle View hospital in New York in 1919 and when he arrived back at the Carmelite Church on 29th street he discovered de Valera in his bed. De Valera who shortly before had escaped from Lincoln jail had come to America to raise funds for the Irish cause and to counteract English propaganda. De Valera recalls the occasion.

"The night before I appeared at the Waldorf hotel, in June 1919 when I was being sought for by the journalists all over America, I spent at 29th Street. It was at 29th Street that Liam Mellows stayed, and it was there that he found his most steadfast friends when he arrived in America after 1916. Fr. Mc Guinness and he regarded each other as comrades in the campaign for Irish Independence." Fr. McGuinness was a true Irishman, who loved his country and his people. He won the regard of everyone.

His speeches and his writings were an inspiration. His death was an incalculable loss.

After his death, however, the Fathers in 29th Street continued the work for the Irish cause. Liam Mellows, Harry Boland, Sean Nunan, Liam Pedler, and I were constant visitors there, and were accepted almost as members of the community. Harry and I had our games of handball and Liam Mellows used us as a butt for some of his practical jokes."

The Irish Carmelites arrived in New York in 1889 at the invitation of the Archbishop of New York. It is now a separate province but has always kept close ties with Ireland. Some days after Fr. Flanagan's arrival, Fr. McGrath came to me and asked me would I drive them up to the Phoenix Park to meet the President. We stopped at the gate to get the go ahead from the security guards. After a quick call to the Aras we were waived through. I said I would wait in the car. The next thing I saw was de Valera coming towards me. "You can't stay here, you must come in and join us," he said. He led me into a beautiful drawing room where Sinéad was waiting to greet us. We sat around an open fire and De Valera and Sinéad recalled old times. De Valera was in his element recalling his youth. Fr. Flanagan remembered their exploits in Blackrock especially on the rugby field. There was a table beside Dev. on which were placed three or four telephones of different colour. They rang every now and then and he dealt promptly with the call. When the green phone rang he spoke in Irish. He then asked did anyone speak Irish. Fr. McGrath went to school in Belfast and never studied Irish, Fr. Flanagan had long forgotten the little he knew. I was the only one who spoke Irish. Sinéad who was sitting beside me showed her approval. It didn't take Dev long to get around to his escape from Lincoln jail. "We began making plans" he said "from the moment we arrived. It was Peter De Loughry who planned the escape. His mother had told him stories about the man who helped the Fenian chief to escape from Richmond jail. A volunteer had infiltrated the prison staff by becoming a prison guard. "We spent all day sitting around with nothing to do except think of ways to escape," said Dev. "Peter came up with the idea of a key. The Chaplain had a master key and all the doors had double locks, so the master key was necessary. I got some candles and melted them down and awaited my opportunity to get an impression. I smuggled it out of the prison and sent it to Gerry Boland in Dublin. Gerry sent the key back in a Christmas cake but to our consternation it didn't work. I made another impression and sent it to an expert in Manchester but when it came back it didn't work. At this point Peter said "get them to send in a blank key and file and I'll cut it myself." The blank key and the file arrived in a birthday cake. Peter cut a perfect replica. On the day of the escape Michael Collins and Harry Boland were waiting outside. Myself, Milroy, and McGarry passed through door after door until we reached the outer door. Collins had another replica which he inserted in the door and gave it a turn. The key broke in the lock. What are we going to do now? I inserted my key in the lock and gave it a turn.

The door opened and we were free. We shook hands with the others and disappeared into the night. I had to lie low for a few days until things died down before returning to Dublin on what we called the Presidential Yacht to meet Cathal Brugha. At that time it was important to get American public opinion on our side. It was decided that I go to America. I went back to Liverpool and waited for a boat. While I was there news came through that all prisoners had been released. I was no longer on the run. I came back to Dublin on the Presidential yacht. Cathal Brugha resigned and I was appointed President. I appointed Countess Markievicz to the cabinet as minister of Labour. Shortly after I left for America where I spent 18 months promoting the Irish Free State and organising bonds. It was a difficult time coping with all the different factions in the States." "It was difficult for me too," said Sinéad. "I was bringing up the children in Greystones." Fr. McGrath as usual said very little. Fr. Flanagan was happy to recall old times. Sinéad spoke about the family and showed us photos. "You know Dr. Eamon goes to Mass in Whitefriar St. every morning on his way to the Mater," "he goes to communion with all the women from York St." "I'm sure they haven't a notion who he is." "I'm glad to hear that" she said, "I didn't know. They then showed us the various presents that had been given to the President by different heads of government. Among them was a lovely sword presented by President John Kennedy. As we left, De Valera presented us with a beautiful red leather bound prayer book, compiled by himself in Irish and Latin. I asked Dev would he mind signing it. He said he would be delighted but I would have to guide his hand as he found it hard to see. Sinéad was coming behind and I also asked her would she sign it and shyly she began to sign. De Valera turned around and said. "Don't tell me she is signing it, she never signs anything." It's my most treasured possession.

***

Later that year I gave a mission in Pennyburn in Derry with Fr Pat Russell. Fr. Russel was a perfect gentleman. He had spent most of his life in America ending up Provincial in the New York Province. He returned to Ireland to retire but he was happy to join the mission band. He never raised his voice while preaching. He told long winded stories with no punch line. When they were over you wondered what the point was. He was a delight to be with. After two strenuous weeks we make our way back to Dublin on the bus. As we reached the city he suggested we go to the Gresham for lunch. I was happy to accept. It was the afternoon by the time I got back to Whitefriar St. As I reached the top of the stairs, there was Fr. McGrath to meet me. "Could you come in for a minute" he said. As I sat down, he said "I have a favour to ask you." I looked surprised not knowing what it could be. "The Archbishop has asked each Order to release one man to work with the Irish in England." I said nothing. "I think you would be the best man for the job," he said. "That's about the last thing on earth I would want to do" I said. "I am very happy here." "It's a volunteering job" he said "but you have the experience of giving missions in England. It's only for a year and you don't have to decide now, think about it for a few days." I came back to my room deflated. My bubble had burst. I went upstairs to have a chat with Mick Carroll. He was delighted to see me back. "I had no-one to talk to during the last two weeks" he said. "You might have to get used to it" I said and I told him what the Provincial had said. "There's no way, you can't do that to me" he said. I thought about it for the next couple of days. This was the first difficult thing I had been asked to do. Suddenly I went back to the Provincial and said "yes."

"I don't know what is involved," he said, "you will have to play it by ear." I was going out into the great unknown.

Before I left I married my brother Richie and Lyla in Ashford with a wonderful reception at the Roundwood Inn. Richie was a keen motor racing driver and he competed in a race the following Saturday while on his honeymoon.

Richie in his first self built midget car at the Copse

21

Birmingham Bound

"Would you like to dance, Father?" came the melodic sounds of an Irish voice as I sat in the Shamrock ballroom in Birmingham. The dance floor was packed with couples as they danced to the strains of 'Lovely Leitrim' sung by Larry Cunningham to the accompaniment of The Mighty Avons. I looked up to see a pretty girl with a Mayo accent standing in front of me. "I think I'll sit this one out " I said with a blush. The Novice Master never told me what to do in a situation like this. She sat down beside me. "Are you over long, Father?" she asked. "The day before yesterday " I said, "I've been sent over as Chaplain to the Irish here. This is my first night . Fr. Maguire said this was a good place to meet the Irish." "Where are you from?" she asked. " I'm a Wicklow man," I said. "Larry sings a song about the Wicklow hills" she said, " I'll ask him to sing it for you, he always takes requests." "Have you been here long?" I asked. "Nearly three years now" she said. "I'm a waitress in the Midland hotel." "What part of Mayo are you from?" I asked. "Is my accent that bad?" she said, I'm from Claremorris". "I gave a mission there a few years ago" I said, "it's a lovely place." "I would have liked to stay at home" she said, "but there was no work." "Everyone has to leave, there are people here from every county in Ireland." With that another girl sat down and asked me could she have a word with me. "Certainly" I said. The noise of the music and the dancing made talking very difficult. "Could we go

Johnny McEvoy at the Shramrock Birmingham. 1967.

up to the balcony" she said, "it's quieter up there." I bought two bottles of orange and we made our way up the stairs. There was a wonderful view of the whole dance floor. She began to sob. "What's the matter?" I asked. "I had a row with my boyfriend" she said. "What happened?" I asked. "He danced with another girl., and to make it worse she's my best friend." "Have you been long together?" I asked. "About two years," she said. "We were thinking of getting engaged. I'm from Down and he's from Galway." "There he is down there dancing with her." As he glanced up, I beckoned to him to come up. Sheepishly he made his way up. "I don't know what to say to him" she said. "Don't worry" I said, "I'll do the talking." He just put his arms around her and said nothing. The less said the better. They went off together and danced the rest of the night away. We had come a long way from the time of the parish priest with the blackthorn stick separating couples on country roads after a dance. It was after one o'clock by the time I arrived back at St. Catherine's, a lovely round church near the Horsefair. Fr. Maguire, the parish priest had collected me from the airport, the day before and showed me around the parish. This was to be my base in Birmingham. The emigrant chaplaincy scheme was the brainchild of John Charles McQuaid who set up the Episcopal Committee for Emigrants with the Archbishops of Tuam, Kerry, Ferns, and Raphoe. Priests were sent to England from these Dioceses to help the young Irish boys and girls who had come to England in search of work. Most had left school at 15 and with no prospect of work in Ireland , had crossed the water to where there was a post-war boom in the construction of houses, motorways, power stations, hospitals. There was a great demand for labourers, nurses, domestic personnel and hotel workers. Like their ancestors of old they left family and home with a sense of hope and adventure. They went through loss, break with family and friends, excitement and isolation and a feeling of loneliness and sometimes homesickness. They experienced hostility, misunderstanding, exploitation and discrimination. They were greeted with signs No Blacks, No dogs, No Irish. One hundred and fifty thousand Irish emigrated in the 60's mainly from Cavan, Roscommon, Sligo, Limerick, Waterford, Galway, Dundalk and Drogheda. Most were ordinary decent people with no particular problems, but they needed help, material, personal, and spiritual. This is where the Chaplain comes in. He also has left home and family and understands from personal experience what they are going through. Up to this time, the Chaplains were sent mainly to London but now the scheme was extended to Birmingham.

On the Monday after arriving I joined a group of other religious, Jesuits, Capuchins, Passionists, and a Dominican for a meeting with the Archbishop of Birmingham, George Patrick Dwyer at St Catherine's. All seventeen sat in a circle like the Apostles to be welcomed by the Archbishop to his diocese. He pointed out the importance of the work we were being asked to do and that he would be available to meet us at any time. "Each of you will be appointed to different parishes around the city." he said as he read out the names of the parishes. I was the youngest of the group and I found myself sitting beside the Archbishop. He hadn't mentioned me. Then he turned to me and said "Would you like to be Chaplain to the hotels?" "What would that involve?" I asked. "I don't know" he said, "no one has been chaplain to hotels before. You will find the various hotels in a tourist guide and you can start from there." With that he wished me luck.

I duly made out a long list and discovered there were hundreds of them. The next morning I set out in fear and trembling to the Albany, a large twenty storey hotel near the Horsefair. I walked up to the reception desk and asked for the manager. The girl looked at me with a quizzical look on her face, probably thinking I was going to stay a month and said "Certainly sir , take a seat for a moment ." I sat in the lobby and watched the busy life of a hotel: porters in uniforms like sergeant majors carrying various coloured leather bound cases, proceeded by elegant ladies and gentlemen to the reception desk. After a while I saw a stout dark skinned man wearing a pin stripped suit coming down the Stairs, with a black moustache . He went to the receptionist and then came towards me. "I am the manager" he said, "you wanted to see me?" I stood up and said. "I'm Fr. Christopher Conroy , I'm very pleased to meet you." We shook hands. "What can I do for you ?" he asked. "It's what I can do for you" I said. "the Archbishop has appointed me as chaplain to your hotel." He took a deep breath, stuck out his chest and drew himself up to his full height. "What do I have to do?" he asked. "You don't have to do anything," I said, "I'll look after everything." "What do you need, do you want a room?" "That won't be necessary" I said. "I'd just like to move around freely and meet the staff." "You are very welcome" he said "and if you need anything let me know." I thanked him and said goodbye. As he went back up the stairs he turned around and said. "You will be welcome to stay for lunch whenever you wish." This was the approach I took with all the hotels. No one refused, and the only ones that questioned the idea was when there was Catholic management. They didn't see the need for a Chaplain. I persuaded them to give it a try. So in those first weeks I went from hotel to hotel seeking approval. I soon discovered there was a certain hierarchy among the staff which had to be observed. There were the doormen, the house-keepers, bartenders, waitresses, kitchen staff, washers up, and last of all the lowly chambermaids. Even their name was humiliating. I didn't just seek out the Catholics but spoke to everyone as I walked around the various floors. On the first morning in the Midland I spoke to the girl cleaning the carpet on the stairs. "Good morning, how are you?" I said. "I'm fine, thank you, sir" she said thinking I was one of the guests. "I'm the chaplain to this hotel" let me know if I can help you" "I'm not of your faith" she said, "I'm a Jewess." "That's great "I said, "you are the first Jewess I have met today. I can still help you if you wish." I moved along up the stairs and spoke to the chambermaids, as they made the beds and cleaned the rooms. Most of them were Irish and were delighted to see me.

Hotels were the ideal places for young girls coming from Ireland with no place to stay. They continued to talk as they worked as they had to have twelve rooms done before one o'clock. The housekeepers controlled the sheets and other supplies for the rooms. They also inspected the rooms after they had been cleaned. God help the chambermaid if a piece of fluff was discovered underneath the bed or hair was found in the washbasin or the shower. The dining room and the kitchen area was another hive of activity to which I had access. I was careful not to appear around mealtimes when it became a war zone. Otherwise I could walk leisurely around talking to the chefs about the exotic dishes they were cooking. The Grand Hotel was an old style hotel where the Lords and Ladies of the realm wined and dined. It was here that the Kings and Queens stayed when they came to Birmingham. The kitchen spread over the whole basement area. In my time the head chef was French. He was a wonderful chef but a bit eccentric. He parked his car in a 'no parking' zone every day and promptly received a parking ticket. . He showed me 365 tickets which he swore he would never pay. One day when I arrived he had a major problem. An Irish Organisation was having their annual dinner in the hotel the following week and they wanted Carrageen moss for desert. "How was that prepared ?" he asked. "I can't help you there" I said, "but they had their dinner in the Midland last year, so I'll ask the chef down there." The following day I returned with the recipe. He kissed me on both cheeks. The pastry kitchen was unbelievable . A whole team of chefs concocted the most wonderful desserts one could ever imagine. Then I moved on to the washing up area. There was an immense trough full of greasy water with pots and pans floating around. Paddy was the head bottle washer. He was a great character from Donegal. He was perfectly content to spend all day washing the pots and pans. His clothes were sopping wet and covered in grease. Every week he gave me money for a Mass for his mother who died the previous year. The chef in the Midland was always happy to see me. He considered it his duty to round up all the sinners and have them ready for when I arrived. "I have a big fish for you today , Father" he said one day as he led me down to the staff dining room. I stood outside as he went in. "John , the priest is here to see you" he shouted over the din. "I don't want to see any f..... ing priest" came the angry reply. "Tell him to go to hell and leave me in peace." I made a quick exit and disappeared. This was not the time or the place to say hello to John. I met him afterwards and he was happy to chat. Soon I became a familiar figure around the hotels and the staff realised what I was there for, not to pry or interfere but to help. The corridors were long and never ending. "Is there anyone else working down this end?" "Yes, Julia is cleaning the toilets at the very end, she is not a Catholic, but she is a lovely girl., she would love to see you." I began to arrange weddings and to say Mass for their deceased families. I attended the funeral of members of the staff irrespective of their religion. I often heard their confession quietly in a room without any formality. Sometimes they would ask me to write home to their family to assure them that they were alright. I always reminded them of the importance of writing home. I was reminded of the story that Fr. Browne S.J tells about cycling up a hill in Donegal. It was a beautiful sunny day and as he reached the top there was an old woman standing at the gate of her thatched cottage. As he came nearer she said. "Ah , Father, I thought you were the postman." "Were you expecting a letter" he asked. "Yes, Father, from my son John in America." "Does he write often" he asked. "Ah, no, Father, he's gone now twenty years and hasn't written yet." she said sadly.

I arranged to say Mass in the hotels once a year. The manager was happy for me to use the ballroom or the conference room. As many of the staff as possible gathered together and the hotel supplied tea and sandwiches afterwards. Did my work in the hotels always run smoothly? Nothing in life runs smoothly. Sometimes I was asked to settle rows between members of the staff. Others who were anti-Church or anti-religion resented my presence. I was thrown out of one hotel. I was up on the top floor talking to a chambermaid when two porters arrived in all their splendour . They were big strong men that could have been mistaken for bouncers in a night club. "Sir," they began, " the manageress has told us to remove you from the hotel." "But I have been visiting this hotel for over two years." I protested, "You, yourselves have opened the door for me and welcomed me" "We have our orders" they said. "Would you please come with us." I walked quietly between them as they led me down the lift to the door. They ushered me out onto the street with the same courtesy as they had welcomed me in. I returned the following week to see the manageress. She welcomed me into her office with open arms and couldn't have been more apologetic. "It was all a terrible mistake," she said "It was my first day here and nobody had told me anything about the Chaplain." She had tea and biscuits sent to the office. "You do understand," she continued, "we can't be too careful we often get undesirables wandering around the hotel." "It's the first time I've been mistaken for one of them" I said jokingly. "I'm really sorry" she said. "the staff really like you coming to visit them and I hope you will continue. You can go wherever you wish and I apologise again." When I went up to the top corridor the chambermaid told me what had happened. Immediately after I left she went to all the other chambermaids and told them how I had been thrown out. They downed tools and all marched down to the manageress. "The priest is our friend" they said, "and he has been coming in here a long time. It was disgraceful the way you had him evicted from the hotel. If you don't let him come back we are going on strike." She readily agreed and said she was not aware of the situation. That was the reason for my generous welcome back. I always got a great kick afterwards in saying 'good morning' to the porters on the way in. A few weeks later I had a letter from the owners of the hotel apologising for the misunderstanding.

Back at St. Catherine's I had settled in to my new surroundings. I helped out with Masses at the weekends and took charge of a Praesidium of the Legion of Mary. They visited the houses and flats in the parish and sought out the destitute and down and outs. Most of these were Irish and I too went on visitation most evenings. Birmingham city had built large blocks of flats like Ballymun. You could spend over a month visiting just one block. I discovered something that I didn't think was possible. Even the families in the top flats over thirty stories high had mice. I could never understand how they got up that far. Late in the evening after visiting families or the Shamrock or Harp dance halls I came back to any empty room alone. This was something I could never have imagined when I joined the Carmelites. We were meant to live together in Community. How I missed the knock on the door in the middle of the night and Mick Carroll coming in for a chat. " Oh, good God, you're asleep, don't you go to bed early," or Fr. McGrath coming to tell me his problems. I soon had to learn how to live alone as a Carmelite.

After a couple of years Fr. Maguire said he had a probem, Fr. Griffith in St Peter's Parish was very lonely and he would love me to go and live with him. I readily agreed. St Peter's was not far away. It is the oldest Catholic Church in Birmingham. It was off Broad St and originally built as a factory when it was forbidden to build a Catholic Church. It still looked like a factory from the outside but when you stepped in you discovered a little gem. The Presbytery was old and dilapidated but there was plenty of room. I had my own bedroom and sitting room. Fr. Griffith was from Mayo and never lost his Mayo accent. The people didn't understand a word he said . Although that worked both ways it took me a long time to get the hang of the Birmingham accent. He was a perfect gentleman with simple tastes. He said he was soon due a plum parish after serving his time here. He had a dog called "Stumpy" and I never discovered why. It was a beautiful collie sheepdog I soon realised that the dog was more important than I was. Fr. Griffith sat at the top of the table and carved the joint of meat. The first slice went to Stumpy who was lying peacefully underneath the table. One day Stumpy began to growl for apparently no reason. Fr. Griffith suddenly ducked underneath the table with him as there was an unmerciful clap of thunder followed by lightning I sat there mesmerised not knowing whether to laugh or cry. I soon realised it was no laughing matter when Fr. Griffith emerged shaking like a leaf. He told me he had a terrible phobia about thunder and lightning. Fr. Griffith had a housekeeper called Agnes. She was a wonderful old lady from Co. Fermanagh. She had been years with Fr. Griffith. She was small and chubby with no dress sense whatsoever. She sometimes dressed like a teenager. Coloured tights were all the go and Agnes got a pair with all the colours of the rainbow. She went shopping one day and I met her coming back sobbing away to herself. "What's the matter Agnes?" I asked. "I met Fr.Griffith up the street" she said., "and he asked me where did I think I was going dressed like that. You look like you came out of the circus" he said. "you're a disgrace. You'll get the Parish a bad name. Go home and put on something respectable." "Maybe you're a bit too modern for him"

I said. "he's not up with the youth of today." Agnes was a hopeless cook. It was a terrible contrast for me to see all the lovely meals being prepared in the big hotels and then coming back to Agnes and her burnt offering. The first Christmas I was with Fr. Griffith I couldn't come home. There was an outbreak of foot and mouth disease and all the Irish were asked not to come home for fear of bringing it to Ireland. Agnes prepared the Christmas dinner. I went into the kitchen to see how things were going and Agnes had a crisis. Fr. Griffith had received a big ham from Mayo and she had no pot big enough to put it in. There it was turning round and round in the washing machine. "I had no pot" she said, "but its doing fine in the washing machine." Normally on a Monday morning I saw Agnes's nick knacks going round and round Now it was the ham. It put me off ham for life. When it arrived at the table all covered with breadcrumbs and cloves. I said. "I'm allergic to ham " I won't be able to have any." "That's a pity" he said, as he tucked into it. "You don't know what you are missing." If he only knew.

***

I came home on holidays each summer and spent some time in Whitefriar St. On one of these occasions Fr. McGrath asked me would I like to go on a pilgrimage to Lough Derg. We set off fasting early the first morning and parked the car near the lake where we got the boat across. Lough Derg is a place of pilgrimage since the sixth century. It was here that St.Patrick came to do penance and is known as St. Patrick's purgatory. There is a wonderful spiritual atmosphere of peace on the little island where you spend three days, fasting, walking around in circles barefoot and reciting the station prayers. There is also a twenty four hour vigil in the Basilica. Fr. McGrath and myself gave a holy hour and recited the Rosary during the first night in the Basilica. During the day we walked round and round praying. There were hundreds of boys and girls who had just finished their Leaving Cert. on the island to give thanks. The American Pilots during the war when they gazed down on this strange phenomenon called it 'Dev's Concentration Camp.' Whenever we weren't praying we had long chats about life in Birmingham while he poured out all his worries about being Provincial. By the end of the second day I was starving. All there was to eat was dry toast and tea or coffee. Although it was a wonderful experience I was happy to leave the third day. I said farewell to Fr. McGrath in Dublin, he was off to Kerry the next day to spend some time with friends in Kerry. I came home to Wicklow and waited up until midnight when my mother prepared a large fry of sausages, rashers and eggs. The following week when I received a telegram to say Fr. McGrath had died suddenly in Kerry. I was devastated. I had lost a wonderful friend. I had a great chat with Mick Carroll after the funeral. He said he wasn't feeling too good himself. He said he spent most of the time in his room reading. His desk was littered with papers and books. When I suggested he should tidy it up he said that was the way he liked it, he knew where everything was and that if he tidied it up that happy situation would end. As I left I reminded him about the poem for Christmas. "Oh God," he said, "I don't think I have the energy." One evening in Birmingham just before Christmas the phone rang, and it was Fr. Ryan, the new Provincial, to tell me that Mick Carroll died peacefully in his sleep the night before. Within a short time I had lost two wonderful friends. But good friends never really go away. Every day I chuckle to myself as I recall the funny things he did and said. Sometimes I feel lonely for his presence. He helped more people than he will ever know.

The following morning I received a letter in the post. I could not believe my eyes when I discovered it was from Mick. The last thing he did was write to me

Dear Christie,

" A happy Christmas to you, my dear friend, I enclose the poem you asked me to write, changes and all. I did it the day you asked me."

Happy Xmas,

M.O.C.

He also enclosed an ordination card. "In Remembrance of my First Holy Mass at the Carmelite Church , Whitefriar St. Dublin on Trinity Sunday, June 12th, 1927.

This is his final poem.

"Active no more, the muse will not be silent,
It's greeting still the same as once we knew,
Of fallen leaves of Xmas and of sentiment
The old attachments in a setting new
Feast of the Crib so dear to Christian homes
Reflecting the gifts so prized from loving hands,
Reminders of the days we blew balloons
And left our precious footprints in the sands
Strange as it seems, the many years between
Seem nothing as the dying year dips low
As though the actors on the earthly scene
Were mascots in a fleeting passing show

God Bless, my friend ,Our Lady guide your way

To another, grander, nicer, Xmas day."

And so he died.

***

Just up the road from St Peter's on the Hagley Rd. is the Birmingham Oratory founded by Cardinal Newman. John Henry Cardinal Newman was an Anglican priest who converted to Catholicism. He was brought up in the Anglican Church with its emphasis on the Bible to Roman Catholicism which bases the Faith on dogmas and Sacraments. In 1854 he was invited by the Irish Bishops to be Rector of the Catholic University of Ireland, the present University College Dublin. He spent four years here giving many talks and lectures which were later published under the title of 'The Idea of a University'. This was an important part of the curriculum when I studied English for my B.A. He spent four years in Ireland returning to England to found the Oratory school beside the church on the Hagley Rd. It was a school for the education of the sons of gentlemen on the lines of English Public schools. It is still the most famous Catholic school in Birmingham. Towards the end of his life he suffered many difficulties and problems, then out of the blue Pope Leo XIII made him a Cardinal, much to everyone's surprise. He was just a simple priest and not even residing in Rome. His elevation to Cardinal was received with great acclaim throughout the Catholic world. He continued to live as an Oratorian in Birmingham The Oratory was founded by St Philip Neri and it is a group of Catholic priests living together in Community. They do not take any formal vows but live together in a bond of Charity. Fr. Geoffrey was parish priest of the Oratory in my time. He rode around the parish on a bike. There were many Irish living in flats and sometimes four or five families living in the one house. Fr. Geoffrey who was an English gentleman and a convert found it very difficult to communicate with them so he enlisted my help. Every week he gave me a long list of houses to visit. I said Masses in houses and arranged marriages and baptisms. He was very conservative like all converts. Having left one faith, he couldn't cope with another faith in a state of flux. He didn't like the changes after the Vatican Council. He was looking for stability. After Cardinal Newman's death the Oratorian's built a magnificent church in his honour. One day Fr. Geoffrey asked me if I would like to see Cardinal Newman's room. The room had not been disturbed since the day he died. There was dust and cobwebs everywhere. It was surrounded with book shelves filled with large tomes. His desk was exactly as he left it. I sat down at his desk and looked around. His Cardinal's hat was hanging on the back of the door, exactly where he left it. As I was leaving the room I took down his Cardinal's hat from behind the door and put it on.. Fr. Geoffrey turned around and nearly had a seizure . "How do I look?" I asked, "would I make a good Cardinal?" "No one has ever worn that since he died" he said. I quickly replaced it on the back of the door.

There was never a dull moment in Birmingham. A girl was in distress in the Norfolk hotel. She was from Connemara and her father had thrown her out of the house when she got pregnant. She took the boat to England and ended up in Birmingham where she got a job as chambermaid in the Norfolk. At least she had board and lodgings. She had worked as long as she could and then went in to have the baby. She had just returned to the hotel distraught . They took the baby away from her immediately after birth and she never even saw it. I will never forget the anguish on the poor girls face as she sobbed. " If only they had let me see her." She had signed the forms for adoption before the birth.

There was panic in the Shamrock last Friday night. They had booked a young singer from Ireland called Johnny McEvoy and he hadn't arrived. "What hotel did you book for him?" I asked. "The Albany," they said, "just up the road." I went up to discover he had fallen asleep on the bed. He arrived at the Shamrock out of breath. He rushed on the stage like Bob Dylan with his guitar and mouth organ. He sang 'Mursheen Durkin' and 'Brown Eyes' to rapturous applause and then came off the stage to shouts of 'more more'. "That's all I have" he said as he came into the dressing room. "Just go out and sing the same again" I said. He was later to go on to greater things.

One morning at St. Peters I woke up to a crackling noise. As I looked up bleary eyed the ceiling was ablaze. I jumped out of bed and ran down the stairs to phone the fire brigade. On the way I met Fr. Griffith coming out of his room holding up his pyjamas with one hand.. "What's wrong? " he asked with a yawn. "The house is on fire" I said , "get out as quickly as possible." He ran to put on his dressing gown and get Stumpy. Agnes, by now had heard the commotion and was on her way. As we stood on the other side of the street in our bare feet looking up, the fire brigade arrived. The flames were roaring from the roof as the firemen extended their ladders and began to hose it down. A large crowd had gathered and the police were keeping everyone back. Luckily the blaze was confined to the roof of the house and didn't reach the church. After a couple of hours it was out. We went back in to the smoke filled rooms to salvage what we could. All the damage was confined to the top of the house but there was water everywhere. I brought my bed down to the sitting room where I slept for the next couple of months. Poor Fr. Griffith went into a state of shock. When the 'Evening Mail' arrived he couldn't read it. There was a picture on the front page with a full account of the fire. "What does it say?" he asked , "read it out to me." "There was a large fire this morning in one of the oldest Catholic churches in the city. The fire spread rapidly but was prevented from reaching the historic church by the prompt action of the fire brigade. Three units of the fire brigade attended the scene. There were two priests and a housekeeper. in the house at the time. All escaped unhurt, (Then I decided to read out things that weren't there). Fr. Griffith, the parish priest said the fire took place at about 9 o'clock in the morning, but he wasn't sure because he was asleep in bed at the time. "Good God" he said, " does it say that?, what's the Bishop going to say, my reputation is ruined, 9 o'clock in the morning, I didn't say that." "The press never gets anything right." I really had him worried, but after a while I told him I was joking, much to his relief.

A short time after the fire Fr. Griffith received a letter from the Bishop. Like most parish Priests he was in fear and dread of what it might contain. He needn't have worried, it was good news. He was offering him the parish of Bromsgrove, one of the most beautiful parishes in the Diocese. "Would you like to come with me?" he asked. "I'd love to," I said but how would I do my work here in Birmingham. "It's less than half an hour on the motorway." he said. "You could come in every day and help me at the weekends. I'll be seeing the Bishop tomorrow and I'll put it to him." The Bishop said he couldn't make any decision until he had talked to me. I went to see George Patrick Dwyer at St. Chad's cathedral. "You get on very well with Fr. Griffith," he said "he would like you to go with him to Bromsgrove. How do you feel about that?" "I would love it" I said. "Do you think you could do your work in the hotels?" " I think I could" I said, "it wouldn't take long to come in." "Half an hour" he said, "I live in Bromsgrove and come in every day." "That's settled then," he said, "as far as I'm concerned you can go."

St. Peter's Church, Bromsgrove was built in 1858 and opened by Bishop Ullathorne in 1862. He was the one who's autobiography we read for months in Gort Muire. The Faith survived many persecutions against Catholics when priests were on the run and constantly harassed by priest hunters. The faith survived due to local Catholic Nobility. Each big house had its priest's hole where the priest remained hidden. One of these was Harvington Hall where I was asked to say Mass and preach in remembrance of penal times. In Ireland it was the poor who kept the faith. Mass was celebrated on Mass rocks on the mountainside. The high altar in St. Peter's was a work of art by the famous architect Pugin. It was adorned with beautiful artefacts that Pugin collected in France after the Revolution. Bromsgrove is in Worcestershire and my first Sunday saying Mass I made a terrible mistake. Reading the notices I pronounced it Worcester-shire. I felt a right fool when I discovered it was pronounced Woster I also found myself praying for her majesty the Queen at the prayers of the faithful. That doesn't come naturally to an Irishman. The parish house was a beautiful modern building surrounded by fields where Stumpy was in his element. Fr. Griffith loved Bromsgrove and soon settled in. He was a man of simple tastes and he seldom did any exercise. On his free day he just sat by the motorway and watched the cars go by. He hated the solemn celebration of the Liturgy and the Holy Week ceremonies. He was happy to let me do the lot. He would assist me as the altar boy. We watched the landing on the moon together and just as Neil Armstrong was making 'one small step for man, one giant leap for mankind,' the doorbell rang. "Good God" he said, "do they not know we're landing on the moon?"

The whole area around Bromsgrove was full of green fields and rolling hills, big farms and the homes of the aristocracy. I loved going for long walks around the nearby Lickey hills. The first thing that Fr. Griffith asked me to do was give a mission. I visited all the homes in the parish and preached and heard confessions in the evening. I preached in St John's protestant church. This was originally a Catholic church and I was the first priest that preached there since the Reformation. I also preached at the Presbyterian Church. There were three hospitals in the parish and I filled in when Fr. Griffith was away. One night I was called out three times to accidents on the motorway and each time the person died. I will never know how one is supposed to come home and go to sleep after that. Then one night I had an urgent call from Ireland, from Davy my brother. My father was watching a car race in Rathdrum in which my brother Richie was competing when he suddenly collapsed with a stroke. He was taken by ambulance to Loughlinstown hospital where he was recovering well. There was no need to return home for the moment.

One evening as I arrived home from Birmingham I was greeted with the terrible news that Fr. Griffith had suffered a heart attack and he was in the intensive care ward in Daisy Hill hospital. Even Stumpy was in mourning. I went immediately to the hospital and found him all wired up in a private ward. He lay unconscious on the bed with the blue monitor showing his weakening heart beat. I anointed him and said some prayers. I held his hand and he seemed to hold it tight. I sat there for hours and watched him slowly dying. Its an awful sight to see the lines going up and down like mountain peaks then slowly descending to foot hills until suddenly there is a straight line across the screen. He is gone. He is dead. I closed his eyes and blessed him. Priests are laid out in their vestments so I returned to the sacristy to get them. I chose the ones he had used the Sunday before. When I arrived back at the hospital a male and female nurse had prepared the body. As I entered the room and they saw the vestments they immediately left. I was left alone to put them on. He was a big man and it was difficult to put on the Alb, then the Stole, and lastly the Chasuble. Stumpy was pining away when I returned to the Church. He lay beside Fr.Griffith's car and didn't come to greet me as usual. It was just before Christmas and I was due to go home the following week. The Archbishop came to see me the next day. "I won't be able to appoint anyone before Christmas," he said "Could I possibly ask you to take over until January or February?" My heart sank for a moment because my parents were looking forward to my coming home for Christmas. "Of course," I said, "I will be happy to stay as long as you wish."

I came to Birmingham for a year and stayed for eight. It was all a wonderful experience and I loved every minute of it. But now I felt it was time to move on. After the Vatican Council everything had changed. The old theology that I studied at Milltown Park was now completely out of date. I wanted to renew , not only my theology but my whole way of thinking. I looked around and was attracted to Lumen Vitae, a Jesuit run international college in Brussels. It is part of the University of Louvain and offers training in Catechetical Pastoral Ministry and Christian Education adapted to today's world. Just what I was looking for. There was just one problem: all the lectures were in French.

22

BRUSSELS

During the summer I enrolled in the University of Lyon to study French for two months before going to Brussels. The Archbishop of Birmingham had written to his friend the Archbishop of Lyons and told him I was coming. He kindly invited me to stay with him but I found it much more convenient to take a room at the University. I had enrolled for an intensive course with a small group of international students. I had five hours of classes each day with study and homework No English was used, it was a question of being totally immersed in the French language and customs. The Olympic games were on in Munich that year. Between classes everyone was glued to the T.V. I watched with disbelief as members of the Israeli Olympic team were taken hostage by Black September. There was an air of tension as the drama unfolded. Then the killing of 11 Israeli athletes and coaches in a frustrated attempt to free them. The episode cast a shadow over the whole Olympics.

The two months went by very quickly and I was soon on my way up the motorway, past Paris to Brussels. As the Eiffel Tower guides you into Paris, the giant Atomium in Heysel park does the same for Brussels. It is one of the most astonishing buildings in the world. Nine giant spheres built in the form of a molecule magnified 150 million times. It was built for the World Fair in 1958 and was not meant to be permanent. It proved so popular that it was decided to keep it on and it has become a special landmark for the city. Soon I was in the Grand Place in the centre of the city. It is the most beautiful town square in Europe if not the world. I eventually found Lumen Vitae in rue Washington. There was a wonderful friendly atmosphere about the place and I was welcomed by the secretariat who showed me around. There are never many Irish students here because of the language problem. Many opt for Berkeley in California. With my University degrees and my theology in Milltown I was able to enrol for a Masters Degree in Catechetics and Pastoral Theology. It is a two year course. They gave me the name of a family who would put me up for a short time until I got permanent accommodation. I was accepted into the Morelle family with open arms. I soon learned that you don't just have to learn the language but the customs as well. To shake hands is considered very formal and British. You put your arms around the person and kiss them on both cheeks. I soon settled in.

They brought me for a drive on the Sunday to visit their relatives in the country. It was out near Ypres where my father had fought in the war. It seemed strange seeing the places my father had so often talked about in the garden at the Copse as we picked the potatoes. That all seemed so long and far away now. We also visited a war cemetery where I saw the graves of brave heroes, many young Irishman of eighteen and nineteen years of age. Belgium is the battleground of Europe. I would have been happy to stay with that family but I needed my own space to study. I found a nice little apartment on Ave. Mozart just beside a supermarket. On my first day in Lumen Vitae I was interviewed by one of the Jesuit professors to test my proficiency in French and see what course I would be able to take. I passed with flying colours and he told me I could take whatever course I wished. I was really delighted and realised that all the hard work in Lyon had paid off. As well as Belgian Jesuits there were professors from all over the world. There were students from fifty different countries and it was the interchange of nationalities that gave the place its special character. Most were mature students, priests and nuns and lay people who came to renew their faith. You devise your own personal programme with the professors from a variety of courses and subjects. One of the most interesting courses that I followed was on Biblical anthropology under a Belgian Jesuit, Pere Jean Radermakers. Jean was one of the best known professors and had become a legend in his lifetime. He spoke ten languages and when he spoke about the Bible he made it come alive. We were transported to the Holy Land in the time of Jesus with all its customs and traditions. During my study of Theology I only used the Bible to prove a dogma or thesis. Now Jean Radermakers separated the myth from the reality. When we read the Bible we take it too literally and we miss the real meaning. We celebrated the Eucharist each day in the Chapel. Each country brought its own customs to bear in the celebration of the different liturgies. The second year at Lumen Vitae is taken up with the writing of a thesis. You can choose your own subject under the direction of a Professor. I choose "Communicating the Faith to adolescents today."

One day while looking for a bank on Ave Mozart I decided to try out my French on a girl coming home from school. "Pardon Mademoiselle, Ou est le banc? s'il vous plait." "Viens avec moi " she said. As we walked along I continued to practise my French by telling her who I was and what I was doing in Brussels. She told me where she went to school and what she had studied that day. I thanked her and waved "Au revoir." The next day she arrived at my door with a group of young people and said I was the very person they were looking for. They explained that they all belonged to a new Christian community called La Communaute Rodenbach and they had no priest to celebrate the Mass on Saturday evenings. I said I hadn't celebrated Mass in French yet and I didn't think I could preach in French. They all burst out laughing and said that would not be a problem. There wouldn't be a sermon. So long as I said the words of Consecration they would do the rest. I was intrigued and mystified but I said I would go along anyway. It wasn't a church but the parish hall. There were about two hundred people, men women , teenagers, and children sitting around a table with the candles lit. There was a ceramic chalice in the centre with two baskets of bread each side. They were singing beautiful French hymns with great Gusto, only stopping when I arrived to welcome me. I was received with warm hugs and kisses on both cheeks. The head of the community gave a long speech of welcome.

The Mass began with more singing. Then various people stood up and asked God for forgiveness. The whole community stretched out their hands and asked for forgiveness. A special theme for the Mass had been prepared. They then read a prayer. We sang the ' Lord have mercy ' and afterwards a joyful hymn of praise. There were various readings from scripture, which everyone discussed. This was the sermon. Patricia in the front row looked up at me with a smile A young lad got up and read a letter from two of the Community who had gone on missionary work to the Belgian Congo. Everyone was enthralled. Bidding prayers were then read out by the young and old. They sang again as the bread and wine was offered up. I then proceeded to the Consecration. We all stood up and held hands for the Our Father. The kiss of peace was a very happy affair. Everyone hugged and kissed and looked as if they meant it. The two baskets were passed around and each one took Communion. After a moment of reflection we sang the final hymn. When the celebration was over it continued on in a different way. Tea or coffee and cakes were passed around and everyone sat in little groups chatting away. For me it was the most wonderful and meaningful celebration of the Eucharist I had ever taken part in. It had lasted over two hours. They wanted to put into practice the teachings of the Vatican Council. Their Cardinal Suenens had been the great liberal voice and advocate for reform at the Council. Cardinal Suenens when he was Rector of Louvain was only saved from execution by the Nazis by the arrival of the Allied troops. Pope John XXIII confessed that he saved the Council from collapse when he proposed setting aside the 70 Conservative schemas and replaced them with 18 progressivist ones. He was the inspiration of two of the most important documents of the Council, Lumen Gentium and Gaudium et Spes. Now he wanted this reform to take place in his own diocese. He gave great encouragement to the Charismatic Renewal and to new forms of celebration. These families met in each other's houses and read the bible and tried to put it into practice in their daily lives. They were soon joined by other families of like mind. After a while they discovered there was something missing. They needed the Celebration of the Eucharist, and for that they needed a priest. The local clergy were too busy and could not help but they gave them the parish hall. Then they got me. I celebrated Mass with them for two years.

I also gave English lessons in my spare time. This was how I met the la Croix family. Madame la Croix was a famous painter and had an exhibition of her work twice a year in the Art Gallery. She lived with her two children Pierre and Isobel in a big house near the Observatory. She was divorced and wanted me to teach English to Pierre. He was a lad of about sixteen and was also a painter. The only problem was that he wasn't interested in learning English. After about ten minutes he got bored; let's play tennis, let's go horse riding, let's go for a cycle in the forest. I was very happy to do all three. The mother thought this was a great way of learning English. She was happy so long as Pierre was happy. The only one that wasn't happy was Isobel. She was attending the University and was very jealous of Pierre having a private English teacher. Her mother agreed that I should give her lessons as well. Then Pierre got jealous. Each day I stayed for lunch with the family. On one occasion the father arrived unexpectedly. The mother quickly explained that I was a priest and that I was giving English lessons to the children. He was an author and a lecturer at the university and a perfect gentleman. The children loved him and he had a cordial relationship with his former wife. Pierre told me afterwards that he had another girlfriend. The mother gave me a blank cheque every month to fill in myself. The University of Louvain asked me to teach English during the summer months, which I did for about seven years.

While I was in Brussels the President of Ireland, Erskine Childers, came on a state visit. All the Irish received a special invitation to the King's Palace to meet him. Because of the Common Market there were a large number of Irish in the city. It was the only time in my life that the butler read out my invitation as I entered the gilded reception room at the Kings palace, FR. CHRISTOPHER CONROY O CARM.

I also visited Waterloo where Napolean met his downfall. It is just outside Brussels and the position of the various armies are marked out so that you can easily follow the course of the battle.

There was never a dull moment during my time in Brussels. I was learning new things and having experiences that I could never have had in Ireland. The learning of French opened up a whole new world to me. Nowhere was this more evident than at Lumen Vitae. My personal faith took on a whole new meaning. It was as if I had to unlearn a lot of the things I studied at Milltown Park and begin again. It wasn't a question of proving dogmas and doctrines as part of the teaching of the Church. The one great lesson I had learned was not to defend a position but to seek the TRUTH. I was reminded of the story of the American who drove up outside a church in Kerry, just as Mass was ending. He pulled down the window and shouted to an old farmer with his pipe and stick who was sitting on the wall "Sir, am I on the right road to Killarney?" "Ah, you are alright," said the farmer pulling on his pipe, "but you are going the wrong way." That's exactly how I felt sometimes I was on the right road but going in the wrong direction. Delving into the Documents of Vatican II renewed my faith . All the professors were experts in their field and had a great freedom to express and teach their ideas. They had the support of Cardinal Suenens, who was not afraid to rock the boat and say what he thought. He criticised the Roman Curia for being too conservative and behind the times. They had shown their true colours when they tried to control the information coming from the Council. Cardinal Tisserand demanded a retraction of the criticism. Suenens refused saying that Tisserand's reaction was unacceptable and unfounded. "There are times when loyalty demands more than keeping in step with an old piece of music. As far as I am concerned Loyalty is a different kind of love. And this demands that we accept responsibility for the whole and serve the Church with as much courage and candour as possible." He also opposed the encyclical Humanae Vitae of Pope Paul VI as did many loyal Catholics around the world. Any priest who signed a petition against it was never made a Bishop. Rome never forgets. I spent my second year writing my thesis on "Communicating the Faith to Adolescents Today."

Fr. Robert Bosc S. J. came to Lumen Vitae to conduct a course on International relations. He was a professor at the University of Paris and had travelled around the world. Each student had to write a paper on some particular problem in their country. Naturally I wrote about the problems in Northern Ireland. He was very interested in this and asked me to his room to discuss the situation. We became good friends and towards the end of the year I received a letter from Paris. He was taking twenty professors from Paris university on a study tour of Russia, Japan, Korea, and Taiwan He asked me would I like to join them with all expenses paid. I wrote back immediately saying I would be delighted.

This experience could be the subject of another book. Suffice it to say here that for the next three months we toured each country studying the customs and history of each.

At the last minute Fr. Bosc was refused a Visa to enter Russia because they suspected he was a spy. He asked me to lead the group throught Russia. Each day we had lectures in the morning, and in the afternoon we visited, schools, factories, hospitals etc. It was a revelation to see how Communism didn't work. We took the Trans Siberian Railway across Russia, stopping along the way to visit the important towns. From here we took a boat to Japan and continued our tour. My greatest experience in Japan was staying in a Buddist monastery and living like a monk for three days. Up each morning at four o'clock to go to the Temple for Zen meditation. I also visited Hiroshima . From Japan we continued on to Korea and Taiwan.

23
Trans Siberian Journey

I stayed with Fr. Bosc at the Jesuit house in Paris the night before my departure for Russia. While I was there he had just received bad news. The Russians had refused him a visa. He had been to Russia many times with various groups and the K.G.B. had compiled a dossier on him and had concluded he was a spy. He had applied for a visa weeks before but they kept him waiting until the last minute to say no. He had already told me not to say I was a priest on my application form for a visa. I was an English professor (which was true). Priests or anything to do with religion were not welcome in Russia.

"You'll have to take over the Russian leg of the tour" he said, "I'll meet you in Tokyo." "But I don't know anything about it," I said with a note of fear in my voice. "There is no problem," he assured me. All the journey is planned and booked, the tickets are bought. When you arrive in Moscow you will have a guide from 'Intourist' (the State tourist agency). They will travel with you everywhere. They are usually connected with the K.G.B. so don't discuss anything openly in front of them." "What language will they speak?" I asked. "French, of course, this is a French group," he said. "But you are lucky you also speak English. Most of the Professors in the Universities speak good English. There are twenty three in the group, mature men and women, all experts in their own field. I have given them all a bible in Russian. I have one here for you too." "That won't be much use because I don't understand a word," I said. "They are not for you," he said. "They will be collected in Moscow. There is a group here in Paris that smuggle bibles into Russia and I told them we would help." "Thanks very much," I said. "Hide it in your luggage and hope they don't find it," he said. "A word of advice, The K.G.B. will follow you everywhere. All your rooms will be bugged. The Russians are very cagey about talking to foreigners. Ask people before you take their photos and don't take photos of soldiers or military installations."

I was up at 4.30 am the next morning. Fr. Bosc drove me to Le Bourget airport where we met the others. All were excited and anxious about the trip. We waited for a couple of hours to be told we had to go to Orly. At last we were on our way. The plane was Luftansa and very basic but comfortable. The hostesses spoke English and French fluently. I found myself sitting beside a Russian diplomat returning home from Washington. He was looking forward to seeing his family again. As we approached Moscow I looked out to get my first glimpse of Russia. It appeared poor and barren with the odd shanty town planted in the wilderness with brightly painted corrugated roofs. We touched down smoothly and made our way to the airport building. It looked old and dingy and half finished. I put my watch forward two hours. We approached the customs with fear and trembling. A stout woman customs officer handed me a form and asked me where had I come from and how long I would be staying in the Soviet Union. "Fill out the form with all the valuables you are carrying and the amount of money you have." Next came the opening of the case. I kept my fingers crossed. She examined my camera, my clothes, shoes, she didn't notice the bible. I passed through safely. Looking back I noticed they had found the bible in one woman's case. Everything stopped. The superior was called. "Why have you got a Russian Bible?" he asked. "It's for my own use" she said, "I hope to learn Russian while I'm here." "In two weeks?" he said, "you must be very clever." We were delayed for two hours while he decided what to do. I couldn't help thinking a great super power was afraid of a little book. Eventually he confiscated the Bible and let her through. Our guide was waiting for us. She was a young girl called Olga and spoke French fluently. We all climbed into an old dingy bus and made our way to the Hotel Bucharest opposite Red Square. The cars were painted grey and green and looked very drab. There were many empty lorries painted green and blue like army lorries. A group of women were busy repairing the street with shovels and picks. The people seemed to walk along without speaking and there seemed to be very few young people. There were no window displays in the shops. The hotel was very comfortable and I had a single room with a shower.

We all gathered in the Restaurant for our first Russian supper. The entree was potato salad and cucumber. Then came a bowl of soup with a hard boiled egg in the middle of it. The main course was meat balls and rice. The dessert of course was ice cream. Ice cream is very popular in Moscow. It is not up to Italian standard but it is very good. One ton of ice cream is eaten every day in Gorky St. We finished up with a complimentary drink of vodka which was very strong but it cheered us up after the meal.

After supper I went for a walk with Jacques and Pierre Magendie, two of our group. They were very keen photographers and had a couple of cameras each, one with telephoto lens. Jacques took thousands of photos on the trip. As soon as we stepped outside the hotel a man came up to us wanting to buy French francs. Russians cannot buy foreign currency and roubles cannot be bought outside Russia. He was prepared to give us 35 roubles for 100 francs which was twice the bank rate. We crossed the square to the tomb of the unknown soldier. A lorry passed by with a drawing of Donald Duck on the side which looked funny in Moscow. There were many buses and cars broken down on the side of the road. Many cars were stolen, so when you parked your car you took out the distributor and took off the windscreen wipers. There didn't seem to be any garages or petrol pumps. There were many drunks slumped on the side of the street. As we looked over at the Kremlin the onion domed church was lit up against the sky. It was Ivan the Great Bell Tower, the tallest structure in the city. It was forbidden to build higher. There are twenty one bells in the tower which sounded the alarm down through the years when the enemy was approaching. On the top was a cross lit up against the night sky. A country which professed atheism had signs of religion everywhere. Their scientists could build rockets to penetrate outer space and yet they couldn't build a house or make a car that doesn't break down. They fought a revolution for freedom and nobody is free. All the men are in the army or the police and the women do all the manual labour. It doesn't take a visitor to Russia long to realise it is a country of contradictions, of contrasts and ambiguity.

Olga was waiting for us early next morning after breakfast to take us on a tour of the city. She spoke in glowing terms of everything Soviet. She always corrected us when we referred to it as Russia. "There are 15 Soviet Republics and Russia is just one of them," she would say." After a visit to the bank to change our money she took us to the Museum of the Revolution. She was in her element. She steered us through the events of the Revolution in great detail. The Romanov Dynasty was overthrown with the murder of the Tszar and his family and the founding of the Soviet regime. There was no mention of Trotsky or any photo of him. There was a photo of Lenin giving a speech with Trotsky at his side but Trotsky had been removed. All the photos were doctored. This was the period of de-Stalinization. All photos of him had been removed. "Did Lenin appoint his successor?" I asked Olga. "No" she said, "it was the Party." "He really didn't want Stalin to succeed him. He saw his faults. My parents only recognised two leaders, Lenin and Trotsky" she said, which was an extraordinary admission. Had she said that in Stallin's time, she would have been sent to a gulag.

There was a machine there for making noise like a machine gun. They used it in Siberia to make the soldiers on horseback think they were being attacked by machine guns. They immediately descended from their horses. Lenin died of hard work but he wrote many valuable books about the future of the Soviet Union. They are followed to the letter. There was a leather strait jacket which was soaked in water, put on a prisoner and then he was put in a steam room where the jacket shrunk and the skin was torn from his body. They had stones on display that were thrown at policemen in the 1905 Revolution. And an armour car that took part in the street battles of 1917.

From here we went to the State Tretyakov Gallery. It is a national treasury of Russian Art. It contains 130,000 paintings. I was only interested in one: The Holy Trinity by Andre Rublev, painted in 1420. It is a masterpiece of ancient Russian iconography. It shows the Trinity in the form of three Angels. The first is the First Person of the Trinity, God the Father, The second middle Angel is God the Son and the third is God the Holy Spirit. All three are Blessing the Chalice. It is the greatest depiction of the Trinity in the world. (Years later I was to see another depiction of the Trinity in the Church in Yauri, in Peru, three men dressed alike in a glass case.)

Next we walked back to Red Square and entered the Kremlin (citadel). It contains four Palaces, four Cathedrals, surrounded by the giant Kremlin wall. This site has been a fortification for over 2,000 years. It is the official residence of the President of Russia. Leonid Brezhnev was President at the time. It was Lenin who first selected the Kremlin as his residence after the revolution. Napoleon occupied the Kremlin for about six weeks in 1812. The Cathedral of The Dormition is the main Church of Moscow where all the Tszars were crowned. The Tszar bell, the largest bell in the world stands on a pedestal next to the bell Tower. It was never rung. When it was still hot there was a fire in the tower and the water cracked the bell. We usually refer to the Kremlin as the seat of government like Downing St. or the White House.

The Armoury museum in the Kremlin, contains not only weapons but also the vast treasure of the Tszars. Among these are the Faberge eggs created by Gustav Faberge and his son for the Romanov family. These were presented by the Tszar to his daughters at Christmas or on their birthdays. They were lavishly decorated and bejewelled. The eggs when opened contained surprises, such as a mechanical singing bird, blooming flowers, even a tiny Trans-Siberian railroad train that when wound up with a golden key actually moved. There was one egg that caught my eye. A beautiful emerald green decorated with shamrocks. I wouldn't have minded taking that one home.

As we left the Kremlin some of us decided to visit Lenin in his Mausoleum. We joined a long queue. This is the resting place of Vladimir Lenin's embalmed body since he died in 1924. On the day he died on the 21st of January the Soviet Government received 10,000 telegrams from all over Russia asking that his body be preserved for future generations. In the beginning they thought he could be preserved for a few years Then the body was removed and treated and this is repeated every so often. Many people think there is nothing there and it is just a mask. Whatever about the body, the myth lives on. Every child learns that 'Lenin lived, Lenin is still living, Lenin will live forever.' Olga warned us that there was no talking, no photos , no stopping, no smoking, as we entered the Mausoleum. There he was lying in state protected by guards. It was like venerating the relics of a saint. For all I knew it could easily have been a mask. Millions have visited him down through the years. Stalin was placed beside him until he fell out of favour and then he was quickly removed to oblivion.

At the foot of the ramparts of the Kremlin is St. Basil's Cathedral, the most beautiful Russian Orthodox Church in the world. It is easily recognised with its multi-coloured onion domes which gives it a fairy tale atmosphere. Many think it is the Kremlin because foreign correspondents usually stand in front of it while giving their reports. It was commissioned by Ivan the Terrible in 1555. Olga told us the story of how Ivan had the architect Postnik Yakovlev blinded afterwards to prevent him building a more magnificent building for anyone else. Its coloured domes are a great contrast to Moscow's winter snows.

As it was the 14th of July the group decided to go to Mass in the only Catholic church in Moscow , St. Louis de Francais. It is the only

Catholic church permitted to remain open under Communism because it was protected by the French Embassy. It stands in the shadow of the notorious Lubianka's prison and the stronghold of the K.G.B. The Church catered for international diplomats, tourists, and immigrants. Catholics came from far and wide to attend Mass there. Although the Russian government sanctioned St. Louis officially, it kept it under strict control. The K.G.B. bugged the confessional and spied on all foreigners attending Mass there. The priest came to the Altar preceded by two men as altar boys. He wore a biretta which he took off at the foot of the altar. The Mass was in Latin except for the gospel. He then gave a little ferverino (talk). There were about thirty people in the Church. As I looked around there was a Statue of St. Therese, and Our Lady and the stations of the Cross. Communion was received in the mouth. After the Mass I went into the sacristy to meet the priest. He spoke French well and was delighted to see me. He signalled that I should be careful what I said because it might be bugged. He told me about the Russian Orthodox Church. The Russian people are very religious which is evident from the number of churches. Lenin separated Church from State and the majority of the Church was happy with this. Soon there was an internal schism when some wanted to accept the new regime. In the early Twenties there was a famine all over Russia. Lenin ordered the Churches to give up their treasures. The Bishops agreed apart from the sacred vessels. Kruschev persecuted the Church and especially the three seminaries. He limited the liberty of the priests. They could not touch money. They were paid by the State. They could not preach what they thought but must submit their sermons to the Ministry of Culture. Priests could not visit people in their homes. All baptisms must be registered by the State but there are many clandestine baptisms, communions and marriages. Children are not instructed in the faith and the priests are not well educated. There are twenty or thirty priests ordained in Russia every year. During the war Stalin allowed the churches and monasteries to be opened for the benefit of the people but Kruschev closed them again. Large factories were built beside churches and the sulphur destroyed the ceramics and icons. The priest had one request before I left: Could I get him a pair of glasses because he couldn't see very well with the ones he had. Many times on our travels there was evidence of the fact that Communism didn't work very well.

Opposite Lenin's Mausoleum is a large shopping centre called the Goum store, the State universal store in Moscow. It precedes the Revolution having being built in 1893. Its outstanding feature is the huge glass roof which lights up the interior. There are enormous skylights of iron and glass. containing 20,000 panes of glass. Although it was the main source of consumer goods in Communist times everything looked basic and shoddy as we walked around. There were queues everywhere. We followed one queue which extended out on to the square. Out of curiosity I followed it to its source to discover they were selling hats, round felt hats that had all being pressed in the same mould. After a while I noticed a man following me. No doubt the K.G.B. When I walked fast, he walked fast, when I stopped he stopped. He kept following me for a long time and by now I felt very uncomfortable. As I looked in a shop window he came up beside me and whispered "Have you got the message?" I looked puzzled and said "What message?" "The message from Paris" he said. "No" I said, I have no message." "But you came in on flight 708 from Paris on Friday," he said. "yes" I replied, "but I have no message." He disappeared as quickly as he arrived. Maybe he was talking about the Bibles, but they were collected from the Hotel.

In the afternoon we were invited to the French Embassy to a garden party to celebrate Bastille Day. We took the famous Moscow metro. Giant escalators whisked us down to the bowels of the earth to a magnificent train station built like a palace. The walls were made from black and white marble while giant chandeliers illuminated the whole place. There were mosaics and stained glass pictures. The train arrived in two minutes. They are automated so that they cannot crash. The stations are named after different Republics or special events. The fare was very cheap. As we walked to the embassy we passed a free market where people could sell their own produce. All was neatly laid out on tables and crowds of people were buying and selling. There were live chickens, butter, milk, potatoes, onions, tomatoes, pork meat, wild strawberries, bilberries, flowers, mushrooms of all sizes and shapes. They were doing a roaring trade. There were Russian guards at the gate to the Embassy to prevent Russians entering. Olga was very disappointed she could not come with us. We presented our passports. Ordinary Russians did not have passports because they could not travel outside the country. We were warmly greeted by the French Ambassador. All the Ambassadors in Moscow had been invited together with the Charge d'Affaires. The Irish Ambassador was not there but I met the English Charge d'Affaires, who was Irish and from Abbeyleix. Foreign diplomats can only travel 40 km outside Moscow and there are certain cities off limits. We were lavishly entertained on the front lawn with beautiful French food and drink. After all we were now on French territory. The French Ambassador told me that when they took up residence the whole house was bugged. The Russian workmen had placed bugs in all the walls. He brought me to the back to show me a round structure they had built where they could discuss affairs without fear of being bugged. The Russians had developed a kind of beam where they could listen to conversations from a distance. We were all presented with a little French flag as we left.

The main purpose of our visit was to study the Russian way of life under Communism. We went to visit a polyclinic hospital beside a motor factory. Two doctors explained the system to us and showed us around. I felt a bit embarrassed walking around the wards observing sick people in their beds. Ninety per cent of the doctors are women in Russia. The people are treated free. There were abortion wards and contraception clinics in the hospital. All medicine is supplied by the State. The patients in this hospital were all from the nearby factory. The whole place was spotlessly clean.

We then moved to the factory where 30,000 workers were employed by the State. They made cars and lorries on a long production line. They had a quota of 5,000 lorries a month. This quota must be met or the manager will be sacked. One foreman explained what happened one month. A certain part didn't arrive so they went out to the lorries that had already been passed and took the part for the new lot. The workers worked long hours and the pay was low. No worker could afford to buy one of their cars. Cars can only be used in Moscow from April to November because of the snow and ice. Each worker had a right to an apartment: 9 square metres for himself and his family. The average family had two children. Most people share the kitchen and bathroom. The elite Russian families have summer homes outside Moscow called 'dachas'.

We also studied the Russian system of education and visited schools. One large school had 1800 pupils and they operated two shifts, one from 8 - 12 and the other from 12 - 6 pm. They went to school six days a week and studied each subject for a minimum of five hours. The curriculum included Russian, Chemistry, Physics, History, Geography and Social Science. They also had military instruction. An army man comes into the classroom with a machine gun and proceeds to dismantle it and put it back together again. Each pupil must learn to do this in a given time. Each pupil wore a red scarf which indicated that they belonged to the Pioneers. (a youth organisation) There were photos of Lenin in every classroom. Girls also study dressmaking, cookery, and typewriting. They had electric typewriters imported from East Germany. All pupils must go to school in their own district except when they attend a specialised school. At the end of eight or ten years schooling they must do an entrance exam to the University. It is very difficult, but if they pass they are guaranteed a place.

Beside the school was Kruschev's Children's Paradise for young Pioneers. Another great monument to the ideals of Communism. This was a youth centre dedicated to creative work and sports training. In the centre was a magnificent Concert hall where the children learnt Ballet, gymnastics and Theatre. A group of girls were practising theatre as we arrived. They were eager to show off their talents to us. They also wanted to practise their broken English. One girl called Ellen put on a delightful ballet display. All around were rooms where different activities were taking place. The aim was the development of the children's creative abilities. As well as sport there was Cultural, Educational, Technical, Political and Artistic classes. All the children were wearing the red scarf of the Pioneers. They had been initiated into the Pioneers by standing before Lenin's tomb in Red Square and repeating the Pioneer oath:

"Stepping out in the Party's footsteps,

Defending peace and truth

Keep to the path, knowing no bounds

Into the distance of the radiant years,

Be prepared."

It was a very solemn occasion and reminded me of making my first Communion. The motto of the Pioneer's Palace was written all over the walls

"In this house the walls will teach."

Once initiated, the young Pioneers acted like the Sun sending out rays to attract others. The principle was "Having been taught, now teach your comrades." Everything in Russia revolved around Lenin. There were huge photos of him everywhere. After a marriage the Bride and Groom went to Lenin's tomb to dedicate their lives to him. As we watched one wedding group before the mausoleum, the bride in resplendent white. Jacques remarked, "That's the first real Soviet Union I've seen so far."

By now we were familiar with Olga's tactics. She had been completely indoctrinated in the Party line. Everything about Russia was bigger, better, more powerful and more beautiful than anywhere else in the world. Irish people are familiar with the Americans when they come to Ireland, telling us how big everything is in Texas. That was nothing compared to Olga. I'll have to admit that their onion domed churches and massive buildings are wonderful. They don't seem to build anything small, except the peoples house's. As we passed Moscow University she remarked, it has 40,000 undergraduates, and 4,000 Professors, with 15,000 staff to care for them, 33 km of corridors, 5,000 rooms. It has a Concert Hall, Theatre, Museum, Library, swimming pool, Police station, Post office, laundry, hairdressers, canteen, bank, shops, cafeteria and bomb shelter. Its facades are ornamented with giant clocks, barometers, thermometers ,statues, carved wheat sheaves and Soviet crests. The star on top of the building contains a small room and a viewing platform. It weighs twelve tons. As she finished we just looked up to heaven and sighed. Pierre remarked "and no freedom." Actually the only free people in Russia at that time were the prisoners in Lubianka's prison.

Early next morning we left our hotel and headed for Yaraslav station to board the Trans Siberian Express. Everyone was excited at the prospect of travelling on the world's longest and most famous train route. The station was a hive of activity with porters rushing here and there loaded down with luggage. Olga guided us to the platform where the train was waiting for us. It had eighteen carriages with nine compartments in each one. I was in compartment six with Jacques, Pierre and Yves. The compartments were not very spacious but the beds were folded back during the day and there was a small table near the window. There was a long corridor along the carriage with one toilet at the end. The train was packed as tickets had been booked weeks in advance. As the whistle sounded for departure we said farewell to Olga who seemed genuinely sad to see us go. There was a tear in her eye as she waved goodbye. It is hard to believe that this railroad was begun in 1891 and took fifteen years to complete. It brought the Asian territories under Russian control and opened up the development of the vast resources of Siberia. The train is electric as far as Sverdlovsk and then changes to diesel . After leaving the outskirts of Moscow we were travelling through the countryside of Russia. All heads peered out the windows to get a glimpse of this strange and foreign land. We passed through little forests of silver birch trees all along the track. There was a wooden house here and there with corrugated roof. Some old people were cutting hay with a scythe. Every place looked poor and barren. Suddenly we passed a little lake where people were swimming and to our surprise the girls wore bikinis. There were also many saw mills. We didn't see many roads but winding country tracks. There were no cars but an odd motorcycle or bicycle. Each shack had its little garden in front where vegetables were growing. Soon the sameness of the countryside became monotonous and dreary. Lunch was served at one o'clock. We went to our reserved places in the dining car. By now we were feeling hungry. We could almost guess the entrée: cucumber, onion, and cream,

View from Trans-Siberian train in Communist times.

followed by soup. Main course was meat and potatoes. They never served many vegetables in Russia. The dessert was apricots followed by terrible black coffee. Lucky the train stopped at every station where we could get out to stretch our legs and buy something at the little kiosk. There wasn't much choice: post cards, mineral water and hardboiled eggs. Pierre and Jacques had a field day taking pictures. One old babushka tried to clobber them with her bag when they took her photo. Some Russians just don't want their picture taken. It's hard to ask them when you don't speak Russian. The station was crowded with people. It seemed the only bit of excitement they had was to watch the train pass through. There are eighty seven cities between Moscow and Vladivostok 9000 km away. There was a mad rush to clamour aboard as the whistle went and we were off. The train never travelled at more than 60 km an hour. Tea was served in the carriages at 11 am and 4 pm. Supper was at 7 pm. It consisted of fish, soup, meat and potatoes, followed by tea or coffee. There was lights out at 8.30 pm and there was nothing to do but go to bed. We tossed for the bunks and I found myself on top. Although I was very tired I found it hard to sleep with the constant movement of the train. When I did doze off I was awakened by the sound of tapping metal. The train had stopped. We all got up and went out to see what had happened. There was a group of workmen going up and down tapping the wheels with long hammers. Eventually they stuck a hollow sound and the wheel had to be changed. It looked primitive but they managed to put on a new wheel. We all went back to bed as the train continued on its way. We were still speeding along when morning came. We took our towel and toilet bag and joined the queue for the toilet. This was the most difficult part of the journey. The toilet always seemed to be occupied. After breakfast I decided to say Mass in our compartment. Two of our group stood guard at either end of the carriage while the rest gathered for the Mass. Guards came around the carriages from time to time and we had also seen soldiers on the train. It was a beautiful Mass in this strange and unusual situation. The countryside had not changed very much and we began to get restless in our confined space.. When they changed the engine to diesel, the dust and dirt prevented us looking out the window. Lucky we had decided to take a break every two days. Soon we would be in Novosibirsk, the biggest city in Siberia, where we would stay two days. We arrived at the big station at 3.15 pm local time, tired and weary. There to meet us was Raisa our new guide. She had a very comfortable bus to take us to Hotel Novosibirsk The city owes its origin to the Trans-Siberian railway. It was built in 1893 beside the site for the railway bridge across the river Ob. It is a very modern city and the people were younger and happier looking. We couldn't wait to get to our rooms for a shower and clean up. Supper was at seven. There wasn't much variation in the menu: Cucumber and salad, soup with hard boiled egg in it. The main course was a sort of fish ensemble but was very tasty. We finished up with ice cream and coffee. After supper I went for a walk with Jacques and Pierre to stretch our legs.

There was a man on the side of the street with a weighing scales. There was a long queue of men and women waiting to pay three kopecs to have their weight taken. We saw this many times on the streets of Russia. At the side of the hotel a man had set up a barbeque. Again there was a queue buying skewers of meat. The three main attractions in Novosibirsk are the university, the opera and ballet theatre and the zoo with its 4000 species of animals including some endangered species.

Early next morning Raisa took us on a tour of the city. Every Russian city has its statues to its heroes and war dead. Raisa was quick to point out that ten million Russians died in the second World War. First we visited a monument to the brave revolutionaries who were shot by the White Guard when they learned that Moscow had fallen. Next we saw the eternal flame for those killed in the second World War. One tenth of the population of Novosibirsk was killed. Their names are written on a huge monument. It is guarded by two boys and two girls in special uniforms, changing every twenty minutes. We then moved on to the opera house and zoo. In the afternoon we went for a swim in the river Ob. We took a boat up the river to a sandy beach. It was a beautiful day and although there was a strong current most of us ventured in. Afterwards we sunbathed on the sand. I would never have thought it possible in Siberia.

After supper we went to the circus. Almost every city in Russia has its circus. Its not in a tent as you might expect but a permanent building beside the church. Nor were there any wild animals but high flying acrobats doing dare devil stunts, many clowns who needed no translation and performing dogs and conjurors and illusionists.

I decided to concelebrate Mass with the Bishop in the Russian Orthodox Church nearby. He was happy to welcome me. There was much blessing of incense and singing. I didn't understand a word and I said the words of consecration in English. The church was packed and as the average age of the people of Novosibirsk is 35 they were mostly young. Communion was under both species mixed together. The Bishop gave Communion with a spoon even to babies. He baptised some babies after the Mass. Each family had to produce their identity cards to be registered by the State. There were many soldiers in uniform at the Mass. After the Mass I gave some of the women Rosary beads that I had brought with me. They gratefully accepted them but I'm not sure if they knew how to use them.

Raisa warned us that the next day we could visit one of the most unique places in Russia. Up to recently it was off limits to foreigners. The bus was waiting at the hotel to take us the 40kms to Novosibirsk Academgorodoc, an academic town where research teams worked in all fields of basic science. The Russian government in their wisdom built this magnificent University in the middle of nowhere by the banks of the river Ob and placed their greatest scientists to do research here. It was built in a beautiful natural setting amid pine forests and birch groves. It was a powerful scientific complex spread over a vast area. Here they would have researched weapons of war and the rockets to outer space. There were forty research and Design and Technology Institutes . These included an Institute of Mathematics, an Institute of computer Science, and Institute of Nuclear Physics and an Institute of Geology. Naturally they weren't going to let us in on any secrets, especially as we had eminent scientists in our group As I walked up the tree lined avenue there were beautiful red squirrels hopping from tree to tree and some even came down to the ground to get a closer look. They looked so tame you could almost catch them, but I knew that wasn't possible from experience. We were guided to a complex where a group of young technicians were busy at work. They were all teenagers with an I.Q. of 160. They were experimenting with cars, dismantling the engine and working out ways of getting it to go faster. Another group was working with bikes, and another with model aeroplanes. They could speak English perfectly and were happy to explain what they were doing. They had come from all over Russia and had been separated from their families in the cause of science. There was a photo of Neil Armstrong on the wall. He had visited here and left a photo of the moon. We then went to a hall where we had a lecture from Ivan Shcheglov, scientific secretary of the Siberian Department of the Academy of Science of the U.S.S.R. Even his title was impressive. The lecture was on the vast resources of Siberia. Petrol, natural gas, diamonds, coal, iron, marble etc., all illustrated with colour slides. He then took us to the museum of geology where he pointed out the various multicoloured stones. We then had another lecture on the Social aspect of Siberia. All Russians seem to be trained in the same propaganda school where they are at pains to point out the wonderful advantages of Communism. Some years before a group of professors began to question the principles of Communism and they were immediately expelled. One couldn't but be impressed at this great scientific complex in its beautiful surroundings but I was always left with the nagging question "If only they were free to say what they really thought."

Asleep on the Trans-Siberian Train.

After another two days on the Trans-Siberian train we arrived at the city of Irkutsk . The scenery gradually became more interesting with stretches of green fields and many rivers meandering snakelike in the plains. There was vast areas of black forests with rolling hills in the distance. Renata was waiting to greet us at the station. There was a big modern bus to take us to the Hotel Angara, named after the nearby river. The city is named after a tributary called the Irkut river. The first thing that hits you in Siberia is that your image of the place couldn't have been further from the truth. You imagine an unknown territory, unsafe and barbaric, with bears on the streets, drunken men with guns and fur hats. Perhaps it's because for years being exiled to Siberia was used as a punishment for criminals and political offenders. For centuries it was unknown not only to foreigners but to ordinary Russians. Irkutsk is a modern city with coloured neon lights over the shops. Renata was quick to point out that there were five theatres, fifteen cinemas, and thirty four libraries. Although it is 300 yrs old it was burnt to the ground in 1879. There are young people and students everywhere, the average age of the people being thirty two. We were welcomed to the hotel by the chimes of hundreds of bells from the forty Orthodox churches. After the usual supper, there was no menu, you just accepted what they served, I went for a walk around the city with Jacques and Pierre. There was a lot of activity even at that time of night and we felt perfectly safe. As well as the wonderful Russian architectural buildings there was a district with beautiful wooden houses with intricate handcrafted designs. Irkutsk suffers from extreme climatic conditions. We were lucky that it is very warm in summer but in winter it freezes over.

The highlight of our stay in Irkutsk was the visit to Lake Baikal, the longest and deepest fresh water lake on earth. We started off badly as the bus broke down for an hour. The journey passed through forests with quaint little villages of wooden houses with tin roofs along the banks of the river Angara which has its source in Lake Baikal. Suddenly we got our first glimpse of the beautiful lake. It looked so blue, pure and cold. Even in summer it never rises above twelve degrees. Renata told us it was bigger than Belgium and Holland together although she had never seen either country. It contains hundreds of species of fish, one third of which are unique to the lake. One species eats all the dirt in the lake which makes it look so pure. The lake is twenty million years old and is deepening all the time as a result of little earthquakes. There is a species of sturgeon in the lake which produces five kilos of fine Russian caviar. The lake freezes in winter and can be crossed by lorries. Renata looked up into the mountains and declared "There are many eagles up there." We took her word for it as we didn't see any. We visited a wonderful museum at the side of the lake with hundreds of exhibits from the lake. There was one transparent fish and you could read a newspaper through it. Just then a funeral passed by. I asked Olga once in Moscow "What do you think happens when you die?". "Nothing" she said looking into space. There was a large crowd of people looking very solemn and sad. In front a group of men carried large wreaths. Four men carried the lid of the coffin which was red: obviously a high up Communist official. Then came a lorry carrying the headstone pointed at the top with a star. A young boy was in the lorry surrounded by flowers. Then six men carried the open coffin which was also covered with flowers. A large crowd followed. There was no sign of a clergyman or religious symbol. There are two kinds of funerals in Russia, religious and state. This was obviously a state one. We returned to Irkutsk by boat on the river Angara in one hour. Our supper that night was an entrée of onion and carrot, followed by a bowl of chopped fish and rice with a cream biscuit and tea for dessert.

Just outside Irkutsk the Trans-Siberian railway divides into three The oldest the Moscow -Vladevostok line, the second Moscow -Bejing, and the third Moscow - Manchurian - Bejing. We could only go as far as Khabarovsk on the Amour river because Vladevostok was closed to foreigners. From Khabarovsk we must take a local train to the coast. Vadlena our guide was anxious to point out how dangerous the city was because across the river was China. She said there was over one million Russian soldiers guarding the border. Trouble could flare up at any moment. Khabarovsk is a large industrial city of about half a million people. Some early explorers settled here on the banks of the Amour in the seventeenth century. Before 1927 there was one picture house and eleven churches, now there are fourteen cinemas and one church. There were giant photos and statues of Lenin everywhere. Lenin never came here but he wrote a lot about it. We met a girl in a bar called Valentina who spoke French very well. She was very happy to talk to us. She asked us to send books and records which could not be had in Russia. She knew about the Beatles, Tom Jones, the Rolling Stones, and Twiggy. Her one ambition was to visit London. She knew London intimately. That's the way they teach English: by having a model of the city in front of the class. She would love to visit Poets' Corner in Westminster Abbey. She was brave enough to say that it was a mistake to demote Stalin. "In the beginning there was a progression from Stalin to Bulgarin, to Khrushchev" she said. "But now they have gone back to Lenin as if the others didn't exist. They make him into a God. Lenin lived, Lenin lives, Lenin will live for ever. I think Stalin will come back."

I know you are dying to know. Supper that night was : entrée, sardines and tomato, then meat and rice, with ice-cream for dessert.

Before we left we took a boat trip out to the centre of the river Amour to observe the Chinese soldiers on the other side. They had binoculars and guns trained on us and we had the eerie feeling that they could open fire at any moment. It was a beautiful hot day and people were swimming and sun bathing along the bank. There were many Japanese among the crowd. Close by there was an enormous amusement park and we saw children laughing and enjoying themselves for the first time but we had to move on. We took the train to the port of NAKHODKA where we boarded the boat DJERZINSKY for Tokoyo. The customs on the way out was every bit as strict as on the way in. You had to present your form showing every place you had visited in the Soviet Union and what presents you had bought. Then they examined your expenses form where you had to account for every rouble you spent. They then searched your luggage thoroughly to see had you any icons or gold. I'm afraid all they found was dirty laundry.

The boat was luxurious compared to the dust and dirt and lack of toilet facilities on the Trans-Siberian train. There was a wonderful air of freedom as we looked out on the bay of NAKHODKA after the constraints behind the Iron Curtain. The food was magnificent and after supper we sat around the pool and recalled our experiences of the last month. Each one of us had different recollections. The doctors among us were surprised at the level of medical care and how everyone had access to it. The scientists were amazed at some of the advances in the scientific field to the neglect of the ordinary everyday things. The architecture and construction of the magnificent buildings and the people living in wooden huts and nine square metre flats. with shared toilet and kitchen facilities. While we agreed that the natural disposition of the Russian people was dour and serious little was being done to cheer them up. You always got the impression that they weren't free to say what they thought. This was very evident in our guides who , although charming , were completely indoctrinated. All in all, everyone agreed it was the experience of a lifetime. We all gathered in my cabin to celebrate a Mass of thanksgiving.

Mass in secret on the Trans Siberian Train.

24

Exploring Japan, Korea & Taiwan

"There it is," shouted Jacques, as he spotted the coast of Japan in the distance. He was in his element taking pictures. We had just spent three days relaxing on the boat after our exhausting Trans-Siberian experience. We were now entering Tokyo harbour amid thousands of boats of all shapes and sizes. It seemed miraculous that we avoided hitting one. It was here that General Douglas MacArthur accepted the Japanese surrender in 1945. Soon we spotted Pere Bosc on the quayside. "Everyone safe and well?" he asked as we came down the gangway. The place was crawling with people, small Japanese, trotting along as if they were late for something, and carrying cases almost as big as themselves. "I had terrible trouble getting a taxi" remarked Pere Bosc, "today is a holiday in Japan and they are all engaged." We battled our way through the crowds to where six taxis were waiting for us. My first impression was that it could have been any big American city with its neon lights and skyscrapers. Looking closer, the giant advertising boards were in Japanese. Young men were in their immaculate white shirts and slacks, women carrying their babes in haversacks on their backs. There were lines of men sitting on paper or a little mat, on the ground lazily reading, writing , or playing games. Some had dozed off. The men looked pale while the women were elegant and slim. Everyone had black hair. One was left with no doubt that you were in a different country with a different culture. At first glance it didn't strike me as beautiful or ugly but different. Pere Bosc had arranged for us to stay at the residence of the Jesuit Sophia University. St. Francis Xavier came as a missionary to Japan in 1549 to bring Christianity to this pagan people. In one of his first letters to St. Ignatius in Rome he wrote about this high regard for the human qualities of the Japanese people and his hopes to found a university in Tokyo. His dream was not fulfilled until 1913 with the opening of Sophia. It has become one of the most prestigious universities in Japan and Tokyo's top ranked private university. The Japanese are very difficult to convert to Christianity and they say there are about the same number of Christians in Japan today as there was in St. Francis Xavier's time. Pere Bosc had an intensive week of lectures and visits prepared for us. Each morning began with a lecture, an introduction to Japanese life, Japanese economy, Japanese young people and other specific lectures for certain members of our group. He also arranged visits to Mitsu-Bichi naval yard, hospitals, schools and car factories.

Before supper I had my first experience of a Japanese bath. This is performed in every Japanese home before the evening meal. It is an integral part of Japanese life. You enter the ante chamber where you undress and sit on a little stool to wash yourself. Your body must be thoroughly lathered, scrubbed and rinsed with a wooden scoop from a tub of clean water. Then you enter the larger room where there is a large bath of steaming hot water. You enter the water naked and sink into the world of 'ofuro'. There were other Japanese in the bath, strict silence is observed as you relax for about twenty minutes. It's easy to meditate. Then you emerge and rinse yourself with cold water and put on a kinono. It is the custom for all the family to use the same water in the bath.

My French companions in Japan.

We then dressed and went to a restaurant in the Ginza shopping centre. I would have been happy to order European food but the group wanted to sample the local Japanese food. A Japanese girl from the university came with us to explain the customs. All the restaurants display their meals in plastic in the window. The display is very realistic. We had to sit on the floor on a tatami mat around a low table. The men sit with legs crossed while the women sit with their legs to one side. Within a short while we could hardly move. The food arrives in various bowls on a tray. Of course we have to use chopsticks. The girl shows us how to use them by placing them between the fingers of one hand. It is extremely impolite to stick the chopsticks in the food. Before we start instead of the grace before meals we say "Itadakimasu" (I receive this food and give thanks to the person who prepared it.). In one bowl is fish coloured like salmon. It is really the famous Japanese raw fish which is a delicacy. One eats a little from each bowl. There is a bowl of rice This is a real test for the chopsticks. You must lift the bowl to your chin and try to scoop the rice into your mouth. Another bowl has herbs and leaves. There is a separate little bowl of soy sauce. Another bowl has noodles in a meat soup. We finish with a bowl of green tea, boiling hot. After the meal we say "Gochiso- Sama" (thanks for a delicious meal). While we enjoyed the meal we didn't feel full. No wonder the Japanese look slim and healthy.

My room was on the fifth floor of the university. I was woken up in the middle of the night by the bed moving from one side of the room to the other. The whole room was shaking. I jumped up and ran to the window. There were crowds of people in the street below in their night clothes. I heard screeches coming from nearby rooms. Most of our party were in the corridor by now. Jacques had his camera at the ready. A professor came along and calmed us down. Obviously this was a regular occurrence in Tokyo. "The building is constructed to withstand earthquakes," he said, "the people are expecting a big one soon, it's fifty years since the last big one and they say they come every fifty years." It would be just our luck to have come at the wrong time. The earthquake lasted about thirty seconds but it seemed a lifetime . The next day they told us it was 6.2 on the Richter scale, the biggest they had had for some time. There was much damage to the smaller buildings.

The Japanese breakfast was something else: miso soup, rice, nori dried seaweed with pickles and green tea. Jacques and Pierre were starving by this time so after breakfast they decided that we should look for a McDonalds. Although I would grow to like the Japanese food, for the moment I just wanted something familiar to eat. A burger never tasted so good. Afterwards we walked around the shops . It was almost impossible to walk on the street, we just kept bumping into people. The people were extremely polite, they just bowed and smiled. As we passed the entrance to the metro, I suggested we would try it out. What an experience. You pay a few yen for your ticket and after that it's a scrum all the way. Silently the train arrives and the doors slide open crowds emerge and another crowd enters. The train is never full, if you can't get on that's your fault. We just squeezed in but there were many more on the platform trying to get in. The doors won't close. Three guards come along and begin to push. Eventually the doors close. We are like sardines. What a great way to get to know the Japanese people.

After our first week in Tokoyo I began to get more acclimatized. The visit to the shipyard was overwhelming. A giant Greek ship was in the process of being built. The front half was already completed even down to the name on the side. Another section was working on the other half. Then there were giant cranes to bring the two halves together where they were welded. Parents in Japan will go to any lengths to get the best education for their children. They usually have only one or two children. Although the schools were on holidays there were large groups doing special courses. The children are very friendly and when I went into the school yard they all gathered around me to talk. I asked if anyone could speak English and one little lad was hauled to the front. "Do you speak English?" I asked. "My name is Naoiki, I live in Tokyo" he said. "You speak English very well, where did you learn it?" "My name is Naoiki, I live in Tokyo."

That was the extent of his English.

My experience of the Japanese people as kind and friendly was completely different to my preconceived ideas. I had been brought up on war films where the Japanese were always the bad guys. They were experts at cruelty and torture. I read about the rape of Nanking in 1937 when the capital fell to the Japanese. There was indiscriminate rape, looting, arson and the shooting of prisoners of war over 200,000 men, women and children were killed. The surprise attack on Pearl Harbour on December 7th 1941 brought the Americans into the Second World War. Roosevelt called it "a date which will live in infamy". The cruelty of their treatment of the prisoners they forced to build the Thailand Burma railway and the Bridge on the river Kwai. The Kamakazi pilots diving on the American ships in the Pacific when they knew the war was lost. It was hard to believe that these could possibly be the same people.

Soon we were to leave the great metropolis of Tokyo and go south to the land of religion. There are two major religions in Japan, Shinto and Buddhism. They compliment each other and most Japanese would say that they are both. Religion doesn't play a big part in everyday life , only for weddings, funerals, and an odd visit to a shrine or temple (much like many present day Catholics). Shinto is the native religion of Japan dating back to 500 B.C. It is a polytheistic religion with many spirits called KAMI. They venerate mountains, rivers, water, rocks, trees. Their principle deity is the sun goddess. The imperial family originated from the Sun. The Japanese flag has the rising sun with the rays going out in all directions. A Kami can exist in a grove of trees, a waterfall, a town, a village, or a valley. The three central principles of Shinto are: the family, love of nature, and physical cleanliness. Festivals are for entertaining the Kami, especially Sumo wrestling.

Buddhism on the other hand originated in India in the sixth century with the teachings of the Buddha,Gautama Siddhartha. There are many different branches. It was imported into Japan via China and Korea. It was immediately welcomed by the ruling nobles as Japan's new State religion. Soon the two religions co-existed. Now Shinto is overshadowed by Buddhism.

Early in the morning we took the bullet train to the city of Kyoto, the ancient capital of Japan from 794 to 1867. We glided through the lush countryside at 200 miles an hour in an air-conditioned carriage drinking tea and munching nuts and ice cream. Not an inch of Japanese arable land goes uncultivated. The city is divided in two with a population of one and a half million people. One side is a modern industrial city while the ancient part stretches up the wooded mountainside with 2,000 Buddhist temples and Shinto shrines. It is one of the few Japanese cities that was spared bombing during the war. It would have been unthinkable to destroy such an ancient culture. There is an abundance of water and this is used very artistically in the lay out of the temples. At first sight the temples take your breath away, wonderful wooden structures with stairs and gardens and pagoda shaped roofs. It would be impossible to give an impression of them all, each representing a different aspect of Buddhism.

Let me try to bring you through the Ryoanjii Temple with its famous rock garden. On entering, you pass a mirror shaped pond with water birds and Manderin ducks, swimming peacefully around. These ducks only choose one mate in the their lifetime and if one dies the other does not mate with other birds. Newly married couples are attracted to them for good luck. The temple itself is an enormous wooden structure with six tatami matted rooms surrounding the image of the Buddha. As in all Japanese houses you must take off your shoes before entering. There is a large bell at the entrance with a pole suspended on rope which can be pulled back to ring the bell. Then there is a square stone water basin with Zen spiritual sayings on the side. You contemplate them as you walk around in silence.

"I learn only to be contented"
"I just know satisfaction"
"Someone who learns contentment is rich in spirit and character."
"Someone who is materially wealthy is spiritually poor, if they do not learn contentment."

You feel perfectly at peace as you approach the rock garden. It is an extraordinary expression of simplicity. A large area covered with white sand and gravel. It is neatly raked every day. Fifteen rocks of different sizes are placed around the sand. They say the secret is to see the distance between the rocks. No matter from what angle you look at the garden, you only see fourteen rocks until you reach enlightenment, then you see the fifteenth. It is like abstract art, an absolute masterpiece of Japanese culture.

For the next few days as I went from Temple to Temple each one more beautiful than the other, I felt a great sense of calm and contentment. There was something about this place that brought me closer to God: the rising and setting of the Sun, the gentle flowing water, the beauty of nature, the tree covered mountains, even the monks with their shaved heads and brightly orange coloured garments. It was so easy to pray and meditate here. As I looked up over the entrance to one Temple, there were the three wise monkeys. Kikazarn; hear no evil, Iwazarn; speak no evil, Mizaru; see no evil. So this is where they came from, an old Buddhist legend. As I sat there in contemplation a thought suddenly came to me. I'd love to live with those monks for a day and experience their lifestyle. I mentioned it to Jacques and Pierre and they said they would love to come with me. One of the monks spoke a little English. I asked him if it would be possible to live with them for a day. He looked at me without the slightest expression on his face and said. "Not possible." He began to walk away. When he had gone a little way he turned and came back.

"Perhaps on Mt. Hiei" he said, "many monks, but not for one day. Must become Novice for three days." The next day we decided to head for Mt. Hiei.

Three Wise Monkeys, so this is where they came from.

We took the funicular railway up the slopes of Hiezan to the Temple. Mt Hiei is a sacred mountain and is known as the mother of Japanese Buddhism. It is not just one temple but a whole complex covering the summit of the mountain. There were hundreds of monks here in various stages of formation. The head monk met us and welcomed us to Mt Hiei with a gracious bow. He led us into a great hall and told us the basics of Buddhism. The three mysteries of Buddhism are Body, Speech and Mind. The body must be brought under the control of speech and the mind. Speech seeks true words. True words transcend speech. Speech is not always the best means of communication. Other artistic skills are encouraged like painting, music, and gesture. The mind is a way of perceiving the truth. As he stood in front of a giant golden Buddha he did not appear to be pronouncing articles of Faith. I was not inspired by the image of the Buddha but I found nothing in what he said that I could not agree with as a Christian. He pointed out how important it was for the monks to keep their bodies in the best physical shape possible. All monks practiced the martial arts. In passing he mentioned that he had a black belt in Judo and a fourth Dan in karate. As we came to a large hall he said we could not enter but we could listen at the door. We heard the sound of running inside. These were the famous marathon monks of Mt. Hiei. I have always been amazed on reading in the Guinness Book of Records of the mysterious and amazing feats that human beings can endure. This was the most unbelievable . There were monks inside running marathons of 40 km a day for 100 days. It is a religious experience called Kaihoyo. Only a small number of monks can attempt it. It comprises sacred worship, ritual, austere meditation, repentance, asceticism and miraculous cures. The runners begin at midnight. They run until 7 in the morning. They bathe, eat a small meal, rest for an hour. Sleep from 8 until midnight when they begin again. The rules are:

- During the run the robe and hat must be worn.
- There must be no deviation from the course.
- No stopping.
- All chants, prayers must be performed.
- No smoking or drinking.

In the beginning they experience pain in their feet and legs. They also get diarrhoea and haemorrhoids. The present group of monks had completed 90 days. When they have completed their 100 days they can petition 1000 days. Only a handful of monks have ever attempted this.

The evening meal was an extraordinary affair. All the monks gathered in front of little tables in two long lines. There was absolute silence. One monk intoned the chant. Everyone joined in. This went on for quite a while. Suddenly it stops. All sit down on tatami mat in front of a table with legs crossed. A tray with several bowls in front of you. On the top left hand corner, salad of tomato and onion, next a bowl of vegetables, to the right green tea, underneath, a bowl of rice, green beans and a bowl of soup. The meal is a form of Zen meditation and must be eaten in silence. When you lift a bowl, you must put one hand underneath as you replace it so as not to make noise. Buddhists don't eat meat or fish or any living thing. They believe in reincarnation, so they might be eating their friends who have come back. Everyone must finish eating at the same time. No food must be left on the plate. The washing up is done at the table. With a glass of water you rinse out each bowl and dry it with a napkin. Then everyone rises for more chant.

Before going to bed, there is the bathing ritual which I have already described. I then slept on the floor of a room with absolutely no furniture. My bed consisted of a small solid pillow. I was woken up at 4.30 a m. to be in the meditation temple by 5 o clock. The head monk had explained the ritual of Zen meditation the night before. He had excused us of the obligation of having our heads shaved and wearing the orange garment. That would happen when we passed the initiation test. We processed to the Temple in a long line and took our places in front of a giant Buddha. First the body must be prepared. The three essential parts were the position of the body, breathing and the heart. We must relax and breathe in and out slowly about one hundred times. Then we must clear the mind completely. This is done by placing one hand over another with the thumbs almost touching. Just a hair's breadth between. Then we contemplate, "How square is a circle?" "How deep is a hole?" The mind very quickly goes blank. Then we are receptive to positive thoughts. One monk walks around with a huge wooden pallet. If you feel like dozing off you bow to him and he gives you six whacks across each shoulder. The noise resounds around the Temple as if you are being flogged. Actually it is quite relaxing and I asked for it twice.

After meditation, all the monks form a long line and process through the forest to the temple of the founder. He is a Chinese priest called Saicho who founded the monastery in the 9th century. He is preserved in a mausoleum surrounded by a temple. Like Lenin , they pay him homage as if he is still alive but unlike Lenin he must be fed three times a day. One monk is appointed to look after him for a two year period. It is considered a great honour. He prepares the meals and places them underneath an opening in the bottom of the door. The old meal, which obviously hasn't been touched is removed and the fresh one put in its place. The monks gather around the Temple and chant his praises.

Mass with Fr. Kim in Korea.
I loved celebrating Mass in foreign countries.

I don't know whether I reached Enlightenment, which is the aim of every Buddhist, but I did feel much more enlightened and came away with a great admiration for their way of life. They have a wonderful respect for nature and every living thing. They do not contribute to the pollution of the earth or the atmosphere. The sea, the rivers, and lakes are sacred and their purity must be preserved. Is it any wonder then that Buddha has passed the boundaries of Christianity and is commemorated in the Roman Martyrology.

***

On August 6th 1945 three U.S. B29 military bombers arrived in formation over Hiroshima city at 8.15 am. Flying at an altitude of 24,000 ft. one of them called the ENOLA GAY flown by Colonel Paul Tibbets headed for the heart of the city, released one single atomic bomb and immediately banked sharply and darted away to the northwest at top speed. The people of Hiroshima were already at work on this lovely summer's day. The children had gone to school. The troops stationed in the city were on parade. The communication centre had received a call to say that three enemy aircraft was passing over but they were probably on reconnaissance, no need to alert the anti-aircraft guns. Some people were fishing in the river. Suddenly there were mysterious flashes in the sky and then a gigantic fireball, which swelled rapidly into a tremendous explosion. A horrifying column of flames hit the earth and rose up in the form of a bulging mushroom cloud to a height of 27,000 feet almost instantaneously. Hiroshima was no more. As Paul Tibbets and his crew looked back they cheer for joy at the success of their mission. One of them took a picture of the mushroom cloud.

Pere Bosc and the group had no plans to visit Hiroshima. Early one morning I set out alone to take the train. It was a daunting journey as no one spoke English and all the signs were in Japanese. At the ticket desk I had to make sounds of a bomb dropping and with my hands a giant cloud. To make matters worse I had to change trains half way. I soon found that it was very easy to tell the Japanese you wanted to go to Hiroshima. The very name is embedded in their minds for ever. It was a lovely journey through the lush Japanese countryside but I was a bit on edge not knowing if I would recognise the station. As I came near I asked a fellow passenger if this was it. He just bowed and smiled and said "Ari" For all he knew I could have been an American.

Again at the station all I had to do was to point to a bomb falling from the sky and the taxi driver brought me straight to the spot. There are many heartbreaking symbols of the event scattered around the Peace Memorial Park. The cenotaph is designed in the form of pre-historic clay figure denoting an ancient Japanese house. This is where an annual Peace Ceremony takes place each year on August 6th. The stone chest in the centre houses the Books of the Past recording the names of the victims.

The number of those who suffered from the bombing is estimated at around 400,000 including both military and civilians.

On the chest is inscribed

"Let all the souls here rest in peace

For we shall not repeat the evil."

Atomic bomb exploded over this building in Hiroshima.

A little further on is a beautiful memorial to honour the memory of the children killed by the A bomb and to appeal for world peace. As I walked around I was overwhelmed by the enormity of the terrible tragedy. At the far end is the burnt out shell of the building over which the bomb exploded. The bomb never hit the ground but was detonated 1,800 feet above this building. In the dark clouds of dust not a house was left standing and fires broke out everywhere and engulfed the whole city. Why was Hiroshima chosen to be the victim of this terrible atrocity? It was because it was the site of the largest army base in the whole of western Japan with numerous military installations, large depots of military supplies, and massive concentrations of army personnel. It is also thought that Hiroshima was chosen because it was surrounded on three sides by mountains and its dense population would make the attack highly effective. Other cities had also been considered, Kyoto and Yokohama. Kyoto was ruled out because of its culture and also the Secretary of War, Henry Stimson had spent his honeymoon in Kyoto. Japan first heard of the Bomb from Washington. Two days later Radio Tokyo broadcast,

> "Practically all living things, human and animal were literally seared to the earth."

Next I made my way to the Hiroshima Peace Memorial Hall which is a vast Museum. First I went to the projection room where a documentary of the dropping of the bomb is shown five times a day. Then to the thousands of pictures of the aftermath of the bomb. An oxidized tram was completely destroyed with its occupants where it stood. Ceramic objects, glass, metallic and other items melted, were deformed or fused with others by the high temperatures of the conflagration. The bones of the people who perished in the raging flames were melted and fused with rubbish. There are hundreds of objects from the many school children who died in their classrooms. Lunch boxes, charred remains of a boys uniform, a wrist watch stopped at 8.15 a m. I read the account of an eye witness :

> "The bomb exploded some 2000 feet above the centre of Hiroshima with a heaven splitting flash and an earth- shaking roar, demolishing the city in an instant. A huge column of flame rose into the air and clouds of smoke billowed up and covered the sky, bringing sudden night. The city below was an inferno. Bodies of the dead and the dying lay where they had been flung. Fires started up everywhere and in minutes joined into a conflagration. From out of the flames naked, blackened, ghoulish figures came staggering and falling, haunted by the hopeless cries of victims caught under fallen stone and timber behind them. Soon these cries were silenced, replaced by a pandemonium of groans. Shrieks of agony and fearful calls for lost loved ones."

There were hundreds of school children visiting the museum. They were in tears as they went from glass case to glass case. Yet as soon as they saw me they immediately gathered around and wanted to talk. I was the only foreigner there that day and I could easily have been an American. It is extraordinary how the young people of Japan don't seem to hold any anger or resentment against the people who caused this terrible atrocity. President Harry S. Truman was asked in later life if he knew the consequences would he still have dropped the bomb. He said " I would ." If only he had come to Hiroshima. As I came back in the train to Kyoto I was in pensive mood. What a contrast: living with monks on Mt. Hiei and the experience of the destruction of Hiroshima. I had plenty of food for thought.

***

Six days after the dropping of the second atomic bomb on Nagasaki, Japan surrendered The war was over. This had a profound effect on the warring nations but on another occupied country which was now celebrating their liberation. Japan had occupied Korea from 1910 to 1945. During the occupation they had tried to impose everything Japanese on the Koreans. Now a vacuum was created and the old division of North and South returned. The Soviets and Chinese entered the North and had ambitions to make the whole country Communist. It was inevitable that the Korean war would break out in `1950 when the North invaded the South. General Mc Arthur and the U.N. forces were to drive them back to the 38th parallel three years later. An armistice was signed rather than a peace treaty, so the two sides are still at war. A state of tension has existed ever since.

All seemed peaceful and calm as we flew into Kimpo airport in Seoul. As we passed the formality of the customs there was a news flash on the many T.V. screens around the airport. Lord Louis Mountbatten had been assassinated by the I.R.A., who planted a bomb in his boat at Mullaghmore, Co. Sligo. People gathered around the screens in utter dismay. Fr. Price S.J. met us and brought us to Sogang University, the Catholic university run by the Jesuits. Here we began a series of talks and lectures on the various aspects of the country. The next day two Korean girls from the university took me on a tour of the city. We also visited a Korean village on the outskirts. The one thing that struck me immediately was the friendliness of the people. They wanted to talk, they invited me into their houses, they offered me food. This was like the Ireland of the past. No wonder the Koreans are called the Irish of the East. Seoul is a modern city with wonderful shops. Here I had my first taste of Ginseng made from the roots of a plant with miraculous cures. It is made as a drink, a capsule or a powder. For the next couple of weeks I drank lots of Ginseng but I'm not sure if it cured me. On the way back the girls took me to a park where we took a boat out onto the lake. One of the girls began to recite:

"I will arise and go now, and go to Innisfree,

And a small cabin build there, of clay and wattles made,

Nine bean rows will I have there, a hive for the honey bee,

And live alone in the bee-loud glade."

I couldn't believe my ears. One of the girls was studying Yeats at the university

"This is what I imagine 'Innisfree' to be like.

Each day we visited hospitals, schools, factories. I paid a very moving visit to the Korean War Museum. It is situated beside the U.S. army garrison at Yongsan. It is a massive display of armoury including vintage planes and tanks from the war. One of the most extraordinary things was a statue of two brothers, one from the North, the other from the South meeting on the battlefield. Everywhere there was evidence of the deep hatred that exists between the South and the North. This was also evident when we visited the boundry at the 38th parallel. It is the most heavily fortified border in the world,with one million soldiers facing each other. They eye each other through powerful binoculars all the time. It seems to be a question of who blinks first. The border is firmly closed with no movement either way.

Korean folklore village.

Mass in Seoul, Korea 15th.Aug. 1979.

My biggest surprise in South Korea was the number of Christians in the country. There are eleven million Protestants and three million Catholics. This is the greatest number of Christians in any Asian country. There are many missioners in the country including the Columbans from Ireland. I had the opportunity of concelebrating Mass in many parishes and in one it was First Holy Communion for hundreds of children. The Catholic population is increasing every year. Japan tried to impose Shintoism on the Koreans but they resisted it as the religion of the invader. We visited many Buddhist temples but only a quarter of the population is Buddhist. it's a different form of Buddhism from that of Japan. Most Buddhists have a huge swastika on their side. My guide pointed out that this was an ancient Buddhist symbol. It is a sign of good fortune and the footprints and the heart of the Buddha. It is also a symbol of abundance, prosperity and long life. The arms of the Buddhist swastika are clockwise, while the Nazi swastika is anti-clockwise, a symbol of the cult. My lasting impression of Korea is of a beautiful country with wonderful friendly people.

From Korea we flew to the island of Taiwan, formerly called 'Formosa' which means beautiful. Again we were looked after by the Jesuits. They had organised the usual lectures and visits to the various parts of the island. Unlike Korea there are very few Catholics in Taiwan. The majority of the people are Chinese who escaped from China with Chian Kai-Shek in 1949. In Taipei there is the most wonderful museum in the world, the National Palace museum. It contains all the treasures brought from China. There are thousands of precious objects on display. Chinese bronze, calligraphy, paintings, and porcelan. I spent hours admiring some of the finest art in the world.

I was anxious to meet the native aborigines of which there are 400,000 still on the island. We took a treacherous journey by bus down the mountainous road to the south. My heart was in my mouth as the driver negotiated the many twist and turns within inches of the great abyss below. The aborigines gathered around in their thousands dressed in their native costumes to welcome us. These were the Ami tribe who lived in the sub-tropical jungle. They had been converted to Catholism by French foreign missioners. The women performed a beautiful native dance. I had the great privilege of celebrating Mass with these wonderful people. Afterwards they produced a meal from the big brown pot. A chicken cooked whole with feathers and all. It required a great act of faith to partake in their generosity (Many years later I experienced the big brown pot while living with the Inca Indians in Peru).

As I flew back to Paris I brought with me many wonderful memories and many hours of material for my Zen meditation. I had experienced many different cultures and a sincere expression of different faiths. My own faith too had been put to the test and come through it much stronger. I never lost sight of the God that I believe in and saw many different expressions of his presence in other religions. I also met many wonderful friends. I bid them a fond farewell in Paris and took the ferry back to Ireland to a new horizon. Tomorrow to fresh fields and pastures new.

25

Back To Gort Muire

On my first Saturday back in Ireland I went for a walk up the Three Rock mountain behind Gort Muire. As I walked along I was wondering how I would go about getting started with youth retreats. I was anxious to put into practice my thesis of "Communicating the Faith to Adolescents Today." Bishop Dermot Ryan came towards me and said "Hello" not knowing who I was as by now I had dispensed with clerical dress. Next three women came along and we began to talk. I introduced myself as Fr. Conroy and they introduced themselves as three Sisters of St Louis from Rathmines. They too had dispensed with their habits. I explained that I had just come back from Lumen Vitae and hoped to start giving youth retreats. "You are the very person we are looking for," said one who was teaching in the school in Rathmines. "It is very difficult to get a priest for retreats" she said, "I will send you up a group on Monday at nine o' clock."

When I arrived home from my travels my parents informed me that Davy was very ill. The wound that he had received in the motor bike accident never really healed up. Now he had developed cancer and he was in St Michael's hospital, Dun Laoghaire having his leg amputated below the knee. The doctor was hopeful that he had caught the cancer in time. By now he had five wonderful children, John, Mary, Richard, Cormac and Gráinne. It was a difficult time for all the family.

Gort Muire at this time was being transformed into a Conference Centre but had not opened yet. There were very few students and most of the rooms were empty. It was now over ten years since the end of the Vatican Council and many areas of the Church was experiencing difficulties in putting into effect the recommendations of the Council. Archbishop McQuaid had taken the stance that nothing had changed and you can't disturb the faith of the good lay people. The Mass is in English, and the altars are facing the people and communion is given under both species. In general the people took the changes in their stride. Very often it was the clergy who had the problems and nowhere was this more evident than in religious life. The habit as a symbol of leaving the world was gone. Religious gave up their religious names and reverted back to their Christian names. The older men who had spent their whole lives living the rule and constitutions to the letter of the law now found that the young priests were getting away with murder. It wasn't fair. Before it was a mortal sin to eat meat on Friday and now you could eat what you like. Priests could go to the theatre and to the races, they could even go to the dogs. The Carmelites decided to set up a Conference Centre where priests and religious could come for renewal courses and retreats. Courses were also given in all aspects of theology and the liturgy and especially folk Masses, which had become very popular at the time.

Early one morning I got a phone call from the hospital to say that Davy had passed away in his sleep. He was 46 years of age. I was devastated as were all the family. I couldn't imagine how my parents could endure losing two sons. Margaret and the children were inconsolable. I said the funeral Mass in the presence of a large crowd in the Church in Rathdrum. Many Carmelites arrived to support the family. He was buried in the cemetery outside Rathdrum alongside his brother Eddie.

The Retreat was centred on my special room. It had lush carpet on the floor, with posters and paintings on the walls. Soon each group had its artists and poets to add to the collection. A girl called Donna left her wooden cross that she wore around her neck. There was a record player with hundreds of LPs. It immediately created a wonderful friendly atmosphere.

My famous retreat room at Gort Muire 1978, remembered by thousands.

Sitting around in my special room I introduced myself. You are very welcome to my home here in Gort Muire. First of all I want to say there are no rules and regulations here. I expect each one of you to behave in a responsible manner. I would ask you to pull down the blinds in your rooms before switching on the light. We don't want to frighten the cows, because they don't give as much milk the next morning. There is no programme. The only thing we are sure of is meal times. There is just one thing you can't do under any circumstances. ASK QUESTIONS. I haven't got the answers. Lets explore and look for the truth together. We won't contradict each other. Let each one begin by saying "I think ." Human beings are the only creatures who can communicate by speech. Yet the lowest form of communication is language. Very often when we have a great experience in life we cannot talk about it. There are no right words. People sometimes speak to one another in dance halls but they don't communicate

"Do you come here often?"

"Only when there's a dance on."

"Do you feel like an orange?"

"Do I look like one?"

"Do you often dance here?"

"No, sometimes I dance over there."

"You're very light on your feet."

"You're very heavy on mine."

The greatest questions in life like: what is love?, what is friendship? what is faith?, cannot be answered in words. So we will search together. There are much higher forms of communication besides language. Some can express their deep feelings in poetry, or art. After the tea break we met in the retreat room where we sat around in a circle. There are three kinds of people in this group that I want you to beware of.

Your friends; you are probably sitting beside your best friend. You will want to stay with your friend and not mix with the others. You will learn nothing new about yourself.

Your enemies; you will try to avoid them. You create a cool atmosphere.

Those you are indifferent to. These are the most important of all. We have lived together for years and don't really know one another.

There are two things I would like you to keep in mind during these two days. Sincerity and the importance of other people in our lives. Each one of us came out different doors this morning. You know what happens behind those doors. Happiness, sadness, rows, problems, Love. We are all affected by the family situation we live in. Try and be yourself. Be sincere to yourself. Accept yourself as you are. This is not easy. We are always pretending we are different to what we are. We wear masks.

Don't be fooled by me,

Don't be fooled by the face I wear.

For I wear a mask, I wear a thousand masks,

masks that I'm afraid to take off

and none of them are me.

"You are important", a girl said to me once. "No one likes me, I'm no good."

I said something to her that an old priest once said to me. "No matter how ugly a specimen of humanity that you think you are, there is always someone else who thinks you are wonderful." She wrote to me later and told me it was true. She had met her boyfriend and fallen in love. Someone is happy because you exist. We all have our own personalities and talents. Put a ball in front of one person and they walk over it and for another it becomes magic. Some can write wonderful poetry while others can paint beautiful images.

Next the importance of others in my life.

No man is an island. We all need other people in our lives and they make us the kind of people we are.. Even before we are born we are affected by our mother. Is she nervous, emotional? This can rub off on us. Our early years are very important. Are we self-confident? Everyone has always told you that you were great. You were loved. In school your confidence can be built up or destroyed. Did you ever have a teacher that didn't like you for no particular reason? The teacher is writing on the blackboard and everyone is having a little natter. Suddenly she turns around and points to you and says "Would you please stop talking." Why me? Everyone was talking. She doesn't like me (and I don't like her either). We put people into little pigeon holes very quickly. A new teacher, look at the way she walks, look at the clothes she wears. We don't see the real person. That person you can't stand, someone else loves them. God loves them. Not just nice people but everyone. Now I want to tell you something you will never forget.

"Each one of you has inside you a LOVELY LITTLE CHILD. A little child that loves, that has feelings, that is easily hurt, that needs other people, that wants to come close to people, someone else to put their arms around you and say they like you, that you are nice. And that little child is the real YOU. Everyone has a little child inside them, even the most formidable of people like policemen, judges, your father, your mother, even the headmistress. I'm sure you were often in a situation where someone hurt you but you didn't pretend. Or perhaps you are not talking to someone - outwardly. "I don't care if they never talk to me" But the little child inside you says "I wish they would talk to me." It's a terrible thing to hurt the little child inside another person. It's easy to understand the little child inside yourself but remember other people have a little child too. Do you really believe you have a little child inside you? Come and take me into your home. Take me upstairs and into your bedroom. Would I notice anything that would tell me you have a little child inside you. Perhaps a teddy bear, some dolls, etc.

Next I place a Bible in the centre of the circle.

"Do you know what that is.?" Ah, you say I knew he would get around to it. You know what happens when you are coming on retreat. You are rushing out the door and your mother shouts after you. "Did you bring your rosary beads?" and all you are thinking of is "Have I got the sweets and chocolate in case the food is terrible?" Aileen Lyons came on retreat about three years ago from Waterford and when the group was coming the Rev. Mother told them to bring their Bibles. Well, she left the Bible behind her. There it is. Look at it. You know that means NOTHING like that. It's made of wood, like the floor with black print. It means nothing, unless you make it mean something. There are two very important things missing from that book which you cannot put into a book. The TONE of voice in which Christ spoke and the EXPRESSION on his face. Each one of you is an expert at reading the expression on your mother's face when you want something. A little child soon gets to know the tone of voice of its mother when she is happy and when she is sad. Jesus Christ must have had a wonderful tone of voice and a wonderful expression on his face. Even the little children came to Him and loved Him. And you can't fool children. They see with their hearts and not only with their eyes, like the little Prince. Put Miss World beside a little child and if she is not a nice person they are not interested. Did you ever see a little child sitting on their grandfather's knee? The grandfather is old with crimpled wizen skin like leather and probably no teeth. The child puts its arms around him and loves him. A child sees with its heart. To make that book mean something you must make it come alive. You must give it an expression and a tone of voice and there is only one expression and tone of voice that you can give it and that is YOURS. You must give it your heart and soul. I look for the heart of Christ within you. I look for His image deep in your hearts. I told you a short time ago that each one of you has a wonderful little child inside them. Well now I want to tell you something else. That little child is not a normal child. It is a handicapped child. We are all handicapped in some way. Who is as clever as they would like to be? Did you ever feel stupid in class and the girl beside you understands everything? Or you might have a physical handicap. Why didn't you get on the basketball team? Why can't you run fast ?

The walls in the retreat room were covered with posters and sayings. I used these to illustrate things during the retreat. These were made by groups from other retreats. One group had made a big question mark. At one end a baby and at the other a dead person. In between all the events of a human life. And the question was WHY?

I had placed a poster of Romeo and Juliet in the central window. Now I want you to look at that poster for two minutes and tell me what you see. I know its Romeo and Juliet but forget about them . What does the picture say to you. LOVE, FRIENDSHIP, HAPPINESS, JOY, TOGETHERNESS, UNITY, ECSTASY. That picture never opened its mouth and yet it has said things to you that language cannot. How can you tell someone what love is in words? The picture is SYMBOLIC. This is a higher form of communication. Like poetry, images, and music. Now I want to play you a piece of music which will be the theme of our retreat. It is in French and we used to play it during Communion in our Community.

"Je cherche le visage, le visage du Seigneur

Je cherche son image tout au fond de mon Coeur

Vous etes le corps du Christ

Vous etes le sang du Christ

Vous etes l'Amour du Christ

Qu'avez vous fait de Lui."

"I look for the face of Christ within you,

I look for his image right at the bottom of my heart,

Because now you are the Body of Christ,

You are the Blood of Christ,

You are the Love of Christ,

Well, what have you done with Him."

Tolstoy said something very interesting

"When primitive people stop believing in their wooden Gods that doesn't mean the God does not exist, it just means He is not made of wood." When we stop believing in God 'up there on a throne in Heaven ' that doesn't mean He doesn't exist. We learned all about our faith when we were young - all the facts. Sometimes we just keep to the facts when we can symbolize and make it personal. I don't know when it is going to happen to you. Walking down some country lane on a summer's evening. The birds are singing, the bees are humming, and you get the scent of the newmown hay. He will give you a dig in the ribs and say " Tell me why do you love me?" And you won't be able to tell him. You will mumble something like "You know." or "I told you before." Jim Reeves used to sing a song

"I love you because..........

But most of all I love you because you are you."

You are eating an ice-cream on a hot summer's day and your friend asks you "What does it taste like?" "It's nice, it's cold, it's smooth, ah here take a lick." Some things can't be explained, they have to be experienced. You must experience your faith. And you can communicate it but not in words.

No one has ever seen God. No one knows what He is like. So sometimes we create our own God. We think God is like us. Some mornings he gets up and he is in great form. You would get away with murder that day. Other days He is in bad form. He is ready to pounce on you for the slightest thing. SIN IS TURNING YOUR BACK ON GOD.

Now we come to a part of the retreat that you will love. So far I've done all the talking. Now each one of you has an opportunity to introduce themselves (An expression of fear and dread comes over everyone). If you could just mention two things. 1. Your Christian Name. 2. How would you describe your faith. Only your Christian name. Often people are known as the son or daughter of Mr. and Mrs. Smith. Not as you. Now you have an opportunity to talk freely and be yourself. Say what you think. What do people normally talk about? Their family, how many brothers and sisters. Do you get on well with your parents? What makes you happy, What makes you sad? What annoys you? You may talk about your Faith, Mass, Prayer, Priests, Nuns, Church etc.

I'll begin. My father and mother are still alive and I have two brothers. I always wished I had a sister but the lads tell me I'm better off and they would be happy to give me one of theirs. I love the country and nature. If I wasn't a priest I would have loved to be a farmer. I love animals. My eldest brother was killed in a motor bike accident. I had to face death in the family. As a priest I often see people dying. It is never easy. The priest has to break the news to the relatives. What should you say? There are no right words.

Now it is your turn. Someone usually begins and the rest follows. I listen to their names carefully and write them down. When they are finished I put away the piece of paper and go around each one and tell them their name. They are surprised and astounded that I can remember all their names, (I'm in school six years and the teacher still doesn't know my name). From then on the whole atmosphere changes. They feel happy and at home.

I drew a triangle on the board. Now lets start at the beginning. Where does faith come in? Why do we believe? Everyone sees things from their own point of view. Some people will look at the board and immediately say. "I know what that is, it's a triangle." Two lads look over the cliffs of Moher. The older lad looks out across the ocean at the beautiful scene and can't find words to describe it. The other looks out and says "If I spit out there it would go a mile.Two men looked out from prison bars, one saw mud , the other saw stars. I'd like to suggest that that is not a triangle but each one of you. Well, I could have drawn a square and you would not have liked that. Let's fill in the corners.

1. Who have we been talking about so far? ourselves. Right so let's put myself on one corner.

2. Who else is there in our lives besides ourselves? Other people. Good. We live with other people. We form relations with others. Lets put 'others' on another corner.

3. Before we fill in the other corner we must answer three questions.

(i) WHO AM I.?

(ii) WHY AM I HERE.?

(iii) WHAT'S GOING TO HAPPEN WHEN I DIE.?

Let's look again at Patricia's question mark. What does it mean. She said she was always puzzled by certain questions. Who really am I? What is the purpose of my life? I often think about death. What happens after death.

Many young people get frustrated with their lives and they imagine death would solve the problem. Often attempting suicide can be a cry for help. A girl on retreat once told me she was going to commit suicide the following Friday. I didn't believe her. On Saturday her mother rang me to tell me she was in St Patrick's. She heard her falling out of bed in the middle of the night. She had taken forty sleeping pills. She was rushed to hospital and had her stomach pumped. She wanted to see me. She was sitting up in bed when I arrived. "Do you remember what you told me when I said I was going to commit suicide?" she asked. "You said I should ring you if I felt low." "Wouldn't that be very stupid? It would be like the robber going to rob a bank and ringing up the manager beforehand to tell him he was coming." "Well, it didn't work this time but the next time I'm going to hang myself. There's a clothes line in the bathroom and I'm going to use that." I didn't know what to do. On the way out I looked in the bathroom but there was no clothes line. She is perfectly happy now. She was going through a period of depression. Sometimes young people get very depressed.

A girl goes to her room and locks the door. She lies on the bed and cries and cries for about two hours. She doesn't know why. As she comes down the stairs she bumps into her father. What are you crying for? She can't tell him. She makes up a story. "My friend's dog got killed." Her father consoles her and tells her she will get another dog.

Let's go back to the question mark. Let Patricia explain. "I first came into existence inside my mother's womb. I lived there for nine months and then I was born. I depended on my mother for everything, nourishment, care, love. Then I began to talk. Soon she came to the WHY stage.

"Mammy, why is the grass green?" Mother explains how colour works. White light enters the eye and we have rods and cones in the retina and the brain tells us it is green." But why does it do that? Is the green in my eye, in the grass or in between? Is the grass green at night when it dark? I don't know.

At the end of the question mark there was a gap and then a dot. I'm going to have to pass over that gap to reach the other side. That gap is DEATH. I'm going to have to go over that gap. One of the great certainties in life is that we must die. We don't know what's on the other side. No-one has ever come back to tell us.

Let us go back to the triangle. There is still one corner to fill. This depends on the answer we give to the three questions. Who am I, why am I here, and what is going to happen when I die. Every human being must answer them. The answer that you give depends on your FAITH. A Muslim will say Mohammad and a Buddhist will say Buddha. As Catholics our answer is God. We believe God created the world and everything in it. He sent His Son Jesus Christ to show us how to live and to die for us. "I am the way the truth and the life." But Jesus Christ rose again from the dead. We too will rise with him after death. St. Paul said that "if Christ be not risen then our faith is in vain." We need to believe. Our faith is a gift from God.

One girl wrote back to me after the retreat to tell me about her experience of faith. "When I went on that retreat my faith was very weak. I thought you would have a magic wand and I would come away believing. Now it is three weeks since I was there and I know there is no magic wand. I am at home in bed with the flu. The sun is shining through the window and there is a sycamore tree outside with all the colours of autumn. How could I not believe that God exists? My family is very clever. My father is a professor in the university. My mother is a secondary teacher. My sister is teaching down the country. My brother is at the university. We have some very intelligent conversations at table. At the moment we are discussing Existentialism Camus and Sartre are all the rage. I wish to God we could talk about ourselves. Oh we don't have rows. Everyone is very polite. We always say 'please' when we want the salt. But sometimes you could cut the atmosphere with a knife. I know now there is no magic wand to give me faith. I will always be a blind man walking with confidence. But now I feel I have found the white stick to tap the path as I go through life."

We all gathered again in the retreat room. We began to talk about relationships, about getting on with people. We often judge other people without really knowing them. We are going to perform an exercise in getting to know people. Most of you have been together for a long time and some of you don't really know one another. We are going to break up into groups of five. We will go to the recreation room sit on the carpet and talk to one another. I want you to say five things to each one in the group. What are you to say.? You say four nice things that you admire about them and one thing you don't like. I counted around the circle one to five. All the ones formed a group etc. You now have two hours to perform this exercise. For most people this was the best part of the retreat and they formed a solidarity with the group that they never had before. The best part was what they learned about themselves

And so to bed.

We woke up next morning to the soothing sounds of Cat Stevens singing "Morning has broken." By the sleepy faces it would seem they hadn't slept much.. They continued to talk through the night. The second day would concentrate more on our relationship with God. On our personal faith. So we gathered around again in the retreat room. You have seen how wonderful it can be to speak sincerely to one another. Now let's see how important it is to speak to God.

"Charlie , how's the wife?

She's fine, I think

What do you mean, you think don't you know?

Well, we're not talking,

Did you have a row, are you not getting along?

Oh no, everything is fine, we just don't talk

How can you be fine, if you don't talk

Really, everything is perfect

She goes her way and I go mine."

If you heard that conversation you would say that their marriage is heading for the rocks. The more closely we are related to a person the more deeply we want to communicate with them.

"Do you have a relationship with Jesus"?

Most of you would answer "Yes"

When did you last speak with Him.?

If there was a computer in the centre of this room and I put into it all the Gospels and everything that Jesus Christ ever did or said. Press the button to discover what was the one perfect way to follow Jesus. Even the computer can't answer that. There is NO one way of following Jesus. Look at the history of Christianity. Various Religious Orders and Congregations in the Church. Each one puts a different emphasis on the best way to follow Jesus. For the Franciscans it's poverty, for the Jesuits its teaching, the Dominicans it's preaching. And for the Carmelites it's Prayer. The Carmelites speak about the importance of prayer in the life of the church. All the Carmelite saints were Saints of prayer. St. John of the Cross, St. Teresa, St. Therese of Lisieux.

Look at the Carmelite nuns, they spend their lives enclosed in prayer. Let me tell you about the first time I went to say Mass in the Carmelite convent in Kilmacud. I rang the bell. The door opened. No-one there. I hear a voice. The key is in the urn. I take the key and open the sacristy. No one there. Vestments laid out; I hear a voice saying the ciborium is ready for Consecration. I say Mass. I get a glimpse of the Nuns as I give them Communion. I come back to the parlour where breakfast is already laid out. A voice talks to me during breakfast from behind the grill. You may say what in the name of God are they doing in there.?

They know what they are doing. They wonder what you are doing out here.

One girl said. " Oh, I know why they are there. They failed the leaving, they are stupid so they had to go to the convent" Another said ." They are disappointed in love, they couldn't get married." I explained. "One nun has an M.A. and she is translating a book from Latin to English. Another nun is over 80 years of age. She has been in the convent for over 60 years. She prayed she would not have to go to hospital before she dies. They pray. If I really wanted something very badly I would ask them to pray for me.

Jesus told us about two people a Pharisee and a publican. They went into the temple to pray. The Pharisee went up to the front of the church and told God what a great fellow he was. The other knelt at the back and without looking up asked God to forgive him. We are told he went home more justified.

Or the story of the two disciples on their way to Emmaus. Jesus walked with them as a stranger and didn't reveal Himself until the end of the journey in the breaking of the Bread. He wanted them just to speak freely with Him. He revealed Himself in the Eucharist.

Prayer is just talking to God in your own words. Sometimes it's enough just to be in His presence. The Cure of Ars tells us a lovely story. An old man came to the church every day and sat at the back looking up at the Tabernacle. One day the Cure asked him. "What do you say to Jesus all the time you are there."? The man looked surprised. "I don't say anything to Him. He looks at me and I look at Him."

We should pray every day, in every way and put our trust and confidence in God.

Don't leave it too late. Tommy Mackem sings a song.

"the man who sat by the road and weeps,
Of all the songs he didn't sing.
And the promises he didn't keep."

After the morning tea break we come to a very important part of retreat. Confession. The one thing everyone says about going to Confession is "I hate confession." Confession is a Sacrament. It was instituted by Christ. We receive absolution and our sins are forgiven. No one has a problem with that. When we were prepared for Confession the most important part was the formula. That's not what Confession is about. It should be a meeting with Christ. In the afternoon you have an opportunity to come and talk in my room. You don't have to come if you don't want to.

You can come just to talk or to receive absolution. So what do I have to do. The first thing is you don't give a laundry list. Just come in, sit down and we'll have a chat. Is there anything worrying you? If you were to die tomorrow what would you want to say to God.

There is one thing I can't take away and that is nervousness. It is natural to be nervous. It goes away as soon as you come in. I have seen people who crawled under the door coming in and they hit their heads off the top of the door going out. It's a wonderful feeling to be at peace with God and with yourself. I'm afraid I can only spend ten minutes with each one but it could be the best ten minutes of you life.

The grand finale and the highlight of the whole retreat was the Celebration of the Eucharist at the end. We all gathered around the Mass table in the retreat room. Everyone felt happy and relieved after their Confession. Not all Masses are the same. Young people often say the Mass is boring. It can be very boring when you don't take part. Today's Mass is very special. We have gathered to Celebrate the Passion, Death and Resurrection of Jesus Christ. You will never understand the Mass. It is a mystery. It is not something that happened two thousand years ago. The Passion, Death and Resurrection of Christ is taking place here today. That is the mystery. We need faith to believe that. That's why I say not all Masses are the same. I said Mass once in Dachau concentration camp. There was a priest's block in the camp which held over 2720 priests. They secretly celebrated Mass and passed around Communion. One of our priests, Fr. Titus Bransma died there of a lethal injection.

There is a Carmelite convent there and that's where I said Mass using a chalice which had been made by one of the prisoners out of wood. That was a special Mass for me. I said Mass in the train on the Trans-Siberian railway. I also said Mass in a Buddhist monastery in Japan. Today we may receive Communion under both species. You may also receive Communion in your hand if you wish. We are receiving the Body and Blood of Jesus Christ.

We sang hymns and songs. We played Mary Magdalene's song "I don't know how to Love Him, " from Jesus Christ Superstar. The readings were picked especially by the young people themselves. And we finished up with Communion.

"Je cherche le visage, le visage du Seigneur."

I spent seven years giving youth retreats in the Conference Centre before going on the Missions in Peru. During that time over ten thousand young people came on a two day retreat. All my years of education and experience was brought to bear on these two days. I soon became an expert in dealing with young people and their problems. They shared with me the inside as well as the outside of their lives. I soon learned that although they looked innocent they had all the problems of the world. I also learned not to judge them by their appearance. It was often the not so good looking ones that had the most beautiful little children inside them. I received thousands of letters with their reflections on the retreat.

Cartoon given to me after a school retreat.

Could I quote from one?

Dear Christophe,

You will have to excuse the 'notepaper' because I am writing this letter during a study class at school. We found it hard to settle into school after the retreat and the atmosphere of friendliness is really great. We have you to thank for that, because you really helped us to know one another better and having shared the experience together means that we all have something personal in common.

I waited until today to write to you because I was still on retreat over the weekend and this morning the 'ripples' from the two days spread out, affecting my family and friends so that I couldn't really say "The retreat is over , how do you feel?" until now. We nearly all half cried half laughed on the way home, sorry to leave the retreat itself behind, but so very grateful for the experience. There the 'something in common' ended because each one had her own feelings and thoughts, private and personal. When I arrived home, my face really 'blotchy and weepy, my mother asked what was wrong. I said, 'nothing' and the conversation went like this. What are you sad for? You shouldn't be so upset. " Sr. Rosemary said the experience was traumatic but if I'd known you wouldn't have gone." "Don't be silly Mam, it was wonderful, just wonderful" Then she put her arms around me and I really felt great. Mam didn't understand fully but she knew I needed that comfort more than I needed words. Then my old Dad came in, thinking the worst as usual. "What's happened? Have you been attacked?" At that moment I felt a warm rush of love for them all, my parents, my sister who was sitting quietly in a corner, watching , and my brother who had gone out, leaving his school books all over the place. I spent the next while trying to explain, but even with the love they couldn't understand. "The whole retreat was one continual prayer, and as the priest said, the two days were part of and leading up to the Mass. They asked about the Mass itself and I said that we had Communion under both forms and that we took Christ's Body in our hands" My Dad exploded. "What do you mean? your hands should have been consecrated, that's something only a priest should do." I tried to change the subject but it didn't work My Dad kept on and on until I turned my back and began to show my sister the poster of Romeo and Juliet. Then my Mam said "Leave her alone Seán, she will grow up someday and see where she is going wrong." Then I exploded. "What do you mean - wrong?" I shouted "Just because I fail to see the point you're making. I took the Eucharist that way because I wanted to. I don't tell you you're wrong when you use your tongue, do I?" Seeing my Mam's upset face I said "Look, I'm sorry - let's leave it." Then I showed them the poster. My sister with all the honesty of a twelve year old said. "Soppy, but he's good looking." My parents wanted to know what Romeo and Juliet had to do with a retreat. I said "They symbolize love, and unity, and isn't that what God is all about. I saw their perplexed faces and gave up. "I'm tired, I'm going to bed." As I went up the stairs I heard a niggling little voice inside me saying "What about all those good resolutions?" so I turned back and said "Good night -- you know something -- I love you all." I went up the stairs chuckling to myself at their surprised faces. Maybe I should say that more often. As I lay in bed looking at the poster the whole retreat seemed to flash back again. I thought, "You know God, you really looked after me, of all the girls in Ireland and in the world who needed such a retreat I got one You gave me the courage to go to Confession when I needed it most. You gave me a priest who understood. Rather than being despised for what I had to say I was understood and really helped. For the first time I found a priest whom I could really compare to Jesus. A priest I could see as Jesus. Then I cried and cried. All the tension and tears bottled up for three years came out. My father's illness, which started in 1972 and which has only just begun to clear up, all the strain it caused my mother and I most of all because my mother is semi-invalid and I had to try to cope, it all came out. My young cousin dying earlier this year. I cried myself to sleep and you know something? Saturday morning dawned bright and beautiful and I jumped out of bed eager to start a new day.

Thank you for just being there. With your understanding you put in the key piece of the jigsaw that is me. Because you set me free of guilt.

Thank you once again,

Mary.

One morning on my way to say Mass at the Carmelite convent I got news that my father had died. He had been taken to Leopardstown Hospital for ex British service men, a short time before. I had been with him the previous night. I continued on to say the Mass with the nuns. I don't know how I got through it, but I felt their prayers gave me strength. After the Mass I made my way to Wicklow to break the news to my mother and Richie. They were just about to come to the hospital. My mother couldn't express her grief but her heart was broken. What was there left to live for? Her life partner is gone. There was a terrible feeling of emptiness around the house. Even the flowers in the garden that he loved looked sad. My mother made a cup of tea and the three of us just sat there and talked. We looked back at all the wonderful times we had together. The Copse and the rabbits and wood pigeons. the walks in the woods, swimming in the river and his wonderful support at every stage of my life. The grandchildren were a great help to my mother. Richie was now in the Irish Army and stationed at Cathal Brugha Barracks.

When I arrived at Leopardstown for the removal I got a great shock. They had placed the Union Jack on the coffin. This indeed was a great honour but not for an Irishman. Although my father had fought in the British Army during the First World War, his loyalties were always in Ireland. He joined the I.R.A. when he returned after the war and was District Transport Officer for Wicklow during the Second World War. Richie arrived with a contingent of soldiers from Cathal Brugha Barracks to perform a guard of honour. He brought with him the Tricolour. I had to act quickly. I removed the Union Jack and placed the Irish flag on the coffin. The soldiers stood to attention as the coffin left the church. The hospital provided the hearse and four cars for the funeral. We made our way amid a fall of snow to the Church in Rathdrum. The Mass was difficult. A priest often says Mass at funerals but when it is your father or mother it is different. He was buried in Rathdrum cemetery beside Eddie and Davy.

***

26

To the Mountains of Peru

It was during one of these school retreats in Gort Muire that I made one of the biggest decision of my life. The girls were sitting around in my special room, listening to my records and looking at the pictures on the wall (most of the pictures were gifts from former girls and boys who had been on retreat). Most groups had talented artists and writers who loved to make a contribution to the room. As they sat on the lush carpet one girl, Jo Sheridan , asked a simple question.

"Have you got a vow of poverty?"

I began to give her the usual theological answer. "Poverty does really mean not having things. It means not being attached to them. I could see her eyes glazing over and not understanding the difference between owning something and having the use of it. To her poverty meant not having things, not having enough to eat, not being able to pay the mortgage or the rent,not having a home or a place to sleep, not having money. That night I began to think: yes I did have a vow of poverty but it didn't really mean anything. I felt my life was passing me by and I wanted to live among the poor.

Next day a fellow Carmelite, Fr. Des Kelleher was home from the missions in Peru where he had worked for years with the Inca Indians, the poorest people in the world. He had just been appointed to a new parish called Yauri, a district the size of Leinster. "It would be wonderful to have another Carmelite with me" he said. I hesitated for a moment. I had one big problem. My mother was still alive and living alone in Wicklow since my father died. How could I leave her now in her old age? I spoke about my difficulty with Des. He just quoted the Gospel.

"Anyone who leaves father or mother, sister or brother for my sake, will receive a reward, a hundredfold."

I was convinced; I would give up everything and go. But how was I going to tell my mother. I was also booked up for retreats for the next two years . I cancelled them. My mother took the news very calmly and with great faith. I promised her I would go to Madrid to learn Spanish and return to spend Christmas at home with her. She was overjoyed. That was the last Christmas we spent together. She died while I was in Peru.

I volunteered to go to Peru for five years. The experience was more than I could ever have expected. It changed my life forever. Yes they are the poorest people in the world, living high in the Andes at an altitude of fifteen thousand feet, just below the snowline. At this altitude nothing grows and it is very difficult to breathe. It is impossible to sleep for more that a couple of hours at night in temperatures thirty degrees below zero. I had to learn Spanish and Quechua, the language of the Indians.There were over fifty communities or villages in the parish of Yauri. This meant long journeys into the mountains to celebrate their fiestas. This involved saying Mass and baptizing the young people and marrying their parents. Sometimes they hadn't seen a priest for over twenty years. I would line the families up in parallel lines and baptize them,as many as five hundred at a time. Afterwards I would do the same for the marriages. I soon realized that the landowners with their extensive haciendas stretching for miles across the mountains were not happy with me visiting the poor Indians. They wanted to keep them in servitude, working like slaves for a pittance on their vast expanses of land. Next came the Shining Path terrorists and everything changed. I was in constant danger of being killed travelling through the mountains. The landowners were quick to avail of the opportunity, accusing me of being a terrorist ,to have me expelled from Peru.

I have written about my time in Peru in my first book, 'A Beggar in Paradise,' which became a best seller. I.T.V. television also did a documentary on my work in Peru called, 'Beggars in Paradise.'

***

Speaking at Mass, Peru, 1995.

In the Mountains of Peru.

On my way to Parupata, Peru.

Knocklyon Parish

On my return from Peru I was appointed parish priest of Knocklyon. There could not have been a greater contrast to my parish in Peru. From the poorest of the poor to the richest of the rich, or so it seemed: a beautiful young parish in the suburbs of Dublin, at the foot of the Dublin mountains. The Carmelites founded the parish in 1974 at the request of the Archbishop of Dublin, Dermot Ryan. They arrived to virgin territory with no church, no schools, no parish hall. But they did have a thriving young community ready to build a parish. By the time I arrived there was a beautiful church, a junior and senior school and every organisation one could imagine. I was installed as parish priest on Sunday the fifteeneth of September 1985, by Bishop Joseph Carroll. In my address to the congregation I said.

"It is with a certain amount of fear and trepidation that I accept the great honour of being your parish priest. I follow in the footsteps of your illustrious former parish priests, Fr.Patrick Staunton, and Fr. David Weakliam. Being Carmelites we are all members of the same family as it were, so the changeover should not be too traumatic.

Parish priest of Knocklyon, a wonderful time.

Nevertheless each of us brings his own individual personality and style. One of the great things about being a parish priest is that everyone else knows how to do the job better than you do. We have a wonderful Carmelite team in the parish, so I will be ably assisted by Fr. Alan Fitzpatrick, Fr. Arthur Fitzpatrick and Fr. Aidan Mcloughlin."

During my years giving school retreats I had learned a very important lesson . Out of a group of thirty girls, there were usually about five who couldn't stand the sight of you. It wasn't anything you said or did, they just didn't like the look of you. Then there were about ten who thought you were the most wonderful person in the world. The rest couldn't care less, one way or the other. After the two days most had come around but there was always a few who stuck to their first opinion. It was the same in the parish, many people loved Fr. Weakliam and didn't want to see him go. Others gave me the benefit of the doubt and waited to see what I would be like. They hung on every word I said in my Sunday sermons. It was the subject of conversation over the breakfast table on a Sunday morning. Because of my enthusiasm about my time in Peru, I spoke a lot about it in the beginning. I could almost hear them shouting back, "oh not again" as I began. I got great encouragement from the many committees and organisations in the parish. The Church was still in debt but there was a wonderful group of collectors from every area of the parish who collected the parish dues every week. But the one thing that struck me from the beginning was the number of young people in the parish. I could see there was a great need for a youth club , but I decided not to do anything for the first six months until I settled in and saw the lie of the land.

My fellow Carmelites also had problems. As soon as I was appointed parish priest I rang Fr. Aidan in Whitefriar St. and asked him to join me. I had seen his expertise in managing schools so I appointed him to the Junior school. Fr. Aidan had been in Terenure College with me and we also joined the Order on the same day. Fr. Alan and Fr. Arthur were many years my senior and had worked in the parish for some time. Naturally they thought that they should have been made parish priest before me. I got a cool reception in the beginning. Fr. Arthur never spoke at our community meetings on Monday mornings for the first year. I could well understand how he felt, but he wasn't mad at me but at the Provincial for appointing me. Soon everything calmed down and we got on very well together.

The people of the parish often said to me,

"How can you settle down in Knocklyon after what you have seen in Peru? We are so well-off. You must find it difficult walking on carpets and living in luxurious conditions."

"Not at all" I said, " I love walking on carpets. In Peru I was living in the first century. Here we live in the twentieth century but that brings its own problems. We have traffic jams on a Sunday morning, there they have never seen a car. Here our Easter dues come in envelopes, there they come in the form of a couple of eggs, a fish, or a smelly piece of meat wrapped up in a rag. The better off brought a guinea pig."

Knocklyon had other problems. Marriages broke down and families separated, the children being the innocent sufferers. Husbands lived in fear of redundancy and not being able to pay the mortgage. Children of good parents who dabbled in drugs and brought sorrow and disgrace on the family. In Knocklyon there were wonderful people who were only too willing to help. There was a lovely spirit of SHARING, GIVING, AND RECEIVING.

The schools were growing year after year. Fr. Alan was manager of the senior school. He was very easy-going and he allowed the school principle to run the school. At the end of his term of office he came to me and said he didn't want to be re-appointed.

There was no one else to appoint, so reluctantly I had to take over. After I became manager, Alan was very annoyed that I hadn't insisted that he remain manager. I couldn't believe it. How could I read someone's mind? Not only that, but he then proceeded to tell the members of the Board of Management that I had sacked him. This is all part of the trials and tribulations of being parish priest.

Probably my greatest achievement as parish priest of Knocklyon happened by accident. One Sunday I announced at all the Masses that there would be a meeting for all new altar servers the following Monday evening at seven thirty. About forty turned up and among them three girls. I looked at the girls and asked were they alright. "Yes," they said, "we want to be altar servers." Without thinking I said, "Alright" and continued with the preparation. (girl altar servers were not allowed at this time). When I came back to the presbytery, I announced to the others that we were going to have altar girls. In unison they said, "You are heading for trouble, you will get the belt of a crosier."

Undeterred, I continued with the preparation of the three girls. Finally they were ready to serve. They had their surplice and soutane made and I decided they could serve my Mass the following Sunday. I hadn't forewarned the people that there would be altar girls but nobody seemed to notice. Everyone just took them for granted. Like all the changes in the liturgy, the people took them in their stride. It was only the Bishops and priests who had a problem. I just made one exception. The girls could serve any of the Masses except the ten o 'clock. Nobody could understand why. It all became clear in June when the Bishop came for Confirmation. The Mass was at ten o 'clock, so there were no girls serving. I didn't want to embarrass the Bishop. These three girls were the first female altar servers in Ireland and now girls have replaced the boys in many churches. The day after they first served Mass I had a call from John Bowman of Radio Eireann asking could he come and interview the girls.

"Not on your life " I said, "I don't want the Bishop getting on to me. Wait until it's the custom."

I loved my time as parish priest of Knocklyon and I met some wonderful people and made great friends. But I couldn't forget the call from Peru. My heart was still there, so I decided to go back. Fr. Arthur was overjoyed. At last he got his wish. He became parish priest.

27

Return From Peru

Having spent fifteen years living with the Inca Indians in the mountains of Peru at an altitude of fifteen thousand feet , it was now time to make another major decision. My time had come to leave. My experience living with these poor Indian people had changed my life. I would never be the same again. I was living the reality of the gospel: living among the poorest people in the world, eating their food from the big brown pot, sleeping on the ground or in their mud huts, enduring the cold, sometimes thirty degrees below zero, or the heat of the midday sun, riding a horse up mountain tracks or through rivers in flood. Then for the last five years the Shining Path guerrillas carried out their war of terror in the mountains. Many poor Indians were murdered and their villages razed to the ground. Foreign gringos were ordered to leave Peru or be shot. The Bishop called all the missioners to a meeting where we were given the option of leaving or staying. Everyone opted to stay.

Eventually my time came to leave Peru. There was no way I could return to live in community in Ireland. I pondered my options. I discussed my plans with many Carmelites including the General, Fr. Falco, on his many visits to me. I wanted to know if it would be possible to remain a Carmelite and live outside community in Ireland. I was assured that not only was it possible but that many Carmelites were living outside community, notable the Chicago Province where there were over fifty Carmelites living in houses, or apartments. I was well aware of the tradition in Ireland of all Carmelites living in community, but I had to face the reality of my situation. When I was sent by the Provincial outside the Province to work as Chaplain to hotels in Birmingham the question of community was never mentioned. By this time I had been living outside community for nearly forty years. I was faced with three options;

1: The Bishop of Sicuani had suggested that i could join the diocese and then retire to Ireland.
2: I could join the Chicago Province where Carmelites can choose where they wish to live on retirement. There are many Carmelites living outside community.
3: I decided to write to the Irish Provincial and ask permission to live in my family home in Wicklow.

THE MISSIONARY

Though miles away he is
At home there
Among the poorest of the poor
He walks and talks
As one of them
He guides and teaches them
Shows his care
And love for them
He blesses them
With his gentle caring hands
He is their link to God
Their lifeline to Christ
He teaches them skills
Has a cure for their ills
Sharing his life
He fights for their freedom
And justice
In a primitive country
Where the poor are forgotten
Fuelled by love and power of the Holy Spirit
He teaches the gospels to them
He has devoted fifteen years
Of his life
Showing concern and humanity

For their well being
His life has been threatened
And yet he is committed
To the Poor
And seeks justice for them
He climbs thousands of feet
On horseback
To celebrate the Eucharist
And is acknowledged
As a celebrity
A great man
Jesus like
Walking among them
They have no church
No community centre
Just the bare fields
And mountains
Around them
As he begins the Mass
They bless themselves
And this is the
Only symbol
That links them with
The Sign of the Cross

Poem written by
Fr. Anselm Corbett O Carm
on reading my book
A Beggar in Paradise

To my delight this was granted.

The peace and quiet of Wicklow was wonderful and just what I needed. I soon settled down to living on my own. I was well used to doing my own cooking and household chores. There was a large garden and once more I returned to my love of gardening. I also appeared on many radio and television programmes talking about my experiences in Peru, including to Pat Kenny and Gay Byrne. Having appeared on the Saturday Night Show with Pat Kenny , his parting remark was "Chris, you should write a book." The next day I was contacted by three publishers. Danny McCarthy of Mentor Press arrived down with a computer and spent a couple of hours showing me how it worked. My book 'A Beggar in Paradise' was published in 1997 and soon became a best seller. I.T.V. had already produced a documentary on my work in Peru and this won first prize for religious broadcasting in Cannes the following year.

Although I did not ask for any assignment in the Dublin diocese I was contacted by many priests in the Wicklow area to help out with Sunday Masses. I soon found myself saying three or four Masses in the surrounding parishes of Wicklow, Arklow, Ashford, Glenealy, Rathdrum and Glendalough. I was living on the old age pension and contributions from the parishes. I received no money from the Carmelites at this time. I was very happy and content.

While I was in Peru, new neighbours had arrived next door. Their house was over a hundred yards away behind a large hedge and separated by a disused laneway which had become overgrown. Word had it that they were not very sociable and had not really settled in. I had never met them. A few years later I was working in the garden when a young twelve year old girl came in on her way home from school. She was very excited and wanted to tell me about what she had learned in school that day. A nurse had come in and told the class all about sex and the difference between boys and girls, where babies came from, and how they arrived in the womb.

"She even showed us diagrams", she said.

She went on and on with great enthusiasm and wanted to tell me every detail as if I didn't know what she was talking about. I just listened and smiled to myself. How things had changed since my day. At least the young people were being taught something about sex.

The next time I saw her was about two years later when she was fourteen years old. There was a ring on the door and when I answered there she was, bawling crying and hyperventilating. When she could talk she told me she had had a row with her father and she hated him and was never going to talk to him again. I tried to console her. Then she noticed that I had Sky television and she loved that. She asked could she come in on Friday evening to watch Buffy the Vampire Slayer and Angel. I told her she must get her parents' permission. She assured me that would be no problem as her father always went to the pub on Friday nights. Her mother would give her permission.

She came in on Friday evenings for the next two years. I never asked her to come in. She sat glued to the television and would only talk during the ad breaks. She told me all about her family and how she got on with them. She had no friends at school and was very lonely. Although she was quite intelligent she had no confidence in herself. I immediately saw her problems through my experience with girls on retreat and she was very unhappy.

She asked me many questions about sex. "The girls at school pretended they know all about sex, but they didn't and they had no one to answer their questions." I tried to answer them as best I could. She said she could not talk to her mother about these things. Her mother just gave her a book before she had her periods and that was that. She shared with me her innermost thoughts and feelings. She recounted her dreams in every detail and spoke about them as if they were reality. They usually involved boys and sex. She had psychological and emotional problems and attended the local doctor for therapy sessions. She was often in bad humour and felt depressed. She thought no one understood her. She was very upset when her granny died. She said she was very close to her. She felt she was excluded from the funeral because she wasn't allowed to sing or read a lesson. She spoke about her own death and said she would not live beyond thirty years of age. She kept a diary at this time and also wrote morbid poems and songs, (afterwards when her parents discovered these writings they thought they were written because of me).

On one occasion during an ad break she said, "you know I could get you into terrible trouble?" "How could you do that"? "All I would have to do is run out of here crying and tell mammy you tried to rape me." I smiled and said "sure no one would believe you". "Ah, they would," she said, "because you are a priest and I am a young girl." I realised she was more aware of what was happening in Ireland than I was.

How the attitude of the Irish people to the Catholic Church had changed since I was away. It all began with Bishop Casey. The people were shocked by the revelations. The old saying "it couldn't happen to a Bishop" lost its meaning over night. Then came the Fr. Smith affair which brought down the government. The gory details were unbelievable. So began an avalanche: Fr. Fortune, Ivan Payne and a long list of other clerical sex abusers. Not a day went by without further revelations. Then came the Magdalene laundries and the industrial schools. Not only the priests but now nuns were reviled. In such an atmosphere it is easy to make an accusation against a priest, especially about anything to do with sex. So she knew that when an elderly priest is accused of sexual assault by a young girl the odds are stacked against him. I had come back to a country that had changed enormously since I was away.

Meanwhile the disused laneway between our two properties became a source of dispute and was to play an important role in subsequent events. The girls father had plans to build a new house at the bottom of his garden, and although he already had an entrance, it would add great value to his property if he could create a separate entrance through the laneway. At this time new houses were being built in the adjoining field to our two houses. He made a long list of objections to the project. He remarked to me one day that the only way to get on in this world was to object to everything. Mr. Redmond , the builder, came to me and asked me did I know my neighbour.

"Not very well," I said, "but I see him now and again."

"Well" he said, "if you could get him to withdraw his objections, I would sell you both the adjoining laneway for a nominal price."

"I'll see what I can do," I said.

I went to visit my neighbour and put the proposition to him. He immediately agreed and we proceeded to draw up a contract to buy the property.

Months went by and nothing happened. Some of my neighbours told me that the laneway was always considered to be part of my family's property. I went to the the land registry in Dublin only to discover that this was the case but it had not been registered in our name, so I proceeded to register it. Consequently the contract with my neighbour became null and void as Mr. Redmond didn't own the laneway. I informed my neighbour that I had registered the laneway in my name but I would still be happy to give them right of way. I immediately began to clear the laneway and he went berserk. He went to the High Court to seek an injunction against me taking possession of the property. In their statement to the Court, he said,

"although I cannot prove it, I believe that the only reason Fr. Conroy wants this laneway is because of allegations made by my daughter." (This was the first I heard of any allegations and I presumed it was a ruse to put the fear of God in me, so that I would give him the laneway). My barrister immediately objected and pointed out to the Judge that the property was registered in my name. The judge responded, "If the property is registered in Fr. Conroy's name he can do what he likes with it."

That was the end of that.

The following week my neighbour went to the H.S.E. and made allegations of sex abuse against me, on behalf of his daughter. The H.S.E. went to the Gardaí and a criminal investigation began.

28

Betrayed

The summer had stretched into September that year and I was looking forward to spending the day in the garden. It was now, Wednesday 18th September 2002. I had spent the previous two weeks on holiday in Nice in the south of France. First I had to go to the supermarket and decide what I would have for dinner. My neighbour's mother had died up the road so I decided to deliver a Mass card to the family. As I passed my next door neighbour's entrance, the mother of the girl was coming out with two gentlemen. As I came near I heard her remark "there he is." One of the gentlemen shouted after me. "Chris, is that you? Could we have a word?" I turned around and said "I'll be with you in a minute I'm just visiting my neighbour." On my return they were waiting at my door. I invited them in. They introduced themselves as Detective Sergeant Fergus O'Brien and Detective Garda Pat Hayes. I immediately thought they were here to discuss the boundary fence which my neighbour was constantly knocking down. The superintendent had told me he would send someone up to investigate.

"Do you want the long or the short version?" I began.

With that Detective Sergeant Fergus O Brien, a tall man (with black hair Brylcreamed back like a fifties teddy boy) read a statement. "Mr. Conroy I am arresting you on suspicion of sexual assault on your neighbour."

I was in total shock I could not believe what I was hearing. He continued "you are not obliged to say anything unless you wish to do so, but whatever you do say will be taken down in writing and may be given in evidence."

Detective Garda Hayes, a kindly gentleman was taking notes. Having recovered my composure I said. "I believe that in situations like this it is better to keep silent. Do you want me to come to the station?" The answer was yes. I sat in the back of the car in silence. On arrival at Wicklow garda station, garda Noel O'Gorman took me into custody and detained me pursuant to Section 4 of the Criminal Justice Act 1984 for the proper investigation of the offence in respect of which I had been arrested. I was requested to empty my pockets of all contents. One handkerchief, keys of car, and some diabetes tablets. I was checked for laces but was wearing sandals. I asked to speak to my solicitor.

Unfortunately he was out of the country so I spoke to his associate who was attending court in Arklow. I asked him a simple question. "Can you be convicted of sexual assault without ever going near anyone?" I expected the simple answer "No don't be stupid." Instead he went into a whole scenario of how it could be shown that you had the intention. At that stage he lost me. He advised me to say as little as possible at the interview.

Garda O'Gorman then led me to cell No. 1. He unlocked the door and showed me in as though it was a five star hotel. As I looked around I was under no illusions. This was primitive: a bare room with a bunk in one corner on which was placed a dirty blanket. There was a strong smell of vomit. This must be where they keep the drunks on a Saturday night. In another corner there was a round hole in the floor which I presumed was the toilet. There was no sign of toilet paper. I was reminded of the toilets in the mountains of Peru. As the guard left he banged the door shut and turned the big key twice with a loud click clonk. As there was no chair I lay down on the bunk bed and stared up at the ceiling. It was covered with graffiti and the names of former prisoners. Why they would want to record their stay here for posterity I couldn't imagine. I was also puzzled as to how they reached the ceiling, because even standing on the bed I didn't come near. There must have been a number of prisoners and they stood on each other's shoulders. I closed my eyes and began to meditate. Now at last I was a real Carmelite. The rule says; "Each one of you is to stay in his own cell or nearby, pondering the Lord's law day and night and keeping watch at his prayers unless attending to some other duty." For the moment I wasn't going anywhere. I was perfectly calm and at peace. My conscience was clear. A terrible mistake had been made and I was prepared to do whatever was necessary to prove my innocence. Every now and then the guard checked on me looking in through a little peep hole in the door. I was on suicide watch.

Suddenly the door opened and Sergeant O'Brien beckoned me to follow him upstairs to the interrogation room. I sat one side of the table and Sergeant O'Brien and Detective Garda Pat Hayes faced me on the other. Again I was cautioned "You are not obliged to say anything unless you wish to do so but whatever you do say will be taken down in writing and may be given in evidence. This interview is being electronically recorded." Sergeant O'Brien asked most of the questions and took everything down in hand writing. Pat Hayes seemed to be there as a witness.

"Do you understand what you were arrested for.?"

"I understand the words you said, that it was for sexual assault. It baffles me to know what that means. I'm absolutely baffled."

"This interview is taking place at Wicklow Garda Station. The time is now 10.19 a.m. on Wednesday the 18th of September 2002."

"You have consulted your solicitor?"

"Yes, on the phone."

"I'll just explain to you, You have been arrested for sexual assault. We have received complaints from your neighbour who lives up on the

Rocky Rd. that you have sexually assaulted her. During the day we will go through the various allegations against you."

Long silence

"Have you anything to say to that?"

"No."

"You might bring us up to speed on your life."

"Born 20/12/1932, native of Rathdrum - the Copse, three brothers, went to school in Rathdrum, De La Salle, Wicklow, Terenure College, Studied for priesthood, went to U.C D, was ordained a Carmelite in 1959. Served in Whitefriar St., Birmingham, Brussels, back to Ireland for seven years. Then to Peru for five years. Parish priest of Knocklyon and back to Peru for ten more years. I returned to Ireland in 1996 and I am living in my parent's house on the Rocky Rd."

"Who are your neighbours?"

"On one side I have the most wonderful neighbours you could ask for. On the other side a family arrived from Dublin while I was in Peru."

"How do you get on with them?"

"Until recently, very well. Their daughter comes in, sometimes with her young brother, they were always looking for something, a lift somewhere, to look at television." Suddenly I realised that I didn't know who had made the allegation against me. "Can I ask you a question? I'm confused. When you said there were allegations made against me I presumed you were talking about the mother." Who were you talking about?"

"The daughter"

I laughed out loud in disbelief. "That's a surprise to me. I thought it was the mother, ah now I understand, it's all about our dispute over the laneway." The father of the girl had taken me to the High Court, where he said "I believe but I cannot prove that the only reason Fr. Conroy wants to buy the laneway, independent of me, is because of allegations made by my daughter."

"What did you make of that?"

"Complete shock and surprise, the proceedings were brought to a halt."

"Why did you think it was the mother?"

"Because of her reaction to the fence, she tried to knock it down. She shouted insults at me and used bad language. Last week she shouted "You are going to get a big surprise." Now I know what she meant."

"Let's go back to the children coming in. When did they come in?"

"About two or three times a week or whenever they wanted something. I never asked them to come in. They came asking if they could watch television. I gave the girl a job doing some housework on Saturdays. I gave her £10 as pocket money. She had to give 10% to her father for her keep. Her older sister came in to book flights on the computer for her and her friend who I never met. She said I was the only one that had a Visa card. She also booked concert tickets for Ronan Keating. She didn't repay me for at least six months. I was not aware of the situation in Ireland when I returned from Peru. I didn't know that you weren't supposed to let children into your house. I was just being a kind neighbour. I certainly would not do it now. The girl was very disturbed. She had no school friends. She explained this by saying she was a nerd. I didn't know what that meant. She was quite often in bad humour and almost never smiled. On one occasion when she was in vile humour, I told her she could carry on like that in her own house but not in my home. I said no wonder you have no friends if you behave like that. With that she got very upset and ran in to her mother bawling crying. That afternoon her brother came in and said she was going to sue me for defamation of character."

"Did she ever come in on her own.?"

"On Friday nights to watch Buffy the Vampire Slayer, she never missed that, also on Saturday mornings to do the housework. She wasn't very fond of work. She spent about an hour cleaning the bath. She didn't do toilets or the sitting room. She'd spend the afternoon singing into my tape recorder. She had notions of becoming a famous singer." One evening while she was watching 'Buffy' she turned to me during the ads and said. "I could get you into terrible trouble." "How could you do that?" I asked. "I could run out of here crying and tell my mother that you tried to rape me." I laughed and said "Sure no one would believe you." "Oh they would," she replied "because you are a priest and I am a girl."

"Are you with me, am I going too fast? You should write in shorthand."

"Ah no"

"It's terrible to have to write down all this stuff."

"How often did she come in after that?"

"She never missed 'Buffy' on Friday nights."

"After that comment, you still allowed her to come in?"

"I had grave reservations. I was really shocked by what she said. Imagine a young girl saying something like that. She passed it off as a joke and I took pity on her as she had no friends. She was lonely. She wanted to get out of her house. If she had a girlfriend like most normal teenagers she would never have come in. Have you got that?"

"I don't understand how you let her come in after that remark."

"I'm afraid that's the kind of person I am. I look for the best in everyone. She needed someone to talk to. She told me everything about her family. She talked about her innermost thoughts and feelings. She got depressed and suffered from panic attacks and she hyperventilated. Her stomach would start shaking. She used to say she was having orgasms. She thought the panic attacks were orgasms. She was a very confused girl, saying one thing and meaning another. She said she was going to sue her teacher for sex abuse because he came into class one day with the button of his fly open. I said "He must have been wearing very old trousers to have buttons. Most of the modern ones have zips.

That was her mentality."

"So that was her mentality."

She had sex on the brain. She was obsessed with it. She told me every dream she ever had and they were all about boys and sex. I'm dying to know what she said about me. Are you going to tell me?" (Up to now the Detective never mentioned directly anything the girl said. He seemed to be hoping to catch me out with innocent questions).

"Surely you don't have to take down everything I say, do you?"

"Yes I do "

"You know I have just thought of something.. When I spoke to my solicitor I thought it was the mother who made the allegations." I said, " I don't know what that woman is talking about. I didn't realize it was the daughter."

With that Detective Pat Hayes butted in. "I made a note. Dectective O'Brien distinctly said it was a complaint about the daughter."

"I didn't hear that. I was so shocked. I saw you talking to the mother in the laneway so I presumed it was her. I was completely under the impression it was the mother."

"Do you want to talk to your solicitor again.?"

"Ah no. He told me in general how things work. I'm just wondering where all this is going. Where is it leading to?"

Detective Hayes explains. "A serious allegation has been made by this girl in relation to things that have happened in your house. She decided to come forward."

"When did this happen?"

"Initially she told her mother"

Detective O'Brien continued. "She made a statement to the guards on the 7th of August this year."

"The girl herself."

"Yes."

"Why did it take so long"?

"What take so long?"

"The investigation. This is September."

"I have been investigating you for the last six weeks."

I think I was supposed to shiver at that remark. "I hope you discovered some interesting things. I'm looking forward to finding out."

"The investigation is a multi- operation. There are other people concerned."

"The 7th of August, that's just after they lost the injunction in the High Court. It's obvious that I would not be here if it wasn't for the dispute about the land."

"Let's continue. When this girl was alone in your house was there any talk about sexual matters."

"Yes, very often, she asked me every question under the sun about sex. I told her to ask her mother but she said her mother would not tell her. She just gave her a book before she had her periods. I was familiar with answering teenagers' questions about sex. I answered all her questions honestly."

"Did you buy this girl articles of intimate clothing?"

"Not that I am aware of, but I'm sure you are going to tell me."

With that he took a large brown paper bag from underneath the table. He proceeded to extract various items of clothing from the bag. He held up a denim skirt. " Did you buy her this.?"

"I paid for it, she bought it. She had a list of things she wanted to buy in Dun Laoghaire. She would pay me back by doing housework."

Next he held up a leather jacket. "What about this?"

"I brought that back from Florida. She had given me a list of what she wanted before I went. All these things were bought at her request. Remember she was a young girl with no friends."

"Didn't she have a girlfriend who lived down the road?

I laughed. "I know what she thought of that girl. She didn't really consider her a close friend."

"Did that girl ever come to your house."?

"Many times they came together."

Next he held up a pair of high boots. "What about these?"

"She bought them in Dun Laoghaire with the other things.

Could I ask you something? If I was doing all these terrible things why did she keep coming back? She was perfectly free. I never asked her to come in."

Next out of the bag was a blue top.

"Also for the disco, I had nothing to do with choosing that. She picked it I paid for it. She said she would pay me back.

"That's everything."

"Let us move on.

When you went to Dun Laoghaire, who went?"

"Just myself and herself."

"In your car - unaccompanied?"

"She had her parents' permission."

"What happened coming back from Dun Laoghaire?"

(We now come to the first allegation that she made against me. That I sexually assaulted her in the car on the journey back from Dun Laoghaire.)

"As we approached the Cullenmore bends, near Ashford she had a panic attack."

"Did you stop the car?"

"No, this was a usual occurrence. I thought what a place for this to happen, coming around sharp bends."

"I put my hand over to try and calm her down."

"Where did you put your hand.?"

"Probably on her shoulder or stomach, it really had no significance to me except to calm her down. After all I was driving the car."

"Did you ever study psychology?"

(To people who never studied Psychology it is a method of studying peoples mental functions and behaviours)

"Yes, it is an important part in the education of a priest. I studied it for four years at the university. It was a wonderful help to me in dealing with teenagers.

I have given Retreats to over 10,000 teenagers, after which you have a good understanding of how they feel and think. The first time I met the girl I recognised she was mixed up and had problems. She was not a normal teenager. Her parents certainly did not understand her and she was attending the doctor for therapy sessions.

With that the interview came to an end for lunch.

The interview was then read over to me and I was asked if I wanted to make any corrections or additions.

"I would like to clarify that the only time I went shopping with the girl was the trip to Dun Laoghaire. Also I'd like to ask why did her parents allow her to come to my house? I had never invited her."

I signed it along with Detective O'Brien and Detective Pat Hayes.

The time was 13.18 p.m. 18th September 2002.

I was then brought downstairs by Detective O ' Brien and placed in Cell No.1. Garda Conor Gilmartin was now on duty. He came on duty at 10.30a.m and checked on my presence in the interview room. All was in order. Detective O' Brien sealed the tapes and handed them to Garda Gilmartin who labelled them and handed them to Sergeant Conway. Garda Gilmartin came to the hatch and asked me what I would like for lunch. "What is on the menu?" I asked. "Whatever you wish" he said "it is on the State. We order it from the hotel." I felt like a condemned man ordering his last meal. I chose fish, potatoes and vegetables. I don't take dessert I have diabetes. I need to take one of my tablets. "What would you like to drink?" he asked. "Just water" I replied.

After a short while the hatch opened and my meal was passed through on paper plate. He then passed in a knife and fork. "I am not meant to give you a proper knife and fork. They should be plastic." I thought perhaps I was getting special treatment. "I will take the plastic ones then as I wouldn't want to get you into trouble." "Well, actually we have run out of plastic ones." he said. I ate my lunch sitting on the dirty bunk and balancing the paper plate on my lap. I was very hungry after a busy morning and really enjoyed it. As I sat there I thought that I had been through far worse situations in Peru. I remembered the day I was arrested and given two weeks to get out of the country. There was no State lunch and for a door there were iron bars. My situation was quickly resolved when the Bishop went to Lima and spoke to the Minister of the Interior who dismissed the Chief of Police. I became a hero to the Indians. As I peed into the hole in the floor I could easily have been back in Peru. The guard opened the little peephole and checked on my welfare. I was still alive.

Garda O'Neill took up duty at 2pm and introduced himself through the hatch as the member in charge. He noted. "I checked on the prisoner and removed dinner utensils. All O.K. Prisoner lying on bunk."

At 2.38pm Detective O'Brien brought me back to the interview room where Detective Pat Hayes was waiting. The interview re-commenced at 2.41 p.m.

"I have to remind you that you are still under caution."

"Yes."

Again he reads from the girl's statement.

"Basically we have an allegation that in the car coming from Dun Laoghaire after shopping, that you touched her whilst she pretended to have an orgasm."

"That's the first I heard of anything like that. It's outrageous. She never mentioned anything like that to me. Its extraordinary how her mind works. She never said anything like that to me."

"Well that is the allegation of sexual assault."

"I understand that. I cannot believe her deviousness. I cannot understand how she can do this after all I did for her. I have no animosity against her family. I can understand them fighting about the land. But this is ridiculous."

"Well that is the allegation."

"What happened when you arrived back at your house.?"

"She couldn't wait to try on the clothes to show me what they looked like."

"How did that go?"

She went upstairs to change. Then went back up to try something else on. She tried everything on."

Detective O 'Brien left the interview room to speak to Superintendent Denis Roche about extending the period of detention. I had already been detained for six hours. He returned at 3.35 p.m. Garda Damien Reilly informed me of the extension of the period of detention for a further six hours. Again he read from her statement. "I told him one day that I thought he would rape me."

"She never said that to me. I have already told you what she said about getting me into trouble."

I did do a meditation with her to relieve stress. She was helping her mother in the supermarket when she let a bottle of Lucozade fall on the floor and it broke into smithereens. She was embarrassed because she thought everyone was laughing at her. She came into me in a terrible state. She was very agitated and finding it difficult to breathe. She could hardly talk. I told her to lie on the sun bed in the conservatory and relax. After about half an hour I asked her did she feel better. She said 'No'. I asked her would she like to do a meditation to take away her stress - to get everything out of her mind. She said she would try anything. I told her to lie back and relax, close her eyes and breathe slowly in and out. Don't think of anything. I learnt this in a Buddhist Temple in Japan. It's about concentrating the mind. I placed my hand on her forehead and asked her to concentrate on her forehead.

"Could you have touched her anywhere then?"

"Certainly not. I have told you what I did."

"What did happen that day?"

"I have just told you she was panicking after dropping a bottle in the supermarket and I tried to relieve her stress. I did not touch her improperly. I am wondering why she makes all this up. It seems she has got help. This is not the girl I knew. She had to fabricate things to make these insinuations and allegations."

"Cast your mind back and tell me what exactly you did that day?"

"I have just told you. I told her I knew something that would help her in her agitated state and get it out of her system. It began as meditation does, by breathing slowly in and out."

(At this point Garda Damien Reilly knocked on door to check that the prisoner was alright.)

"You touched her forehead."

"I did not touch her improperly."

"When you were doing the meditation is it possible you could have touched her on the breasts.?"

"Of course it's possible. But it didn't happen. When you do something intentionally you'd remember."

"Did you perform this meditation in Peru on any of the Indians?"

I laughed out loud. "Good God no, that's so outrageous. It's a different culture and they wouldn't understand anything about meditation. This is the only time I did meditation with that girl, in an effort to help her in her agitated state."

"I'm not finished with this allegation. You touched her on her forehead."

"I did not touch her improperly."

"What do you consider an improper place?"

"Any sexual or private part of her body"

"Such as?"

"Any sexual part of her body, I don't have to specify."

"What do you mean?"

"Now you are being ridiculous. There are parts of the body that are sexual and others that are not."

"Are the breasts sexual?"

"Of course they are."

"Is the crotch/vagina area regarded by you as sexual?

"Of course they are. Everyone knows that."

"She says you touched her sexually"

"Definitely not, she said a lot of things."

"You're definite."

"I'm emphatic. If I had something on my conscience, I'd know about it."

"In all your contact with that girl did it ever cross your mind to have a relationship with her?"

"No, it never crossed my mind. What do you think I am? I am a Catholic priest with three vows. I never thought of her in a sexual way. Had that happened she would never have got past the door."

"So the warning bells would have rung?"

"There were no bells, it just didn't happen.

(I found this line of questioning very insulting, a crude way of trying to catch me out.)

"But buying clothing like that, it goes against her parents."

"Her mother gave her permission to go to Dun Laoghaire to buy clothes. Her mother thanked me afterwards."

"There was another incident -- getting her ears pierced."

"Her mother gave her permission to have her ears pierced. At least that's what she told me. She had the money to pay for it. She came to Dublin with me early in the morning. I didn't give her permission. She got them pierced by herself. What's she complaining about now? Is she blaming me for that too?"

"You still brought her, despite her father?"

"Her father never knew where she was or what she was doing. The only word she ever used with regard to her father was 'hate', she hated him. She told me of an incident when he beat her with a shoe. She found it difficult to talk about it."

(Again Garda Damien Reilly checked that I was alright and I asked for another cup of water)

"Did she ever have a bath in your house?"

"Yes, one Christmas Eve. Her mother gave her permission. She arrived at the door with a towel and soap. She was fascinated by the bath. She spent an hour cleaning it every Saturday. There was no bath in her house. Her mother told her to make sure she locked the door. I remained downstairs while she had a bath."

"During the dispute about the land, did the father and son call in to see you to talk about the dispute?"

"Yes, he came in with his son who had a plan, one Saturday afternoon. There had been a cooling off by the family at this time. I said "Do you think that I am going to share a laneway with you when you won't even bid me the time of day?"

"What about my daughter?" he said. "What?" I asked. "You know" he replied.

"If you gave me a million pounds I could not tell you what you are talking about."

"We have decided not to do anything about it, that's all I'll say."

I wondered what he was talking about. On the Monday I went in to talk with his wife who was alone. I spoke to her for about an hour but she never said a word. "Your husband made certain insinuations and I do not know what he is talking about. I don't know whether it's something I said or did? If your daughter is worried about anything perhaps you could bring her in and we'll have a chat and sort it out. I'm surprised at your husband making allegations and I'm sure he didn't mean it." "No, he didn't." she replied.

"The Mother says that you told her if a priest is accused of sexual abuse, he is immediately suspended from his priestly duties."

"Yes, I said that. She would not have been aware of that."

"But who accused you of sexual abuse?"

"No one, but I am not a fool, I knew by the insinuations that her husband made that it could include sexual abuse."

"Did you ask her what her daughter was complaining about?"

"No. She didn't talk. She kept silent."

"Did you offer her a right of way?"

"No, not on that occasion. The lane wasn't in my name at that time. The registry of the land didn't go through until about a month later. It was then I made the offer. I decided it would only be fair to let my neighbours know. I explained that the land was originally part of our property and now I had rectified the problem. But that would not change matters and I would still give them a right of way."

"Why didn't you resolve the issue?"

"It takes two to resolve a problem and I did try. Now they are trying to say that I was bribing them with the right of way. Nothing could be further from the truth."

With that the interview ended.

The document was read back to me and everyone signed it. The time was 6.11 p.m. 18th September 2002.

Sergeant O'Brien brought me down to cell No. 1 and double locked the door.

Garda Reilly opened the hatch and asked me would I like a meal. I said I would have two rashers, two sausages and an egg with tea.

The hatch was opened at 6.45 p.m. and my meal was passed in on a paper plate with a proper knife and fork. During the meal the hatch opened again and Garda Karen Weymouth informed me that she had taken up duty.

Detective O'Brien returned to inform me that the interview was over and that I was free to go.

Garda Weymouth returned my property (handkerchief, keys and pills).

I was driven home in a Garda car at 7.39 p.m. I had been arrested at 9.45 that morning. I had been in custody for eight hours (Later at the trial the judge was to express surprise at the length of the detention).

***

When I arrived home I just sat down and began to think of the events of the day. I was still in shock but I felt at peace because my conscience was clear. The accusations that had been made against me seemed like a dream. Many priests when they have been falsely accused have said that they would rather have been shot than falsely accused as a priest. Their good name and reputation which had been built up over a lifetime had been destroyed in an instant.

I can only profess my absolute innocence of all the accusations. How could a young girl that I had been so kind to possibly do such a thing? I knew her parents were devastated when they lost the High Court injunction. They were beside themselves with anger and revenge. Now their daughter saw an opportunity to take revenge on me and ingratiate herself to her parents especially her father. She told them how I spoke to her about sex, not mentioning she had asked the questions and I had brought her shopping. Her father persuaded her that all this was wrong. To her parents my kindness could only mean one thing. I was a pervert and I was doing this to take advantage of their daughter. Why should I be so kind to her and not expect anything in return?

When I was arrested her mother could not wait for her to come home from school to tell her the good news. She wasn't prepared for the girl's reaction. Instead of being over the moon she became very upset. She knew the game was up. Now she would have to substantiate all the false accusations in Court. (I could never understand why the detectives went in to inform the mother that they were going to arrest me. Was this really necessary?).

The next day I rang the Provincial Fr. Fintan Burke and informed him that I had been arrested and interrogated for over seven and a half hours. He was completely taken aback and wondered what the Order's response should be. He immediately suspended me from all pastoral and priestly ministry. He would consult the Order's solicitor Ian O' Herlihy to see where we should go from here. I also rang my good friend Fr. David Weakliam and he said he would come to Wicklow right away. It was wonderful to have someone to talk to. We recalled our school days in Terenure College and our times in Gort Muire. David was Provincial when

I volunteered to go to Peru. He came to visit me in Yauri and although he couldn't sleep a wink in the Altitude, he did ride a horse to one of the outlying communities. He could not believe the false accusations made against me. "This is a complete travesty of justice," he said. "The more you speak about that girl the more I realise how kind you were to her."

29

No Good Turn Goes Unpunished

On the 11th.of October 2002 I received a letter from the Provincial ordering me to return to Whitefriar St. by Wednesday 30th 2002. "The Terenure Community and the Gort Muire communities are not options at the moment because of the presence of young people. I reiterate your suspension from all pastoral and priestly ministry. These directives are in line with the policy of the Provence in such a matter."

I arrived in Whitefriar St. and was allocated the same room that I had nearly fifty years before. I was warmly welcomed by the Prior and the community and I explained my situation at a Community meeting. All were sympathetic to my plight knowing that the same could happen to any priest in Ireland today. The more I read the Provincial's letter the more it dawned on me that I was being condemned before a trial, Guilty until proven innocent. I wrote to the Provincial pointing out that he couldn't suspend me from my priestly ministry until I was convicted of some crime. Following the guidelines, I would voluntarily stand aside from my priestly duties. I could not say a public Mass in Whitefriar St. My case had gone to the DPP and now I must await his decision. I spent my time studying in the National Library and visiting all the places of interest around Dublin. I went to the National Gallery and all the museums. I went to Trinity College to see the Book of Kells and Brendan Kennelly kindly showed me around.

I also spent many happy hours visiting the Zoo and the Botanic Gardens in Glasnevin. I returned to Collins Barracks which is now a museum where I had given a Mission to the Army in 1966. I remembered how the soldiers marched to the Church for Mass and as the bugler played at the Consecration the guard of honour drew their swords in salute around the altar.

After two years I suddenly got a call from Detective Sergeant Fergus O'Brien to say that my case was going to trial and I must appear at the court house in Wicklow that afternoon. The accusations were read out before the Judge and I was released on bail of one hundred euro. It was the end of the Court sitting for the day and as I looked around I was the only one left in the room.

During the next few months I was summoned to court on many occasions before the case was heard. Court begins at ten o' clock. On my arrival the first day the Court house was packed , everyone milling around like a cattle market. It was utter confusion. There was no law or order. There were barristers in their gowns and wigs, solicitors laden down with enormous briefs, guards just hanging around and prison guards leading in prisoners in handcuffs. Suddenly the door opened and a young teenager burst out screaming and shouting. He was tackled by two big guards and brought to the ground. They carried him out in great distress. Seemingly he was part of a family case that was being held in camera in the judges rooms. Then the Judge arrived and demanded strict silence. He began to go through the list for the day with the barristers and solicitors. He first heard the minor cases: speeding, drunk and disorderly, drug pushing, possession of pornographic material, abandoning a car on the side of the road, cashing false cheques. He then discussed the days available for hearing with the barristers and how long each case might take. "Is Mr. Conroy present?" he asks. My solicitor just nods. Another barrister asks if a particular case can be transferred to Dublin. The Judge proceeds to give a long speech on how important the Wicklow court is and that he is reluctant to have it transferred but in this case he accedes.

As he proceeds to the next case and assigns it to the next day, a barrister puts up his hand.

"My Lord, I can't be here tomorrow."

"Why not" asks the Judge

"I have a case in the High Court."

"That's the lamest excuse I have heard for a long time." (I thought I was back in school again.) My case was adjourned until the next sitting.

***

The case was heard in July 2004. It was to begin at ten o clock. There had been a lot of publicity beforehand so I knew the press would be there. The cameras clicked as I ascended the steps to the court. I had asked the Provincial if he would come to support me. Having consulted his solicitor he said he couldn't because he might be photographed on the way in or out. Fr.Weakliam was there, not on behalf of the Order but as my friend. Many more of my friends were there together with my family. I felt very relaxed and looked forward to the ordeal at long last. I was dressed in black without my collar. The girl arrived with her parents and they were ushered into a room at the back. Rumours began to spread that the judge Pat McCartan was marooned on his yacht in the Channel Islands. Judge Mathews replaced him, a perfect gentleman.

Next twelve people must be selected for the jury. There was a large panel to choose from. The prosecution and the defence must make the selection. There is a great art in choosing people for the jury on which the case depends. Anyone can be dismissed without explanation. One girl went into hysterics at the thought of it and of course was dismissed. Selection can depend on trivial things like wearing a suit, hair style, clothes, appearing tense. One woman had mauve hair; she was immediately picked by my barrister. At last we had a jury but the case could not begin until Judge McCartan arrived the next day.

Mr. Murray, barrister for the State made the opening statement. "I see my task in this case as being a relatively simple one - I am not here to secure a conviction at all costs, my job is to try and present all the evidence to you members of the jury and let you decide beyond reasonable doubt that the accused is innocent or guilty. You are citizens of Ireland here today to reach a verdict in relation to the evidence presented to you."

The girl was first to be called to the stand. Although nervous she appeared confident, in her best attire and wearing ear rings. The interrogation began with simple and easy questions which lulled her into a sense of security and growing confidence. There was nothing that she wasn't absolutely certain about. This was to prove her downfall. When my barrister began the cross examination she was not so confident.

"Do you remember the day you went shopping in Dun Laoghaire?"

"Yes, it was a Wednesday."

"That was the night you went to the disco?"

"Yes"

"Are you absolutely sure about that?"

"Yes"

"Do you swear with total confidence that is the night you went to the disco?

"Yes"

"I have to suggest to you in terms of credibility that you are completely and utterly wrong about that.- do you understand why you are wrong about that?"

"No".

"Can you consider what you said and reflect was there a disco on the Wednesday night, isn't the disco on a Friday night?"

"No, it was on that day."

"I suggest and it will be established there was no disco on Wednesday 1st."

"Well it was on the Wednesday, I remember."

Mr Kean returned to this line of questioning the following day.

"It now emerges that the 1st of June was not a Wednesday but a Thursday. Do you understand that?"

"Yes".

"Are you saying there was a disco on the Wednesday and the Thursday night?"

"I said there could have been."

"Yesterday you said you went to the disco on the Wednesday and you were certain"

"Yes I was sure"

"Are you still absolutely certain?"

"Yes"

"And if you were wrong about that, you could have been wrong about other things?"

"Well, I am certain."

"You are a hundred per cent certain?"

"Yes, because I rang my friend"

"As a result of questions I asked you yesterday a very assiduous detective went to the Parochial Hall in Wicklow and we now have additional evidence from a Patrick Boyce, who looks after the discos, do you understand that?

"Yes"

"Mr Boyce will give evidence about the discos in the Parochial Hall and he will show you were not at any disco on the 1st of June. Do you understand that?"

"Yes, but that is how I remember it."

"I appreciate you are one hundred per cent certain, but is that your signature second down, No 168."

"And do you see the date on top of that and would you tell the ladies and gentlemen of the jury what that date is?"

"The 2nd of June.

"And the 2nd of June was a Friday, do you accept that?"

"Yes"

"Do you now accept that your one hundred per cent certainty is completely wrong?"

"Yes"

"You do. And yet you were competent enough under oath, you did not say, 'I am not sure about dates', 'I could be wrong' or 'I am a bit unclear' you said you were one hundred per cent sure about it. It is very important that when you make allegations under oath that you are one hundred per cent sure. Remember somebody's freedom is at stake."

"You know that you are in a very unique position here today because for this 72-year old priest who stands accused of these offences, in the thousands of boys and girls that have come to his retreats and that he has counselled and taught, you are unique because you are the only person ever to make an allegation of any form of sexual impropriety against him you know that?"

"Yes"

"He has counselled and educated thousands of young people and made himself available to those people, and always a priest who gave generously to the poor, and you know how he came to go to Peru in 1979. You know from discussions with him and what you have read in his house that he was there for some fifteen years, and that Peru is the poorest country in Latin America?"

"Yes".

This was the way the cross examination went throughout the trial. The girl seemed to believe that she just had to make an accusation and that made it true. This happened again and again. She had to retract many statements that were shown not to be true. Under investigation some of the situations she described could not have happened as she described them. There were only two people who knew the accuracy of her allegations, me and her. She had difficulty in remembering and I couldn't believe what I was hearing. Her witnesses were more of a hindrance than a help to her. The two girls from school were like two frightened rabbits caught in the headlights in the witness box. They did not want to be there and were so nervous that they made no sense of their statements. Her parents were not any better. Her mother presented herself as a lady who never used bad language, whereas when she shouted insults at me over the fence her vocabulary was more like the proverbial fishwife.

Her father was a little man with a small moustache . Like all little men he tried to compensate for his height in other ways. He asked the judge could he make a statement. He then began murmuring at such a gallop that the stenographer could not keep up with him. The judge had to reprimand him on many occasions and ask him to slow down.

"To help her survive would you please slow down a little bit"

"Maybe I am a little anxious"

He spoke of the sad situation he had been through.

"In June my father had a stroke, God bless him, he was 85 years of age and he was a man that had reared me, because my mother died when we were very young, so it was like losing a father and mother at the same time and to put it mildly it was a pretty rough time. The day he died, I had gone into him every day for six days a week, bar Sunday for three months. The day he died, it was a Friday, Manchester United were playing at Old Trafford. Myself and my son were lined up to go over but I went to the hospital"

In cross examination, my barrister questioned him about the land dispute:

"When you discovered that Fr. Conroy was the registered owner of the land you could not have been too happy about that I take it?"

"I was over the moon. I thought it was great."

"Did you?"

"Yes"

"Are you being sarcastic?

"Absolutely. I was shocked at what he had done."

"He became the registered owner and you know you can't be registered as owner of land unless you have title to land."

Shortly after this the trial came to an abrupt end. The judge declared that there had been discrepancies with regard to times and dates and that he would have to excuse the jury and call a mistrial. On the way out the jury were very relieved and happy to be off for the bank holiday weekend. Some remarked 'that girl was like a Walter Mitty character, you couldn't believe a word she said." "We had the priest innocent after an hour the first day." My barrister on his way out of court remarked "If the parents of the girl put her through that ordeal again, they are not human."

But, as expected, the trial did go ahead again, this time just before Christmas on the 15th of December 2004. Raymond Groarke was the judge presiding. A jury of eight men and four women were chosen after many were dismissed for unknown reasons: dress code, hair style, expression on their faces, or some other feature that seemed to say they would not be favourable to one side or the other. Who knows? Choosing a jury seemed a mystery to me. Every aspect of the case had to be repeated as if the first trial had never taken place. I sat alone dressed in dark suit with polo necked jumper. Again I pleaded 'not guilty' to both charges and the trial began.

The first day was mainly taken up with the accusations of the girl. She omitted many things from the first trial which didn't go in her favour. She had prepared her answers to all the questions from the first trial. But this didn't happen. Barristers are very clever in their cross examination and they have a way of extracting the truth through a series of innocent questions. The old adage of 'have you stopped beating your wife always seems to work. The girl's memory had not improved but she didn't have to cope with the date of the disco this time. Instead she was probed deeply about the second accusation of sexual assault in the conservatory which she still insisted was a massage instead of a meditation. There was so many aspects of her evidence which just didn't add up. Was I standing up or kneeling down? She wasn't sure. But she was sure that I was sweating profusely, she could feel the drops of sweat falling on her even though she was fully clothed. How could she flatter herself that she had such an effect on me? What an imagination and how preposterous. One of her young witnesses landed a bombshell when she declared that she wasn't her friend any longer. She now actually hated her, thus nullifying the value of her testimony. The detective was asked if I answered all the questions put to me promptly and directly. He answered yes that I was very co-operative. At the end of the hearing, the State barrister read a summary of my seven and a half hour interrogation with the detective. My barrister then asked the judge for a short recess while he consulted with his client. He suggested that there was no need for me to give evidence. There is no way you could improve on what we have just heard. I agreed. The judge began summing up. He thanked the jury for their care and attention during the trial. He told them before they retired to consider their verdict that they were entitled to bring in a verdict of guilty or not guilty on either or both of the separate charges.

He also directed them to consider the nature of the relationship between the alleged victim, her family and Fr. Conroy. "There are a number of different matters in this mosaic that you have to look at. On the one hand it is open to me to accept that the accused was open, priestly, pastoral, helpful, caring, perhaps lonely, generous with his time and generous with his money.

But the prosecution says something far more sinister was involved here, that he was grooming this young girl potentially to assault her. You have to consider what kind of 14 year old you were dealing with. Was she headstrong, precocious, imaginative, had a capacity to be devious -this on her own account? Was she vulnerable, an immature person albeit sexually advanced, she said she was curious about sexual matters? What was she like at 14?" he asked. With that the jury retired.

The next hour was a very anxious and emotional time. My Barrister asked me how did I feel about going to jail? I replied, "It will be like going on holiday compared with the jail in Peru." My whole life, my good name and reputation was at stake. The time seemed to go very slowly. There was nothing that one could do now. My friends and family were in bits. I remained quite calm, at least externally. Suddenly there was a call from the court that the jury was about to return. They had been out for just over an hour, (afterwards they said they could have returned after five minutes but they were afraid that the Judge might not look kindly on them after all his instructions). You could cut the atmosphere with a knife.

The judge broke the silence by asking the foreman of the jury,

"Has the jury reached a verdict?"
"We have, my Lord "
"What is your verdict on the first charge?"
"Unanimously NOT GUILTY, my Lord."
"What is your verdict on the second charge?"
"Unanimously NOT GUILTY, my Lord."
"I declare Fr. Conroy NOT GUILTY on both counts."

These were the most beautiful words I had ever heard, finally, it was all over. The girl hadn't returned to Court to hear the verdict. She already knew she had lost. Her mother collapsed when the verdict was announced. My friends and family were in tears.

Christmas was great that year.

Reflection.

After the trial many people talked to me about it.

"How could you appear so calm and relaxed when everyone else was in bits?"

"Because I knew I was innocent. I knew all the charges were false, this had nothing to do with the girl, it was about a laneway. I only had to look into my heart. I was at peace and had long since forgiven the girl and her family for what they had done."

"But you weren't declared 'innocent, rather 'not guilty'?

"That's the way the Irish legal system works, I cannot be declared innocent. The jury said afterwards that they had me innocent from the first day. It wasn't a case of being not guilty beyond all reasonable doubt, they had no doubt whatsoever."

"How did you feel about your Provincial not being present in Court to support you?"

"The Provincial was acting on legal advice. How would it have looked had I been found guilty? He would be supporting a lost cause. The Provincial never supported me. He always felt he must defend the good name of the Carmelite Order. To this end an individual can be sacrificed.

He has always said that he believes I am one hundred per cent innocent, but to this day he has never restored my good name and reputation publicly."

"So there will always be people who think you are guilty, there is no smoke without fire. You just had a good lawyer who got you off."

"Of course people will think that but I can't do anything about what people think. Before the trial the Press went into great detail about the false accusations made against me. After the trial when I'm acquitted the Press does not report that all the accusations were false. They are not interested in innocent people, it doesn't sell newspapers.

"In the present climate in Ireland, there are many people think all priests are poedophiles, I know I'm innocent."

"How could you have let that girl into your house?"

"I was not aware of the changed situation in Ireland. I had just returned from living in the first century. I have been dealing with teenagers all my life, the girl was in distress. How could I turn her away? I never asked her to visit me and soon realised she had many problems. The greatest of those being she had no friends at school. She said it was because she was a nerd. If she had girlfriends she would never have come to me. She also had family problems. I knew by her attitude why she didn't have friends and I thought I could help her. That was the biggest mistake I ever made and I failed miserably. I never spoke an unkind word to her and I tried to help her in every way. She betrayed me."

"How did you let her have a bath in your house?"

"I never thought that was a big deal as she didn't have a bath in her house, so she never had a bath in her life. She was fascinated by it as she cleaned it every week. When she arrived at my door on Christmas Eve with soap in one hand and a towel in the other and said her mother told her she could have a bath, I just said, you know where it is, fire ahead." I remained downstairs and when she was finished she went home. She introduced the bath into the court case insinuating that it was my idea and let people's imagination run wild as to why. It backfired."

"Why did you talk to her about sex?"

"Sex as far as she was concerned was 'the facts of life'. She asked many questions about the 'facts of life'. The conversations were very matter of fact. She asked the questions and I answered them honestly. I did say to her to ask her mother if she thought that anything would be embarrassing. Her parents never spoke to her about sex. She also said her mother would not know the answers.

When I was ordained over fifty years ago there was no sex education in school and families never mentioned it. The only one who ever gave sex instruction was the priest. Whenever I gave school retreats there was always a question time at the end. Everyone looked forward to this. All the questions were about sex. I had no problem answering questions on sex to teenagers. The difficulty was that the girl used this as ammunition in court. She made out I was the one who brought up the subject."

"What about the clothes you bought for her.?"

"This was another smokescreen, she was planning to go to a disco and she wanted to buy clothes. She asked me could she have an advance on her wages and she would pay me back. She came to Dun Laoghaire with me and she picked all the clothes. I paid with my Visa card and then deducted it from her wages. Her parents presumed I had bought them for her and the next day her mother thanked me. She tried to use the clothes in the court case to make out that I was grooming her by buying her sexy clothes. This also backfired and the jury quickly saw through it.

All through the trial as the girl was making one false accusation after another I looked forward to my turn when I would take the stand. Like Robert Emmet I would make a speech from the dock. I would carefully go through each accusation and tear it to shreds. I would show how these things never happened, and could not have happened in the way she described them. But my great speech from the dock never happened. The state barrister, when he read out a summary of my evidence, did it for me. I could not have done it better myself. On hearing it my barrister realised that I had already won and there was no need to take the stand. I was found 'not guilty', but I knew in my heart and soul that I was INNOCENT.

30

Betrayed By The Church

Everyone was overjoyed. Justice had been done. My family and friends and the people of Wicklow were generous with their congratulations and support. When they heard who the family was they said they were not surprised. The girl's classmates were her greatest critics. The Wicklow People declared on its front page "Fr. Conroy is looking forward to his best Christmas ever." I went to see the Provincial expecting to be reinstated immediately. He said he had consulted Ian O'Herlihy and he had advised him that although I had been declared innocent I was not out of the wood yet. We should wait and see what the family might do next. Now the family who had falsely accused me were calling the tune and I had to do the dancing.

Indeed the family was devastated. They were like caged wild animals lashing in all directions. The girl went into hibernation and would not go down the town. The father decided that all was not lost and he wasn't going to take this lying down. First of all he would have me removed from Wicklow. He went to the Superintendent in Wicklow on numerous occasions and asked him to get Fr. Conroy out of Wicklow. The Superintendent said "That can't be done, Fr. Conroy is a freer man than I am. He has been acquitted in a court of law." Not to be deterred, the family then decided to go to the Archbishop's House in Dublin where they met Diarmuid Martin and the child protection officer Mr. Garland. The archbishop received them with open arms and they proceeded to repeat all the accusations that had been dealt with in court. Fr. Conroy must be got out of Wicklow.

When the problem of land arose, they said they could not understand how a priest with a vow of poverty could be dealing in land. When money was mentioned the archbishop explained that Fr. Conroy did not come under his jurisdiction and referred them to the Carmelite Provincial. Mr Garland gave them a copy of the guidelines for the archdiocese with regard to sex abuse. The archbishop rang the Provincial, Fintan Burke and read the riot act, speaking to him in a very irate manner and treating him like a little boy. The Provincial was so overwhelmed and overawed by the tone of the Archbishop that he meekly replied:

"Yes, your Grace, and No your Grace."

"I have just come from a meeting with a family from Wicklow and I can't believe what I have just heard."

"Do you have a priest by the name of Fr. Chris Conroy?"

"Yes, your Grace".

"Does he have permission to live in Wicklow?"

"Yes, your Grace"

"Well if he was a secular priest he would be out of there immediately.

Does he say Mass?"

"Yes, your Grace"

"Does he have a vow of poverty?"

"Of course, your Grace."

"Why then is he dealing in property? He must leave Wicklow immediately."

"Yes, your Grace."

The Provincial was shocked at the archbishop's tone and manner. He was also very annoyed that he should interfere in Carmelite affairs. After all Fr. Conroy did not come under his jurisdiction and has no appointment in the diocese. The Archbishop gave instructions to Mr. Garland to write to all the parish priests in the Wicklow area informing them that Fr. Conroy was not available for supply. Moreover if they heard of him operating in the area they must inform the archbishop (So much for my good name and reputation. I felt like an outlaw).

Many of the parish priests had contacted me after the court acquittal to congratulate me. Some enquired "Where did that letter come from? Was it from your Provincial?" "No" I said, it was from Archbishop's House." "Well, in that case you can say Mass here any time you like."

The family arranged a meeting with the Provincial at his office at Gort Muire Dundrum. They had read in the guidelines that they were entitled to a support person so they brought along their best man from their wedding. The Provincial would have a member of the Council as secretary. Neither I nor David Weakliam was asked to attend. How could the Provincial act on my behalf when he knew nothing about the case? He had never asked me anything about it. All he knew was what he read in the papers. Before the meeting he was well coached by Ian O'Herlihy. "You must meet them at the door and sympathise with them on the terrible ordeal they had been through. They should be dealt with in a pastoral way with kindness. On no account antagonise them." The family were in their element. They used their usual choice language and at one stage told the Provincial that it was no wonder people were leaving the Church if all priests were like him. They repeated the accusations that had been dealt with in court. They were adamant that Fr. Conroy must leave Wicklow.

When the Provincial told me what they said, I suggested that we sue them for defamation for repeating false accusations. "Oh, we couldn't do that, Ian O'Herlihy says we shouldn't antagonise them. The Provincial never told me anything after that about the meetings.

In strict trade union tradition, they insisted on meeting on neutral territory and not on Carmelite property. One meeting took place in a hotel. Half way through the meeting the girl was produced in a distressed state. The years before the trial the girl behaved like any normal teenager. She did her Junior Cert. in June 2001 and did extremely well. She was very intelligent. In November 2001 she had a prominent part in "Joseph and His Amazing Technicolour Dreamcoat" which the Convent staged with the boys from the De La Salle School. She also had a boy friend at this time. In April she took part in "Star for a night". She always had an ambition to be a famous singer. Her photo appeared on the front page of the Wicklow People. Her anxiety and nervousness only came about when she lost the court case. Her parents were seeking recompense from the Carmelites. The Provincial insisted that I was innocent of all charges and that not a penny of compensation would be paid. The Provincial assured me and Fr. Weakliam that this was the case. He was not to keep his word.

I didn't know the Provincial, Fr. Fintan Burke very well. He joined the Order some twenty years after me. He was a teacher in Moate and Terenure College while I was outside the Province. He wasn't a very good communicator and found it difficult to talk face to face. Consequently he communicated with me in the form of a letter and because he discussed everything with the Order solicitor it was in the form of a solicitor's letter. First of all, on the instruction of the Archbishop, he revoked my permission to live in Wicklow. I must return to Whitefriar St. My friends and legal team advised against this and said to leave Wicklow at this time would appear an admission of guilt. I had a big decision to make. There was no way I could leave Wicklow in CONSCIENCE, and if he insisted I would be prepared to leave the Order. I would never stop being a Carmelite as long as I live but I would leave the Order. Communication stopped for about two years and then the letters began to arrive. The letters were sent to Whitefriar St. and were always opened as the Prior was also called 'Chris'. This was to cover himself because to send them to Wicklow would be admitting I was there. In one letter he wrote,

"Your membership of the Carmelite Order has implications both for us and for you which would not be the case if you were a private individual. The Order paid for your defence in Court. You have brought the Order into disrepute. While the role of the Provincial and Council may not be acceptable to you, we have a responsibility to act for the good of all."

I responded,

I write this letter to refute the unjust accusations made against me, mainly to be recorded in the Archives because I feel that nothing I say will make any difference. It would appear that you have ceased to communicate with me. You won't talk to me face to face. I am well aware of my obligations to the Carmelite Order. I have been a member for the past sixty years. During that time I have been a faithful member of the Order. I have responded willingly to all requests made to me although at times it was not easy. e.g going to Birmingham and then Peru. During this time there has not been the slightest complaint or allegation made against me.

My first obligation is to my conscience. Being a Carmelite does not take away my human and civil rights. All allegations made against me were proven to be false and I was declared innocent. There is no difference between an innocent Carmelite and an innocent Irish citizen.

I was falsely accused of sexual assault. I was completely vindicated by the Court. It was shown that these allegations did not and could not have taken place. You have said many times that you believe that I am innocent. You have documentary evidence of my good character and priestly ministry. I have only to look into my heart to know that I am innocent. A terrible injustice has been inflicted on me. You continue to crucify me.

The most difficult thing to accept is the complete lack of communication with me. No meeting face to face. So many conclusions have been arrived at without any reference to me. I feel like a little boy being told to 'eat your bun and shut up.' I am condemned to no man's land. I am like a prisoner in Guantanamo Bay. The 'guidelines' state, that when a priest has been found to be innocent, his good name and reputation must be restored in the place where it was taken away. The good people of Wicklow deserve an explanation as to why I am not saying Mass.

All this correspondence came to nothing and next I received a letter threatening me with expulsion from the Order. The Provincial came to Wicklow to see me. As always, meetings between fellow Carmelites are cordial and friendly. I served him strawberries and cream. Then down to business. "I had a long meeting with an eminent Canon Lawyer and we discussed your situation. His opinion is that I would definitely have a right to dismiss you from the Order if you do not move out of Wicklow" he began.

What did he say about CONSCIENCE? I asked. "We didn't discuss that".

"Well, you should have; you know I can't move out of Wicklow and I have taken that decision, knowing what the consequences might be. You can kick me out if you like." "The Archbishop is also not happy with you remaining here" he added.

"I don't come under the jurisdiction of the Archbishop and I haven't asked him for anything." I reminded him what St Francis of Assisi said in the thirteenth century. "If a superior give an order to one that is under him which is against the man's conscience, although he do not obey it, yet he shall not be dismissed." There was no answer to that, and on that note we parted. I would have to wait for the next solicitor's letter.

As the Archbishop Diarmuid Martin had interfered in Carmelite affairs by ringing the Provincial and berating him in an irate manner, I decided to request a meeting with the Archbishop myself.

Your Grace,

I write to you in desperation. It is now over a year since I was acquitted of all allegations brought against me. I was falsely accused by my neighbours with ulterior motives. My Provincial and Council were about to reinstate me when you entered the situation. Now it has come to a standstill. I enclose an analysis of my case by Fr. David Weakliam, parish priest of Whitefriar St. As you seem to have met everyone involved in the case except me, I would like to meet with you and with David Weakliam, to discuss my situation. Please let me know when it would be convenient to meet with you.

A month later I received a reply from the Diocesan Moderator (The Archbishop does not reply personally to letters).

Dear Father Conroy,

I wish to acknowledge receipt of your letter of 23 March 2006 to Archbishop Martin. Archbishop Martin has given careful consideration to your letter and to your request to meet him and Father David Weakliam to discuss your situation. It is Archbishop Martin's view that the matters about which you write are matters primarily for your own religious order. Archbishop Martin has not received any requests in your regard from your religious Superiors.

I found this the height of hypocrisy. He says it is none of his business, and yet he is interfering behind the scenes. In a recent interview he said, "My door is always open to anyone who wishes to see me, as well as to those who bring constructive criticism." His door was closed to me.

Diarmuid Martin was appointed Archbishop of Dublin on the 26th of April 2004.

His appointment came as a surprise and shock to the priests of the Diocese. One old priest who had experience of how the Vatican works remarked, "I wonder how he dirtied his bib in Rome, to be kicked upstairs to Dublin?"

He found the Diocese in turmoil: shortage of priests, fall off in Mass attendance, change in attitude to the Church, and the biggest problem of all child sex abuse. He has described how he has got 'violently angry' on reading the reports of child sex abuse and would throw the papers across the room. In the past a priest was moved from parish to parish and it was the innocent victims who suffered. Now when there is an accusation of child abuse against a priest, no matter how unfounded, no matter how long ago, with no evidence, the priest is publicly humiliated and his good name and reputation destroyed.

While the people of the Diocese applauded his efforts in eliminating the scourge of sex abuse, he alienated the priests because he made no distinction between innocent and guilty.

As Fr. Brendan Hoban wrote,

"More recently priests have discovered a new and even more frightening form of unease. A significant number of false and unsubstantiated allegations of child abuse against innocent priests has brought an unprecedented level of personal vulnerability to the lives of priests. Regardless of how bizarre an allegation is or the credibility of its provenance, reputations of innocent priests are being systematically destroyed because, in the interests of child protection, every allegation automatically demands the withdrawal of a priest from ministry and from home and it would seem the subjugation of his rights - under civil, canon or common law. Nobody would argue that children should not be put at risk or that the highest form of child protection should be in place. But if the perception among priests is that the personal or professional reputations of individual priests seem less important than a bishop covering his own back, then the relationship between priests and their bishops may be irreparably damaged."

In civil law if an Irish citizen is accused of breaking the law, he is innocent until proven guilty. In the Catholic Church, one is guilty until proven innocent. The way I was treated by the Irish State left nothing to be desired. I was accused, interrogated by detectives, brought before the Court, given an opportunity to defend myself, my case was presented by my solicitor and barrister, witnesses were called, the jury deliberated and returned a verdict of NOT GUILTY, and that was the end of the matter.

In the Catholic Church when I presented myself to my Provincial, expecting to be completely exonerated and returned to my former ministry. I was politely informed that this could not be done. "We have to wait and see what the family might do next." Where do I go from here? My Provincial assured me that the Order considered me completely innocent, and proceeded to consign me to Limbo. When I asked him to give me written confirmation that the Order considered me innocent, he refused to do so, not wanting to antagonise the Archbishop. I was sent to 'Guantanamo Bay' where I still remain.

After some years I suggested to the Provincial that he should investigate my past by asking the surviving six Provincials to write a reference with regard to my conduct during their time in office. He received six glowing references.

Fr. David Weakliam wrote,

"I have known Fr. Chris Conroy for more than fifty years: since we were both pupils in Terenure College, Dublin 6W, again as Carmelite students at Gort Muire, Ballinteer, Dublin 14 and thereafter as fellow Carmelites and priests for over forty years. He is four years older than me, and was ordained a priest four years before I was. Even as a boy, he was known for his cheerful, optimistic personality, and approached life with great self discipline, commitment to work and study and a friendly, generous and courageous spirit; all of which traits and attitudes he has consistently manifested in his priestly ministry throughout his life and up to the present time.

His life has been dedicated to the service of people in a variety of ministries, at home in Ireland and abroad. Outstanding in these ministries were his commitment to youth and his work for the poor people of Peru, living high in the mountains of the Andes. Both of these latter ministries brought me in particularly close contact with Fr. Conroy, as I was his Prior Provincial for six years of that time, 1976 - 1982. I lived with him at Gort Muire for three years, where he conducted retreats for boys and girls at Leaving Certificate level. Following our Provincial Chapter of 1979, he volunteered to serve in Peru, where I later visited him and was immensely edified both by the trojan work he was doing and the frugal life he was living.

Earlier, in the seventies, in my capacity as Prior and senior school principle at Terenure College, I sent groups of sixth year boys to Gort Muire for one or two day retreats. Whenever I asked the boys, on their return, how they got on at their retreat, their response was invariably positive and enthusiastic. Later, when I was living in our Gort Muire community and had occasion to witness a constant succession of groups of boys and girls coming on retreat, I was impressed by Fr. Conroy's utter dedication to their welfare. He had ,and has, a rare insight into the teenage mind and a singular gift to meet them at their level and to understand them; a gift to which many of them have borne witness.

Never once - even during my time as Provincial of the Irish Carmelites, a role where one is no stranger to allegations or complaints of one kind or another - did I hear a breath of suspicion, much less complaint, of anything even remotely savouring of impropriety in relation to Fr. Conroy, or the work he did. Similarly, when Fr. Conroy later succeeded me as parish priest in Knocklyon, Dublin, he organised a successful youth club in the parish. Again, his reputation with the youth was altogether impeccable."

My bishop in Peru Albano Quinn wrote,

"I was the Apostolic Administrator (bishop) in Sicuani, Peru, in 1980 when Fr. Chris Conroy arrived to work with us in this mission of the Prelature of Sicuani. This Prelature, high in the Andes of Peru, was entrusted to the Carmelites by the Holy See in 1959.

Fr. Chris Conroy was assigned to a remote parish in Yauri, Espinar, at an altitude of some four thousand metres above sea level. He was a very devout and faithful pastor, visiting the many native villages that belong to this huge parish, about the size of Leinster. In many areas there are no roads and he went on horseback to the different villages. He became quite a proficient horseman. He could easily have kept up with the American cowboys.

When he arrived in these communities, frequently he'd have to sleep on the ground and eat what these good people could share with him. Besides, he was in danger from the Shining Path terrorists, who were in the area. Some land-owners even accused him of being a terrorist.

Fr.Chris carried out his duties at all times with great zeal and personal commitment. He was a faithful, pious priest and loved by the people, especially the more humble ones.

During his time in Peru, I never received one complaint against Fr. Conroy. On the contrary, he was loved by the people he served in the name of Jesus and the Church.

Knowing Fr. Chris Conroy as I do over many years, I cannot believe the allegations brought against him. They must be the product of sick people or of someone who wants to do him harm. Fr. Chris Conroy has always been an exemplary, faithful priest."

By now I was up against a brick wall. It didn't matter what I said, or did, it wouldn't make any difference. I was in a catch 22 situation. The Provincial was like putty in the hands of the archbishop. He must be obeyed at all costs even though he has no jurisdiction over me. He says Fr. Conroy must leave Wicklow. So the Provincial says I must leave Wicklow. The archbishop says it has nothing to do with him because I am a Carmelite. I am stuck in the middle. The fact that I must follow my CONSCIENCE doesn't register with anyone. The Provincial preferred to follow the old system of blind obedience. This meant that you blindly obeyed your superior, no matter what he asked you to do. Very often superiors used obedience to impose their will and whims on their subjects in order to control them. The Second Vatican Council changed all that. One of the chief architects of the Council was Cardinal Suenens of Belgium, whom I got to know when I was in Brussels. Before the Council he conducted a survey of Religious Congregations in France and Belgium. He discovered that some Superiors were like dictators in their Convents. Often the sisters were treated like slaves. One of the first things the Council looked at was obedience in religious life. They rejected the old idea of blind obedience and introduced the notion of Prophetic Obedience. This defined religious obedience as a prayerful listening for the will of God, in all relevant 'voices' and the search for His will in the 'signs of the times'. this may at times involve dissent, not as defiance or disobedience but as a creative contribution to the fuller discernment of and obedience to the will of God in the present situation. In other words obedience is not mindless submission; it's an explicit commitment to mindful discernment. So the whole nature of obedience was changed forever in religious life. It means that a Superior cannot just order someone to do something blindly.

At the heart of obedience is dialogue, communication, talking face to face, not solicitors' letters.

Around this time the ex General, my old friend, Fr. Falco came to Gort Muire to give our annual retreat. At the end of the retreat there was a question and answer session. The Provincial and assistant Provincial were present. The assistant Provincial, Fr. Martin Kilmurray asked him a question. "Fr. Falco, what do you do when someone will not accept a directive from the Provincial?"

"Well, first of all you would discuss the situation with him. Talk it over face to face."

Fr. Martin interrupted him rather impatiently, "Yes, I understand all that, but what do you do, when after discussing it he still won't obey?"

"In that case you have failed" replied Fr. Falco with a smile, "Begin again."

But of course this never happened, there was no discussion, no face to face talks. I continued to get solicitors' letters ordering me what to do. The Provincial would mention meetings he had with the Archbishop and the family. He never informed me about anything that was discussed. Everything took place behind closed doors, in secret.

One of the greatest problems of the Catholic Church is secrecy. This goes back to the time of the conversion of Constantine in 313 A.D. although Constantine converted to Christianity, he never really converted to the Gospel of Jesus Christ. The Church took on Rome's civil order and class system. A great distinction was made between the clergy and laity. Later the Curia committed itself to secrecy to keep the Church ranks in order. The Curia became a big secret society.

The Vatican secret archives date back to this time and occupies fifty miles of shelf space in an underground bunker. Down through the ages the Vatican decided what the faithful should be told (The third secret of Fatima, prophesying the assassination of a "bishop dressed in white", was kept under wraps in the Vatican Doctrinal Office until the year 2000, when it was considered the right time to reveal it).

The Church which is committed to honesty, justice and morality, has a system by which it can tell lies called 'mental reservation'. The clergy can mislead people without being guilty, in the eyes of the Church, of lying. In recent times Vatican leaks have revealed some secrets of the Vatican. In a letter to Pope Benedict, eighty four Archbishops informed him of corruption in the Vatican. It is believed that this was the reason for his resignation. The Church has always followed the principal of loyalty above honesty. The Catholic Church's option for its good name over the truth has nearly destroyed the Church. What the Vatican needs is not secrecy but accountability. The old system of defending its position at all costs must be abandoned and rather seek to find the TRUTH. Secrecy is not just confined to the Vatican, it permeates the whole Church. Carmelite Council meetings are held in secret and the members are forbidden to discuss them outside the meeting. The conclusions of these meetings are often conveyed as though they were defined doctrine and infallible.

In November 2009 the Murphy Report concluded that the Archdiocese of Dublin had covered up sexual abuse in varying degrees. It said "that the archdiocese had an obsessive concern with secrecy and avoidance of scandal and had little or no concern for the welfare of the abused child. In a television interview in October 2006 it would seem that Archbishop Martin has little or no concern for innocent priests. He said,"there have been priests taken out of ministry who are innocent.They can be very angry with me and have a right to be angry with me. Sometimes those who are innocent go through horrendous suffering and the assessments are extremely invasive."

I had to make a decision, to leave the Order that I loved and had dedicated my whole life to, or obey an INJUSTICE. But I must obey my CONSCIENCE. Then the Provincial informed me that I would never be dismissed from the Order after over sixty years of faithful service. Now he tried a different approach. He would try to bribe me.

"Just come back to Whitefriar St. for six months, to get the Archbishop off my back, then you can return to Wicklow and live in peace.

"I don't play games," I said.

Then he offered to buy me a house anywhere in Ireland to the value of one million Euro, if I would move away from Wicklow.

"No thanks" I said, "I am happy where I am."

Next the Archbishop tried a different tactic. I was driving home from Dublin one day listening to Joe Duffy on 'Liveline'. Philip Garland, the child protection officer for the Diocese, was explaining how the archbishop deals with sex abuse cases against priests. I couldn't believe what I was hearing. "The Archbishop always meets with each priest and discusses the accusations."

I immediately rang the programme and said he was talking rubbish. The archbishop refused to meet me. I gave my name and Joe referred to me as Fr. Conroy. Mr Garland refused to discuss my case because I was a member of a religious Order and I didn't come under the jurisdiction of the Archbishop. Next day there was a call from archbishop's house to the H.S.E. in Wicklow instructing them to send me on a six months assessment course to the Granada Institute (This is where people who are accused of any sexual deviation go to be assessed by a psychologist). The H.S.E. are all powerful, so I had no option but to go. So during the course of the next six months I went to the Granada Institute to be assessed by Psychologist, Dr. Jeanne De Volder. She often remarked:

"You should not be here, you are more normal than I am." After six months I received a copy of the report.

"Fr. Conroy is judged to be low risk for future sexual offending as measured by the combined score on the Static-99 and Stable 2007. This is the lowest overall score it is possible to obtain on actuarial risk assessment measures. These findings are consistent with the previous assessment conducted by Dr. Patrick Walsh in 2003."

You will notice I was judged a low risk for future sexual offending. Why wasn't I judged no risk at all? The answer is this cannot be done. The Psychologist must choose between three categories, high risk, medium risk and low risk. I was assured that I was absolutely no risk to anyone. The archbishop received a copy of the report, but of course it didn't make the slightest bit of difference to my situation.

By now, Fintan Burke had come to the end of his term of office (Normally a Provincial's term of office is six years, but Fintan got this extended for three more years, as he considered himself the most competent for the job). His parting words to me were,

"If you had done what I asked you, you would be back in Wicklow now enjoying your retirement."

Fintan Burke, as Provincial, was totally preoccupied with protecting the good name of the Order and in the process was quite happy to sacrifice me and my good name and reputation. He relied completely on the Province solicitor, who seemed to operate under Murphy's Law, "anything that could go wrong will go wrong." Fintan could not talk to me, face to face, as a fellow Carmelite. He did not understand the principle of the primacy of CONSCIENCE. And of course he could not see the elephant in the room, which was the ARCHBISHOP. Fintan hadn't the courage to take a stand against him.

The situation was not to get any better under the new Provincial, Fr.Martin Kilmurray. He had been the Assistant Provincial and close friend of Fintan during the previous nine years. He was well aware of my situation, and most likely was the writer of the solicitor's letters. For the first few months after his election, I heard nothing from him. He was probably hoping I would just go away and get lost. I wrote to him and asked for a meeting. He listened to me in silence for over an hour, as I brought him up to date with my situation. He thanked me for coming and said he would have to consult with the Council. In due course I received another solicitor's letter. It began by citing Canon Law and the Carmelite Constitutions, stating that all Carmelites must live in Community.

NOW HE HAD MOVED THE GOAL POSTS.

Now I was back to the situation I was in before I left Peru. I know Carmelites normally live in Community, but there are exceptions to the rule. In every Province there are Carmelites living outside Community. I had been sent outside community by the Order and by this time I had been forty three years living on my own. But I knew this was just an excuse to please the archbishop.

Another two years went by and I continued to live in Wicklow. Nothing happened. I asked for another meeting with the Provincial. He agreed to meet me with a member of the Council. Again I spoke for over an hour, as they listened in silence. Then the Provincial reached for his briefcase and began to read the same letter he had sent me two years previously. I stopped him and said I knew what was in it.

"You haven't obeyed yet." he said.

"Would you say I am disobedient?"

"Well, technically you are," he said after a long pause.

There is no answer to that. It was just like Vatican II hadn't taken place. Obedience means doing what you are told, and conscience doesn't come into it.

"The archbishop was asking about you last week." he said.

"The archbishop has nothing to do with me." I replied.

With that the meeting was over. He led me to the door.

"Chris, how are you keeping?" he asked

"Fine" I said.

"You know you still have all your priestly faculties, they were never revoked."

"I know," I have done nothing wrong."

"Just carry on as you are," he said, "and everything will be alright."

With that I went back to Guantanamo Bay.

Summary

So I end up in Limbo. It is now ten years since I was acquitted at Wicklow District Court by judge Raymond Groarke. The jury acquitted me, not just beyond reasonable doubt but they had no doubt whatsoever. In other words I was innocent.

Then the Church stepped in and I became guilty until proven innocent. After exhaustive investigations by the Carmelite Order, six former provincials gave written testimony of my exemplary character and how they had never received any accusation or complaint against me during their term in office. At the request of the Archbishop's house, the HSE sent me on a six month assessment course for sexual abuse to the Granada Institute. I was completely exonerated and placed in the lowest risk category possible, which means I was no risk at all. The Bishop of Sicuani, Peru gave a glowing account of my time on the Missions.

All was going well until the Archbishop intervened in the situation and declared that I must be got out of Wicklow at all costs. A weak and incompetent Provincial cowed down before the Archbishop and humbly submitted. In due course I received a solicitor's letter from the Provincial ordering me to leave Wicklow. This is where I had to make a stand. I had gone to jail in Peru because of injustice I could not and would not accept it in the Church. I pointed out that as an exempt religious I did not come under the jurisdiction of the Archbishop. Also by leaving Wicklow I would be admitting guilt. I cannot do this in conscience. I was then threatened with expulsion from the Order. If that is the price I have to pay for justice then so be it. And all the time the Archbishop continues to interfere. He seems to have some kind of vendetta against me to act in such a vindictive way. When I requested a meeting with him, he refused, because I don't come under his jurisdiction.

The present Provincial has not met me during his term in office. He communicates by solicitors letters. I have asked to meet him on two occasions and he just listened in silence. In spite of my situation I live alone in happiness and at peace. I have reached the twilight of my years. I sleep soundly every night and live life to the full. The secret is a clear conscience. And I never felt more a Carmelite, after all we began as hermits on Mt. Carmel.

Epilogue

"There's a divinity that shapes our ends rough-hew them how we will." Hamlet.

Looking back through my life now, it would certainly seem there was a destiny that shaped the important stages of my life. Almost a hundred years ago my father ran away from home to join the British Army and fight in the First World War in France and Belgium. He was one of a team of eight that manned a sixty pound field gun on the front line. He was wounded by shrapnel, smothered by mustard gas, and was the only one of his field gun who survived the Battle of Ypres. I have often thought that if the shrapnel had been a few inches higher, or a stray bullet had his name on it, I would not be here. I asked him once did he ever think he might be killed, "Oh, no," he said, "you couldn't think like that, I knew I would come home."

My early childhood at the Copse was idyllic. Even now when I daydream I go back once more to the fields and woods and helping my father in the garden. I think of the happy times I spent looking for birds' nests, shooting rabbits and woodpigeons and trying to catch squirrels. I loved exploring the mysteries of nature with all its wonders and delights. My trips over the hill to Jack Jordan's farm; watching Lil baking the bread in the iron pot on the open fire, turning the bellows to keep the fire going; churning in the dairy, milking the cows and collecting the eggs from the free range hens (That was the only kind there were). I loved the freedom of roaming through the woods and the fields of barley on a hot summer's day.

Just after my First Communion, the Second World War began. My father read extracts from the paper every day to keep me informed. The war became very real, when a German plane dropped bombs in the garden of the Copse. "They are still trying to get me " remarked my father as he stood in the huge bomb crater. Although the war meant rationing and the lack of luxuries, we still had an abundance of fruit and vegetables. But young people in other countries were not so lucky. I remember feeling so guilty after the war on reading the Diary of Anne Frank, thinking of her locked up in the annexe in Amsterdam, having been betrayed and dying in a concentration camp, just a few weeks before the end of the war. I will never forget her words as she looked out the window of the annexe.

"In spite of everything I still believe that people are really good at heart. I simply can't build up my hopes on a foundation consisting of confusion, misery and death." "I was just about her age, a world away, free and happy and I could do nothing to help her."

Then Alicia came into my life, at last I had a sister, and the joy and happiness she radiated as I tried to sing 'Delaney's Donkey.' But my destiny was soon to take me away from the Copse. Now it was time to leave home. It was beyond my wildest dreams to go to Terenure College. On a big beech tree in the grounds of the Copse I carved a farewell message, "Christy is gone to college, goodbye."

I loved my time in Terenure, the daily life of the boarding school, mixing with boys from all over Ireland, going to class, playing rugby, debating, athletics in the summer, acting on the stage. The friendliness that existed between the priests, the teachers and the pupils; we were just one big happy family. That camaraderie between Terenure boys continues wherever they meet long after they leave the college.

Hitchiking to Rome for the Holy Year and receiving Pope Pius XII's blessing was another highlight .

But now I must say goodbye to all that. In September 1951, I joined the Carmelite Order, put on a brown habit and entered another world. My daily life revolved around prayer and meditation and of course obeying the rules and regulations. The most important rule was blind obedience, giving up my own free will and coming under the will of my superior.

I was ordained a priest in 1959, when an unknown Cardinal was elected Pope and took the name of John XXIII. He shocked the world by calling the Second Vatican Council. The windows of the Church were thrown open and the old system based on rules and regulations was replaced by the primacy of CONSCIENCE. The God of the commandments was replaced by God the carpenter, God the ploughman, God the Shepherd. There were only two great commandments: love God and love your neighbour.

My destiny took another turn when I was asked to leave the monastery and go to England to be chaplain to hotels. I had returned to another world. Then I went to Brussels to Lumen Vitae, a branch of Louvain University, to study in depth the documents of the Second Vatican Council . Here I got the opportunity to run a New Christian Community and travel the world. On my return to Ireland, I organised a new form of youth retreat based on the Second Vatican Council and my experiences in Brussels. Over the next ten years, I gave two day retreats to ten thousand young people.

It was during this time that my destiny took another extraordinary turn. Out of the blue, I volunteered to give up everything and to live and work with the Inca Indians in the mountains of Peru, fifteen thousand feet above sea level. Here my life changed for ever, as I lived the Gospel with the poorest people in the world. I lived a freedom that was not based on rules and regulations. Canon Law does not apply above ten thousand feet. I put my life on the line, fighting for justice for these poor and exploited people. I was put behind bars in jail. I did not return home to Ireland to accept injustice within the Church.

A Beggar in Paradise

My book on my experiences in the mountains of Peru. It was well received and became a best seller. Unfortunately it is out of print. I still have a few copies.

Chris Conroy
10 Rocky Rd.,
Wicklow,
Co. Wicklow;
conroychristopher100@gmail.com

Richie Conroy

1936 2013

"I came that you might have life and have it more abundantly"
John 10.10

Richie certainly lived life to the full
His two great passions were the army'and cars.

He loved the camaraderie of army life and was a crack shot on the rifle range.

He was happiest on the racing track from midget cars to the Phoenix Park.

But his greatest joy was his beloved Morgan's

May he rest in Peace

Richies memorial card